The Critic as Conservator

BOOKS BY GEORGE A. PANICHAS

❧

Adventure in Consciousness:
The Meaning of D. H. Lawrence's Religious Quest (1964)

Epicurus (1967)

The Reverent Discipline:
Essays in Literary Criticism and Culture (1974)

The Burden of Vision: Dostoevsky's Spiritual Art (1977)

The Courage of Judgment:
Essays in Criticism, Culture, and Society (1982)

The Critic as Conservator:
Essays in Literature, Society, and Culture (1992)

Renaissance and Modern Essays:
Presented to Vivian de Sola Pinto in Celebration of His Seventieth
Birthday (edited, with George R. Hibbard
and Allan Rodway) (1966)

Mansions of the Spirit:
Essays in Literature and Religion (editor) (1967)

Promise of Greatness: The War of 1914–1918 (editor) (1968)

The Politics of Twentieth-Century Novelists (editor) (1971)

The Simone Weil Reader (editor) (1977)

Irving Babbitt: Representative Writings (editor) (1981)

Irving Babbitt in Our Time
(edited, with Claes G. Ryn) (1986)

Modern Age: The First Twenty-Five
Years. A Selection (editor) (1988)

George A. Panichas

The Critic as Conservator

Essays in Literature, Society,
and Culture

The Catholic University of America Press
Washington, D.C.
1992

The paper used in this publication meets the minimum requirements of
American National Standards for Information Science—Permanence of Paper
for Printed Library Materials, ANSI z39.48–1984.
∞

Library of Congress Cataloging-in-Publication Data
Panichas, George A.
    The critic as conservator : essays in literature, society, and
culture / George A. Panichas.
        p.   cm.
    Includes bibliographical references and index.
        1. Literature, Modern—History and criticism.   2. Literature and
society.   I. Title.
    PN710.P288   1992
    91-32217
        ISBN 0-8132-0762-2 (alk. paper)

To Henry Regnery

Brave Man of Thought, Publisher, Friend

❧

It will always be so. Every principle is a war-note. Whoever attempts to carry out the rule of right and love and freedom must take his life in his hand.

—RALPH WALDO EMERSON

Prove all things; hold fast that which is good.
—I THESSALONIANS 5:21

He [the critic] has to understand for others, to answer
for them; he is always under arms.
—HENRY JAMES, *"Criticism," in*
Essays in London and Elsewhere (1893)

[F]or life to be large and full, it must contain
the care of the past and of the future in every passing
moment of the present.
—JOSEPH CONRAD, *Nostromo* (1904)

Contents

Preface

What comprises the responsibility of the critic? This is the central and interweaving question this book strives to elucidate. Throughout, the office of the critic is viewed as one that is ultimately rooted in moral concerns and has a high moral calling. How the critic fulfills his responsibility; how he infuses an inwardness into the critical act; how he gives his witness in a modern world that discloses a crisis of consciousness at all levels: these are the dominant concerns in this book.

Here the critic thus registers his conceptions and judgments of those inner and outer features of modern civilization that are now imperilled. The tone of voice heard is urgent, censorious, combative. It cannot be otherwise as the essays in this book, individually and collectively, demonstrate in their assessment of the conditions of modern literature, society, and culture. The primary focus is on Western civilization, especially its American genus; and the time frame is that of the modern age during the past one hundred years or more, with the greatest stress given to the American experience in our time. The personal and autobiographical temper of some of the essays underlines the intensity of the critic's own experience of the dynamics of the American scene.

The needs of religion; the problem of leadership; the testimony, in word and work, of great writers and thinkers; the state of education, of arts and letters, of politics; the consequences of ideas; the moral estate of criticism—these are issues and themes that engage the critic and quicken his responsibility in the following pages. These preoccupations, as they are delineated and conveyed, place this book mainly in the genre of social criticism and intellectual and cultural history. But it should be stated that this book does not try to enforce a specific social-political theory. Its aims are basically diagnostic, even as its critical impulse emerges from anxiety with the conditions—the moral drifting and shifting—of a society that increasingly, even violently, separates itself from metaphysical moorings and from spiritual and religious acceptations. In fact, these deviant conditions induce not only the book's protests and warnings but also its critical unity and ethos. A distinct effort is made, in the cumulative sequence and import of the essays, to measure the losses occasioned by the ongoing assaults on the spiritual idea of human continuity and its ancillary components—faith, tradition, piety, order, decorum, standards.

At the same time, the diagnostic thrust of the book should not preclude a viable corrective transaction. Hence, the critic's invitation to the reader to examine the sum and substance of human character and conscience in a rapidly changing world is inclusive and unconditional. One hopes that this invitation carries with it the challenge and the opportunity for what can be constructive and restorative. One hopes, too, that the critic's responsibility goes beyond that of diagnosing the tendencies and conditions of modern literature, society, and culture; that it is the critic's responsibility to point the way in any manner he can if losses in the ethical and moral life are to be arrested.

The moral constituents of the critic's function and responsibility can never be overestimated when the forces of deconstruction and disorder threaten the foundations of civilization. This aspect of the critic's task is particularly important during a period of history that embodies a total spiritual crisis. It can even be said that the following essays make manifest a state of emergency which must be faced and endured indefinitely. In responding to this state of emergency the critic validates his responsibility in a social and moral framework. He refuses, above all, to settle comfortably into a soulless secularization.

The obsession with prescriptive approaches, with social–political reform, and with the necessity of relating ideas to action and shaping life to a prefigured ideology, has invaded the realm of criticism. This obsession has advanced the belief that the critical function that distances itself from direct political action must end in statism. Politicization has thus also become a major activity in the academy. In this book the essays again and again point to the dangers posed by a critical radicalism that governs the intellectual community and administers policies and curriculum in the academy. On the other hand, a sapiential criticism that surmounts ideology and revolution has little or no place in the academy, and is treated as a dissident phenomenon. This book weighs the effects of a situation in which critics abandon or betray their true calling by dismantling the inheritance that they should guard.

Indeed, this book depicts the exertions of the critic who refuses to subscribe to a modernity which, emptied of Spirit, ends at the frontier of nothingness. But how does the critic deal with this emergency? This is another central question that the critic strives to elucidate here. Inevitably, then, this book identifies the nature of the critic's struggle to apply the checks and disciplines needed to curtail the offshoots of the emergency. Reverence for the religious sense—that is to say, affirming the spirituality of man and the existence of spirituality itself—is the categorical principle that the critic pleads for most in this book. And unfailingly he affirms the absolutes of the creative Logos and loyalty to our sacred patrimony. This affirmation is a moral dimension of the critic's responsibility that rejects the idols of temporality and pragmatism, as well as the anarchy of transition. Accordingly he commends the canons of order and faith that redeem the secular.

As found in some of the essays, the sharp critical censures are prompted by the critic's recognition of moral lapses and deviations from the sacred that lead to the debasement of literature, society, and culture. The essays that follow try to trace and to assess both the symptoms and the consequences of the displacement of the sacred in a mechanistic and technological world. No attempt is made to disguise the gravity of the process of displacement. Neither illusion nor unwarranted optimism diverts the critic from focusing on issues that cry out for attention. In an age addicted to the relative, to unstructured and unrestrained change, to the laws of multiplicity and pluralism as these besiege human existence, there are axiological positions to be taken and standards to defend. The critic's moral responsibility inheres precisely in this plenary need. Such a critic gives his testimony in a state of tension between the responsibility to make inspective and watchful comment and the responsibility to conserve universal values, principles, and truths that give meaning and purpose in a world of flux and confusion.

Today the boasts of change reach shrill and oppressive proportions and become a daily affliction as one hears and experiences them everywhere. Perhaps the most alarming aspect of impieties without number is the way they fast become a habit of mind and a way of life, to such an extent that those who voice dissent are barely heard—or tolerated. The criteria of retention and salvation, of conservation and continuity are routinely glossed over, derided, dismissed. No quality of universality is deemed holy in the face of a rampant relativism. But that we have gone even beyond relativism and find ourselves mired in decadence and nihilism is an emergency that accents spiritual ruin and signals still another darkness in the twentieth century. Insofar as we live at a time when the permanent things are always in the process of being attacked and lost, the role of the critic as conservator is one that this book insists upon. To stem the tide of loss and to recover and thereby to save and retain what has been lost is a responsibility that the critic must actively embrace. To shirk this responsibility is to sanction spiritual disarray.

No doubt what the critic has to report in this book will meet with strong opposition from unrepentant modernists. But the critic who believes that there are enduring things to defend and bequeath—a legacy of values and virtues to be preserved from defilement—has the responsibility to press on with his work, despite the opposition that he must confront in the pursuit of his by no means popular task. Clearly, the antinomian tendency, a powerful and pervasive one in the modern world, needs to be resisted. The necessity for such resistance impels the critical orientation of this book.

Of course, resistance is not the last word: The critic needs to provide paradigms of responsibility that lead to moral and spiritual discrimination and recovery. In pursuing his concerns and in fulfilling his responsibility, the critic must aspire to join the virtue of reverence to the virtue of courage. But there is yet another virtue that the critic needs to practice if he is to complete his mission more effectively, and that is the virtue of loyalty. This virtue signifies faithfulness to responsibility in spite of losses and dangers; and it signifies devotion to those sacred values and transcendent meanings that have come down through the centuries and have acquired spiritual wisdom and insight. In a profane age of unrest and breakdown, it is not enough for the critic to be purely and simply critical. He must work to conserve what is timeless, time-tested, time-honored. He must fight for causes he believes in, even if they appear to be lost causes. The critic's burden of responsibility is also his vision of order.

I

Moral Ascent

༄

Irving Babbitt has been called a "New England Saint" and Simone Weil a "Saint of the Churchless." In their perception of the world and in their conception of the meaning of life there is much to be found that endorses these honoring designations. Yet there is still another path of sympathy that they travelled. It marks a still higher ideational parallelism, and one that instances the highest point of the convergence of their thought. It relates to a definitive ethos, with its complex of civilized ideas and habits, its embodied moral beliefs and certitudes, its reverent apprehension of a spiritual unity and discipline of order, as well as an order of reality with a standard of values. Babbitt and Simone Weil labored to save this ethos from a modern world that, in its Promethean secularism, proclaims "the end of the modern world." Babbitt's moral centrality was born of earnestness, Simone Weil's, of grace—surely compatible and complementary centralities. Each spoke out bravely regarding the modern experience of affliction and shipwreck.

The Christ of Simone Weil

Christ likes us to prefer truth to him because, before being Christ,
he is truth. If one turns aside from him to go toward the truth, one
will not go far before falling into his arms.[1]
—SIMONE WEIL (1909–1943)

These are direct and powerful words of affirmation, the words of a believer. They are now seldom heard in a world in which chronolatry too
easily slips into blasphemy and the whole process of desanctification
whirls on without end. These are also brave and beautiful words worthy of meditation. They help to remind us that a faith without Christ
lacks truth, lacks an added dimension, lacks quintessence of spirit.

Simone Weil's words are forgotten or neglected words, consigned
almost arbitrarily to the realm of an angry silence in an age of disbelief.
Some will no doubt find them painfully embarrassing words and still
others will find them entirely antipathetic. But these are precisely
words that differentiate Simone Weil from her time and contemporaries. For what she says in these two sentences, with an eloquent simplicity and grace, identifies her Christian witness and defines her standard
of faith. Her witness is unassuming, her standard is uncomplicated:
Truth is Christ, Christ is Truth. Above all, she discloses courage of
faith at a time of history when it is far more preferable, even rewarding,
to be either neutral or, as is perhaps the more fashionable choice, hostile to the religious idea.

Ultimately Simone Weil's belief in Christ is mystical and transcendent precisely in those individuating ways that one finds in John 12:44-
49—"He who believes in me, believes not in me but in him who sent
me"; and in 2 Corinthians 1:19, 20—"Jesus Christ . . . was not Yes and
No; but in him it is always Yes. For all the promises of God find their
Yes in him." Hers is not a theology or a philosophy of Christ, since
for Simone Weil there could be no dogmatic or systematic theology or

philosophy. Her perception of Christ, and of Christianity, if it is to be properly fathomed and placed, is remarkably close to, if not a modern continuation of, Christian Hellenism, particularly that form of it that came with the rise of Eclectic Alexandrine Platonism and that was exemplified in the life and work of Clement of Alexandria (about A.D. 150–213), who maintained that Christianity is the heir of the past and the interpreter of the future: "There is one river of Truth; but many streams fall into it on this side and on that."

The Jesus who is Christ has a commanding spiritual and moral presence in Simone Weil's life. Her first mystic experience of Christ occurred in 1938 (she was then in her twenty-eighth year), when, as she records in her "Spiritual Autobiography," she spent ten days at the Benedictine Abbey of Solesmes, from Palm Sunday to Easter Tuesday, following all the liturgical services. Though suffering from violent headaches, she was able to rise above her affliction by finding "pure and perfect joy in the unimaginable beauty of the chanting and the words." In the course of these services "the thought of the Passion of Christ entered into my being once and for all." On this occasion, too, she chanced to meet a young and devout Roman Catholic from England who introduced her to the English metaphysical poets of the seventeenth century. She found particularly appealing George Herbert's poem "Love," which she memorized. She thought that at first she was merely reciting a beautiful poem, yet "without knowing it the recitation had the virtue of a prayer. It was during one of these recitations that . . . Christ himself came down and took possession of me."

In the midst of this experience she felt a simultaneous sense of love; and, in the fashion of a true Christian Hellenist, she "came to feel that Plato was a mystic, that all the *Iliad* is bathed in Christian light, and that Dionysus and Osiris are in a certain sense Christ himself; and my love was thereby redoubled." She goes on to say in her "Spiritual Autobiography": "I never wondered whether Jesus was or was not the Incarnation of God; but in fact I was incapable of thinking of him without thinking of him as God." Later on, in the summer of 1941, she memorized the Greek version of the Lord's Prayer, eventually reciting it once each morning with absolute attention, the words "tear[ing] my thoughts from my body and transport[ing] it to a place outside space where there is neither perspective nor point of view." During this recitation, or at other moments, she adds, "Christ is present with me in person, but his presence is infinitely more real, more moving, more clear than on that first occasion when he took possession of me."

One comes to see Simone Weil's Christ-experience as profound and consuming, ascetic and ascending. Though occurring towards the end of her life, this experience had all the marks of inevitability, or as she writes of her general religious outlook: "I always adopted the Christian attitude as the only possible one. I might say that I was born, I grew up, and I always remained within the Christian inspiration." Indeed, it seems infused with miracle and mystery in which, to use her own words, "Christ is the key," or, as Dietrich Bonhoeffer would have it, "Christ is the center."[2] A divine effluence pervades her life and thought; her own academic grounding in philosophy is a preparation for the Logos. Simone Weil finds the image of the Mystical Body of Christ appealing and yet one that, in its importance, is also a sign of degeneration. Man's true dignity, she contends, is not to be a part of a mystical body, whether of Christ or some other figure. Her view of Christ in this respect is both higher and of a more demanding standard that relates to one's achieved state of perfection. When one reaches this state, a great transposition takes place and one no longer lives in oneself but rather Christ lives in one, becomes each one of us. The Pauline text comes to mind here: "It is no longer I who live, but Christ who lives in me" (Galatians 2:20). It is Christ's active, immanent presence in existence that means so much to Simone Weil. How one absorbs and projects that presence, that transcendent truth, identifies the true nature of one's transfiguration, which at its highest spiritual point is the attainment of perfection.

Simone Weil writes: "Only the desire for perfection has the virtue of being able to destroy in the soul some part of the evil that defiles it." She stresses that Christ offers God himself as an example of the perfection, at once impersonal and divine, that men should strive to achieve. That perfection at the same time consists of a full and uncompromising recognition of one's spiritual destiny, which also includes all those things outside a visible Christianity—"Greece, Egypt, ancient India, and ancient China, the beauty of the world, the pure and authentic reflections of this beauty in art and science." As such, it is a comprehensive and consummate spiritual destiny that, Simone Weil claims, "deliver[s] me into Christ's hands as a captive." For her, Christ is the indwelling Logos of God: "God is present, Christ is present, wherever there is enacted between one man and another an act of supernatural virtue." But what concretizes this virtue? How is it made manifest? Her answer, which she predicates on the basis of her belief that "the virtue of anything is manifested outside the thing," is emphatic and illustrative: "If a man gives bread to a beggar in a certain way or speaks in a certain way about a defeated army, I know that his thought has been outside this world and sat with Christ alongside the Father who is in Heaven."

In describing her possession, or captivity, by Christ, Simone Weil recalls that in the process she felt the presence of love, "like that which one can read in the smile of a beloved face." It is a Christlike love that she cites as being of supreme importance: the "pure love" that one experiences in "moments of grace," when men find their souls. (She finds aspects of this love in Homer's *Iliad*, and specifically in the tradition of hospitality, in paternal and fraternal love, in married love, and in friendship.) As such, this love is "a disposition of the supernatural part of the soul." Love in no form, she is careful to stress, can exist anywhere where Christ is absent. The absence or the presence of Christ is our choice: "Our consent to his presence is the same as his presence." Christ "is always there at the door of our souls, wanting to enter in, though he does not force our consent. If we agree to his entry, he enters; directly we cease to want him, he is gone." Love is the organ in man through which he sees God, whereas the intelligence is the organ through which he sees truth.

Christ's words to his disciples, "Love one another," she considers as a new commandment to be added to the great commandments of love of neighbor and love of God. This commandment, this "asking," contains a form of pure friendship and has in it something of a sacrament. "Pure friendship," she writes, "is an image of the original and perfect friendship that belongs to the Trinity and is the very essence of God." Simone Weil sees love, then, in terms of divine otherness: "Belief in the existence of other human beings as such is love," she writes in *Gravity and Grace* (1952). Her emphasis is on the need to achieve a "supernatural love," a purity rather than an intensity of love that touches only creatures—"loves them as intermediaries"—and goes only to God: "God's love for us is not the reason for which we should love him. God's love for us is the reason for us to love ourselves. How could we love ourselves without this motive?" Love, for Simone Weil, thus takes the form of a bridge, of the Platonic *metaxu*; love, too, is an intermediary leading to God, who "created through love and for love." "The love of God is only an intermediary between the natural and the supernatural love of creatures." Christ embodies the highest spiritual form and function of *metaxu*.

For Simone Weil, the crucifixion of Christ is not only "this supreme tearing apart," "this incomparable agony," but also "this marvel of love." She believes that all men struck down by affliction, that is, an anonymous and indifferent process which deprives them of their personality and turns them into things, are at the foot of the Cross, "almost at the greatest possible distance from God." Christ, she emphasizes, was afflicted: "He did not die like a martyr. He died like a common criminal, in the same class as thieves, only a little more ridiculous. For affliction is ridiculous." The crucifixion signifies the distance placed between the Son and his Father, but this distance is only separation: "For those who love, separation, although painful, is a good, because it is love. Even the distress of the abandoned Christ is a good. There cannot be a greater good for us on earth than to share in it." She maintains that the love that unites Christ on the Cross to his Father, who is at an infinite distance, resides in every saintly soul. Love is an orientation and not a state of soul: "The man whose soul remains oriented towards God while a nail is driven through it finds himself nailed to the very centre of the universe; the true centre, which is not in the middle, which is not in space and time, which is God."

This is not only a point of intersection between creation and creator but also the point of intersection of the two branches of the Cross. It is each man's right to desire to have his part in Christ's Cross, which becomes the substance of man's life and which "is the only source of life that is bright enough to illumine affliction." "The Trinity and the Cross are the two poles of Christianity, the two essential parts: the first, perfect joy; the second, perfect affliction. It is necessary to know both the one and the other and their mysterious unity, but the human condition in this world places us infinitely far from the Trinity, at the very foot of the Cross. Our country is the Cross."

Simone Weil's concern is essentially with the Passion of Christ: the Suffering and Crucified Christ, not the Christ in Glory, the Risen One, dominates her view. In some reminding ways her meditations on Christ have their visual counterparts in the agonizing crucifixions of a

Grunewald—his *Christ on the Cross* (1519); and of a Holbein—his *The Man of Sorrows* (*circa* 1520). Pertinent here, too, is her admiration of F. M. Dostoevsky, for like the great Russian novelist her Christian anthropology emphasized the universal, or what Dostoevsky called the "omni–human," sources of spiritual life; and like him she also focused on the Cross and suffering rather than on the Resurrection and the Ascension. Indeed, the theme of affliction occupies the same place of importance in Simone Weil's thought that the theme of humiliation ("the insulted and injured") occupies in Dostoevsky's. His famous statement, "If anyone could prove to me that Christ is outside the truth, and if the truth really did exclude Christ, I should prefer to stay with Christ and not with the truth," finds a responsive echo in Simone Weil.

Of crucial importance to an understanding of her conception of Christ is her essay "The Love of God and Affliction," written at the very end of her life. From a theological viewpoint, this essay contains, *sine qua non*, her most systematic reflections on suffering and is crucial to an understanding of her religious thought as a whole. Her Christology, the science of the Logos of God, also attains defined clarifications in this essay. It could be said that, as seen in this essay, Simone Weil's view of affliction is tantamount to her encounter with Christ. "The Love of God and Affliction" remains one of her great spiritual meditations in which one is exposed, in T. S. Eliot's words, "to the personality of a woman of genius, of a kind of genius akin to that of the saints."[3] The contemplative voice of a modern mystic speaks eloquently in this essay as Simone Weil gives her witness.

The essay begins simply and directly, and with spiritual cogency: "In the realm of suffering, affliction is something apart, specific and irreducible. It is quite a different thing from simple suffering. It takes possession of the soul and marks it through and through with its own particular mark, the mark of slavery." Simone Weil is careful to point out that affliction is an uprooting of life, a form of death, "made irresistibly present to the soul by the attack or immediate apprehension of physical pain." The afflicted man, like Christ hanging on the Cross, feels both his body and his soul accursed. Though, too, man is a slave of material necessity, he is also the son of its Master. The knowledge of affliction, she insists, is the key of Christianity, even as the Trinity, perfect joy, and the Cross, perfect affliction, are the two poles of Christianity.

The human condition of this world places us a great distance from the Trinity; places us at the foot of the Cross of Christ. To repeat, "Our country is the Cross." Only by looking upon the Cross can one love God. Yet it is an error, Simone Weil also insists, to indict Christianity for having a morbid preoccupation with cruel suffering and grief, which are sensations and psychological states: "Affliction is not a psychological state; it is a pulverization of the soul by the mechanical brutality of circumstances." Since affliction contains the truth about the human condition, "[t]hey alone will see God who prefer to recognize the truth and die, instead of living a long and happy existence in a state of illusion." Only the contemplation of Christ's Cross helps us to accept the reality of affliction, or as she puts it in a paragraph remarkable for its succinctness and deep spiritual insights:

> The Cross of Christ is the only source of light that is bright enough to illumine affliction. Where there is affliction, in any age or any country, the Cross of Christ is the truth of it. Any man, whatever his beliefs may be, has his part in the Cross of Christ if he loves truth to the point of facing affliction rather than escape into the depths of falsehood. If God . . . had been willing to withhold Christ from the men of any given country or epoch, we should know it by an infallible sign; there would be no affliction among them. We know of no such period in history. Wherever there is affliction there is the Cross—concealed, but present to anyone who chooses truth rather than falsehood and love rather than hate. Affliction without the Cross is hell, and God has not placed hell upon the earth.

No amount of quotation or of summary can do justice to Simone Weil's reflections on Christ. A spiritual and prophetic fervor characterizes her reflections, which communicate, reciprocally, poetry of language and beauty of inspiration. What she says about Christ underlines the power of truth that He compels and that she discloses—"to disclose the secrets of the heart," in Simeon's words (at the presentation in the temple)—in her essay on "The Love of God and Affliction." The Christ that one meets in Simone Weil's thought is the Christ who makes the difference between life and death, between salvation and damnation. "Christ is our bread," she writes in her meditation "Concerning the Our Father." One's acceptance of Christ, she declares, is the "yes" of marriage; is an existential yes that is pronounced within and for the present moment, "but spoken as an eternal word, for it is consent to the union of Christ with the eternal part of our soul."

For Simone Weil, Christ is "the bread which is supernatural," the food that constitutes a "transcendent energy." Bonhoeffer's words, "So the question of transcendence is the question of existence and the question of existence is the question of transcendence,"[4] help to capture here the innermost meaning of Simone Weil's own emphasis on the principle that "the bread which is transcendent is the same thing as the divine name." The illusion of man's perspective, however, places man at the center of space, thus rejecting the idea of transcendence. The world is one of unreality and dreams, which too often prompt one to assume a false divinity. Simone Weil stresses that the love of the order and beauty of the world has ultimately both a sacramental and a transcendent character: "God created the universe, and his Son, our first-born brother, created the beauty of it for us. The beauty of the world is Christ's tender smile for us coming through matter."

Simone Weil's affirmation of Christ is all the more exceptional when one considers the years of her life as these encompassed the nightmare of oppression and war—an era when the life of faith and principles of order and belief were collapsing. Human devaluation and spiritual disinheritance are major modern problems that Simone Weil actively confronted; in effect, she was to define and mould her conception of Christ at a time of history when darkness was engulfing the whole of civilization. She was profoundly sensitive to the crisis of civilization that Existentialists image as a shipwreck, which in fact had actually been in the making since the Great War of 1914–1918. Historically, when one views the rise of communism in Russia after 1917 and the triumphs of fascism and nazism in the twenties and thirties, one thinks of the reigns of terror that have mercilessly assaulted and enslaved modern man. At this point of history the *Kyrios Christos* was indeed "the dead Christ in the tomb."

Simone Weil viewed the phenomena of deracination and destruction in terms of what she called "the empire of might." Bravely, she was to give her prophetic witness in the midst of "the shaking of the foundations" and "the reality of the demonic." Her conversional experience of Christ cannot be separated from her experience of the world, and specifically the world that she apprehended in the contexts of these words: "The world is the closed door. It is a barrier. And at the same time it is the way through." Christ is "the way through," the key to the soul's painful journey of purification, which she describes in one of her metaphysical poems, "Threshold": "We want the flowers. Here thirst grips us. / Waiting and suffering, we are here before the door. / If we must, we will break this door with our fists. / We press and push, but the barrier still holds." Simone Weil's accepting vision of Christ, and of the Christ who is "the center of history," must be seen against the backdrop of a world in which "we wander without knowing and find no place."

Once again Bonhoeffer's words help us to pinpoint Simone Weil's view of history: "In faith, history is known in the light of eternity."[5] Of her many essays, none more vividly confirms the applicability of Bonhoeffer's statement than "The *Iliad*, Poem of Might," which she first started to write in 1939. Both in an immediate and in a transcendent sense, this essay illustrates the bondage of history and yet ultimately the salvation in history through Christ. The essay is an astonishing meditation on an epic poem that constitutes a "mirror of reality" and renders the consequences of cruel history on the life of the soul and on human destiny. "The Gospels are the last and most marvellous expression of Greek genius," she declares, "as the *Iliad* is its first expression." And of Homer she writes: "The author of the *Iliad* depicts life as only a man who loves God can see it." Noting that the spirit of Greece reveals human misery in the person of a divine being who is also human, she goes on to observe regarding the spiritual affinity that she believes miraculously connects and unites the *Iliad* and the Gospels, Homer and Christ, Troy and Jerusalem: "The accounts of the Passion show that a divine spirit united to the flesh is altered by affliction, trembles before suffering and death, feels himself, at the moment of deepest agony, separated from men and from God. The sense of human misery gives these accounts of the Passion that accent of simplicity which is the stamp of Greek genius."

The affliction that Simone Weil detects in the destruction of Troy and in the crucifixion of Christ has a universal spiritual significance that goes beyond spatial and temporal restrictions: "For violence so crushes whomever it touches that it appears at least external no less to him who dispenses it than to him who endures it. So the idea was born of a destiny beneath which the aggressors and their victims are equally innocent, the victors and the vanquished brothers in the same misfortune."

Christ on the Cross represents for Simone Weil the greatest harm that is inflicted on the greatest good. At the same time, "On the Cross he rendered unto Caesar what was Caesar's and unto God what was God's." In Christ, she sees the constituents of a spiritual way of life that by its very nature illuminates the things of the world. The Gospel itself, she claims, "contains a conception of human life, not a theology." In that life Christ occupies a central place, even as the Paraclete he enacts, through his presence, words, deeds, and fate, the highest meaning of human destiny and the path to truth. That meaning and that truth must require and contain two purgative, or "decreative," qualities of soul, compassion and humility, which in themselves are active, spiritualizing essences of Christ, the enactments, as well as the immanences, of his divinity and eternity. "Every movement of pure compassion in a soul is a new descent of Christ upon earth to be crucified," she writes. Only Christ's presence in the soul can place true compassion in it and as such is an operative form of charity, "a miraculous gift," a process in which "he who gives from true compassion gives Christ himself."

Compassion is a spiritualization of suffering, a transfiguration on a universal scale, at once sacramental and redemptive: "Compassion is all the more tender, all the more poignant, the more good one is able to discern in the being who forms the object of it, and it predisposes one to discern the good." In Christ compassion attains its acme, as well as its criterion of divinization: "Mankind's crimes didn't diminish Christ's compassion. Thus compassion keeps both eyes open on both the good and the bad and finds in each sufficient reasons for loving. It is the only love on this earth which is true and righteous."

In Christ, Simone Weil sees the supernatural virtue of humility, which is also the root of love and the antecedent to the state of grace. True humility crowns all virtues. "Without humility," she writes, "all the virtues are finite. Only humility makes them infinite." As an attitude and *praxis*, humility is of supreme importance, and is nowhere more visibly symbolized than in the Cross of Christ: "Humility consists of knowing that in this world the whole soul, not only what we term the ego in its totality, but also the supernatural part of the soul, which is God present in it, is subject to time and to the vicissitudes of change." Christ is the Humiliated One; in the crucifixion the God-man is humiliated, or as Simone Weil asserts: "Humility exerts an irresistible power upon God. If God had not been humiliated, in the person of Christ, he would be inferior to us." Humility instances a relation of the soul to time. "It is an acceptance of waiting," she states. In identi-

fying humility with the experience of waiting—"waiting humbly"—
she strives to show how the Christlike inner condition of patience
"transmutes time into eternity": "Humility partakes in God's patience.
The perfected soul waits for the good in silence, immobility and humility like God's own. Christ nailed on the cross is the perfect image of
the Father."

Hence, in the crucifixion of Christ is to be found "the image of the
fixity of God." She continues: "God is attention without distraction.
One must imitate the patience and humility of God. . . . Time which
is our one misery, is the very touch of his hand. It is the abdication by
which he lets us exist." Patience and humility have a dual function,
which Christ epitomizes, particularly as he bravely "endured" the
Cross, symbolizing the truth of affliction and the contemplation of its
reality, which is, in the end, the redemptive function itself. "Twenty
centuries ago," she writes, "in the Roman Empire, slavery was the affliction of the age, and the crucifixion was its extreme expression."

The Cross of Christ ultimately illustrates the Christian idea that
weakness can be a formidable force. But that force, Simone Weil insists, does not relate to temporal strength but "is a force that is not of
this world, that is supernatural." Even Karl Marx, she adds, accepted
this contradiction of strength in weakness, but he refused to accept "the
supernatural which alone renders the contradiction valid." Particularly
in the twentieth century does she see the subordination of the supernatural, in its various ramifications, to the collective industrial machine:
"Now the social mechanism, through its blind functioning, is in the
process—as everything that has happened since August 1914 shows—
of destroying all the conditions for intellectual and cultural development." It is the supernatural truth, incarnate in Christ, that is violated
by the doctrine of social mechanism.

Simone Weil's Christianity, it should be stressed here, is not reclu-
sive, is no escape into the past, even into *historia sacra*; her mystical orientation and contemplations never blind her to the boundary-situation
of history and society—and of Christ in history and society. Hers is
fundamentally a Christian world view, absolute and uncompromising,
even thorny, in its choices and judgment: "If you do not believe in the
remote, silent, secret omnipotence of a spirit, there remains only the
manifest omnipotence of matter." Christ, and the Cross of Christ, represent victory over matter. He brings balance to a civilization in which

"everything is disequilibrium." "Christ is the key," she reflects. "All geometry proceeds from the Cross." This latter sentence returns us again to the abiding place of Christian Hellenism in her religious thought and brings into focus these analogous words of Clement of Alexandria: "All wisdom is summed up in Christ, who is the keystone of the arch of knowledge and its uniting principle."

Christ, as Simone Weil iterates, represents for the catechumen the ultimate lessons of humility and also the ultimate criteria of wisdom. In this respect, above all, he provides for us a divine, a supernatural, perspective. This perspective, she says, and here she hankers back to Hellenism, revolves around the ideas of limit, of measure, of equilibrium, and simultaneously helps one to determine the conduct of one's life and one's thoughts about man and the universe. It enables one to understand the true significance of the world and to accept its true parameters and nature: "To give up our imaginary position as the center, to renounce it, not only intellectually but in the imaginative part of our soul, that means to awaken to what is real and eternal, to see the true light and hear the true silence." What results from this process, which is one's encounter with the divine, and consequently a supernatural discipline, is a transformation that occurs at the roots of one's sensibility and that alters, by purifying and refining and sanctifying, one's conception of the greater spiritual self and the greater spiritual world.

It is with deep poetic feeling that Simone Weil paints some of the interior properties of this transformation in its divine contexts: "It is a transformation analogous to that which takes place in the dusk of evening on a road, where we suddenly discern as a tree what we had at first seen as a stooping man; or where we suddenly recognize as a rustling of leaves what we thought at first was whispering voices. We see the same colors; we hear the same sounds, but not in the same way." This transformation both reveals and identifies the supernatural essences of man; it marks the ascending motion of the soul as it is freed of its burden of illusions, its mortality: "To empty ourselves of our false divinity, to deny ourselves, to give up being the center of the world in imagination, to discern that all points in the world are equally centers and that the true center is outside the world, this is to consent to the rule of mechanical necessity in matter and of free choice at the center of each soul."

Though Simone Weil is concerned with the place of Christ in the modern world, the world which she herself was to experience in its interminable pains and perils and predicaments, she was in no way to modernize her conception of Christ, to compromise his divinity, to temporize his life and fate. An incorruptible reverence characterizes her feelings for Christ; and a permeating spiritual dignity identifies her conception of the Christ who bridges history and eternity. It is Christ's universal attributes, his cosmic presence, and his transcendent *didaskalia* that she celebrates. What remains consistent in her attitude towards Christ is her total respect for his divine ministry and message. Her every reference to him is fraught with awe and fear; she in no way makes him subservient to any modern theories of Christ, to those trivializing pseudonyms of Christ that one finds, for example, in modern fiction, or even in modern theology.

The tendency to diminish the person of Christ, as instanced particularly in contemporary emphases on the "good news" rather than on the Passion of Christ, does not exist in Simone Weil's views. What is always impressive about her views is the sense of mystery and sanctity that she connects with the kenotic person of Christ. Those perverse modern heresies of romanticism and nationalism, as these have been relentlessly applied to Christ and as these have sought to demystify his transcendence and divinity, find no favor in Simone Weil. Nor does she sentimentalize Christ, whom she endows with great internal strength and with resolute compassion.

Simone Weil's is not the Christ of the modern novelist, or of the modern philosopher, or of the modern theologian. He is not, in other words, an exclusive but rather an inclusive Christ who does not judge but who is judgment, and grace. His understanding is an inescapable revelation of truth, a divine radiance. Our own finite understanding of Christ's infinite understanding enables us in the end to confront the immensity of sin itself. "Sin is nothing else," Simone Weil writes, "but the failure to recognize human misery—it is unconscious misery and for that very reason guilty misery. The story of Christ is the experimental proof that human misery is irreducible, that it is as great in the absolutely sinless man as in the sinner."

Not the curse of Christ but the victory of his Cross, his Truth, is at the center of Simone Weil's conception of Christ. She does not fail to warn, in this respect, that "there are many Christians who have no part in Christ because they lack the strength to recognize the blessed Cross in every affliction." The contemplation of Christ's Cross is an implicit acceptance of Christ's Truth: "There is not, there cannot be, any human activity in whatever sphere, of which Christ's Cross is not the supreme and secret truth." But the contemplation of Christ's Cross and thus of Christ's Truth also brings one into the domain of self-contemplation, for "We must look for the secret of our kinship with God in our mortality." Man's search for that "secret" will succeed only insofar as there are, according to Simone Weil, two conditions piercing enough to penetrate man's soul: beauty and affliction. Yet even that search will disclose neither final answers nor final causes, for, as she observes, "If there were finality in the world, the place of the good would not be in the other world."

Beauty compels one to ask: Why? "Why is this thing beautiful?" And affliction, as soon as man falls into it, also compels one to ask: Why? "Christ himself," Simone Weil avers, "asked it: 'Why hast thou forsaken me?'" To the everlastingly accursed questions, she maintains, "Silence is the answer." She goes on to say: "He who is capable not only of listening but also of loving hears this silence as the word of God." In this "eternal silence" resides the Logos, of which *agapē* is the vibration and zenith. Simone Weil's paths of meditation reach a supernal conclusion in the harmony of God's silence. Christ is the omega-point of this silence: "God's secret word of love can be nothing else but silence. Christ is the silence of God."

2

Babbitt and Religion

As a teacher and critic, Irving Babbitt has come to represent a man of character, an Anglo-Saxon moralist, a New England mind, "the last of the great American Puritans." In his person, as in his teaching, Babbitt was to communicate solidity, robustness, austerity, tenacity, integrity. Even his physical appearance identified him as quintessentially Yankee: a man above average height, powerfully built, with a radiant complexion and dark blue eyes. "*Qui est ce monsieur, si beau, si distingué? Il a l'air d'un dieu!*" someone in his Parisian audience was heard to observe.[1] His was essentially a masculine disposition. Ascetical and ethereal traits are not part of this disposition; nor was there anything valetudinarian or epicurean in what he projected. Combativeness was at the center of his character and task. He was a man of immense, tactile energy: a polemical dialectican with a probative mind and prophetic message, working from axiomatic principles to inevitable conclusions. Not the idealism of Plato, but the positivism of Aristotle is what inheres in Babbitt's thought. And what is fundamental and experiential, secular and empirical in the best sense, characterizes the articles of Babbitt's humanist creed.

This creed must be assessed in the contexts of what Babbitt calls "the immediate data of consciousness," that is, those viable and verifiable elements that are distinct and different from the metaphysical and supernatural and from what he termed "a mystical-transcendental mist." In defense of his creed he was indefatigable: "Nor shall my sword sleep in my hand" are words that Babbitt might have easily written. The ancient Greeks used the adjective *gennaios* to designate a man who is high-minded, brave, manly. This word, which describes Babbitt's mission as teacher and critic, is central to "the courage to be" and "the courage of judgment." Irving Babbitt had both.

This profile can hardly do justice to the strength of conviction and "the terrible earnestness" that Babbitt disclosed in his long ministry as a teacher and critic. Even his foes paid him respect for his effort in behalf of what they happily considered to be lost causes. "He was so powerful a teacher that the very presence of him," writes Alfred Kazin in *On Native Grounds*, "the slow stubborn consecration of his ideal, was moving. In the face of so much inertia, cynicism, and triviality in others, the total absence of anything like his force in American criticism, his moral effectiveness was profound."[2]

For the most part, Babbitt has been denied full recognition as a religious man, as a man of spiritual insight. Kazin dismisses Babbitt as "a commonplace skeptic," "a Yankee Republican and a Tory materialist," who lacked religious history and religious sensibility. And Paul Elmer More, Babbitt's coadjutor and friend, opined in his obituary essay that Babbitt's life, though obedient to "the unrelenting exactions of conscience," was not a life of steady growth in Grace. "I can remember him," More reminisces, "in the early days stopping before a church in North Avenue, and, with a gesture of bitter contempt, exclaiming: 'There is the enemy! there is the thing I hate.' "[3] This incident has long influenced a common perception of Babbitt as anti-religious. Nothing could be, or has been, more misrepresentative of Babbitt's religious importance, which a Hindu crystallizes in these words: "Oh, Babbitt, he is a holy man, a great saint!"[4] Austin Warren further defines the special nature of his mentor's saintliness by including Babbitt among the "New England Saints"—Jonathan Edwards, Ralph Waldo Emerson, Edward Taylor, Charles Eliot Norton. "My saints are," Warren emphasizes, "none of them, canonized; but they are, whether priests, and of whatever 'communion,' men I recognize, and celebrate, as those to whom reality was the spiritual life, whose spiritual integrity was their calling and vocation."[5]

But the hagiographic titles assigned to Babbitt by his Oriental admirer and his Harvard pupil have enjoyed little approval. Babbitt has always been a victim of those who, like Kazin, see him as a fanatic reactionary and those who, like F. O. Matthiessen, see his "conception of human nature . . . [as] high principled, but arid and inadequate."[6] These impressions of Babbitt, like More's recollection of Babbitt gesticulating at a Cambridge church, have led to a distorted image. Perhaps his friends and his enemies wanted him to be something more than he could be. To the question, "Does not criticism consist above all in comprehending?" Babbitt was to reply, "No, but in judging." That reply takes the measure of the man. It adumbrates, with economy of emotion and expression, his severe magistrative orientation and his absolute honesty. Babbitt did not fudge; there is an astonishing transparency in his total contribution that makes it difficult to accept the charge that he was plagued by "abstract spiritual manliness." What identifies Babbitt is the absoluteness and the concreteness of his views: the commitment and the pertinacity, the belief and faith, of one who avows principles of life and order. A central quality of his achievement is the absence of corruptions, of anomalies, of fantasies, of roles, of turnings. Babbitt wears no masks. The centrality of his thought is its virtue of honesty, its integrative *gennaiotēs*, to use that informing Greek word.

"The saints come to us," Henri Daniel-Rops tells us, "as the *judges* of their own period and society."[7] One must read Babbitt's particular form of saintliness in the contexts of these words. Daniel-Rops also reminds us that "a saint is a scandal," that he creates "'a troublesome commotion.'" No words better characterize both the treatment and the effects of Babbitt's endeavors. But for Babbitt not to have held any one of these saintly dimensions would have made him merely another humdrum critic.

It was as a teacher-saint that Babbitt was to conduct his dedicated ministry. His arena was his classroom; his pupils were both his catechumens and his concelebrants. No other teacher in this century has more powerfully or memorably exemplified selfless commitment to the art of teaching, to *humanitas*. His writings were the products of his teaching, that is, lectures transposed from the lectern to the printed page, there to become permanent principles of character and conscience. Babbitt was to sanctify the whole process of teaching as a moral act and to elevate it to its maximum point of meaning. "Here was a new kind of teacher: not reducible to a learned expositor, he taught with authority," Warren recalls. "If, to doctrinal 'liberals,' he was patently reactionary, he defended an academic freedom precious and perishable—the freedom to judge. . . . He was concerned with principles, with tracing lines of intellectual development."[8] Babbitt's pupils readily testify to the greatness of his teaching, which he summarized repeatedly with his admonition, "live at the center." Even those pupils who disagreed with him and those adherents who diverted from his ideas testify to the influence Babbitt exerted on them. To read his pupils' reminiscences and tributes is to become aware of one who is, as

the Chinese are wont to say, "a teacher of men." For them his classes
were an intellectual and spiritual experience and, ultimately, "spiritual
exercises." Master of "self-reverence, self-knowledge, self-control,"
he disclosed those gifts and disciplines of the teacher-saint possessing a
great soul, one whom Babbitt's own master of "unsurpassed humanism," Aristotle, speaks of as *megalopsychos*.

Few would deny Babbitt recognition as a teacher-saint. But that recognition is diminished frequently by the concomitant indictment of
Babbitt's humanism as being, at the very least, religiously vacuous and
of Babbitt himself as being a teacher-saint who is also a heretic standing
some distance from or outside of the Church and holding a position
short of a commitment to Christianity. Babbitt's brand of humanism,
as Marion Montgomery has recently charged, is overtly Hellenic and
not New Testament. That is to say, Babbitt represents a gnostic mentality whereby the Greek spirit threatens to engulf faith in speculative
philosophy. "Aristotle without St. Thomas," Montgomery reminds us
in the course of indicting Babbitt, "like Plato without St. Paul, is an incomplete champion against secular relativism."[9] The substance of this
indictment of Babbitt is not new, but goes back to what remains a definitive statement, T. S. Eliot's *After Strange Gods: A Primer of Modern
Heresy* (1934), in which Babbitt is included with D. H. Lawrence, Ezra
Pound, and the early Yeats as modern heretics, that is, men who are
not necessarily unbelievers, but who emphasize a doctrine too strongly
and obsessively, to the point of falsehood. In two earlier essays, "The
Humanism of Irving Babbitt" (1927) and "Second Thoughts about
Humanism" (1928), Eliot had also delineated his critique of Babbitt's
religious position, or what he calls "the weaknesses of humanism."[10]

Eliot's case against Babbitt's doctrine of humanism can be summarized as follows: Insofar as humanism refuses the orthodox religious
view, it seeks to be an alternative to religion; it stresses the role of human reason, not the revelation of the supernatural. As such Babbitt's
humanism is essentially a byproduct of liberal Protestant theology. In
the end, Babbitt is trying to make his form of humanism work without
religion, even as he himself remains detached from any fundamental
religious belief. Babbitt has come to know many philosophies and religions and has assimilated them so thoroughly that he cannot commit
himself to any. Eliot could not accept Babbitt's emphasis on the appli-
ance of the "inner check" in controlling the human personality's cen-

trifugal pull. Orthodox religion alone, he insisted, was capable of providing not only the "external restraints," but also "a single spiritual core and a dogmatic creed." ("Only Christianity helps to reconcile me to life, which is otherwise disgusting," Eliot once wrote to More.) However admirable Babbitt's concern "with the discipline and training of emotion," Eliot says, the end, the *telos*, of humanism is futile: "What is the higher will to *will*, if there is nothing either 'anterior, or superior' to the individual?" What Eliot has to say is underlined by Allen Tate in his essay on "The Fallacy of Humanism" when he observes: "His [Babbitt's] doctrine of restraint does not look to *unity*, but to abstract and external *control*—not to a solution of the moral problem, but to an attempt to get the moral results of unity by main force, by a kind of moral fascism."[11]

The depiction of Babbitt as a heretic who somehow transfigured into a moral fascist has long been with us. It has conspired to strip him of those genuine religious qualities that pervade his humanist faith and that reveal him as a great spiritual figure. If there are seeds of heresy in Babbitt, they are neither perverse nor diabolic. His heresy can be interpreted as a necessary aspect of the life of the church, as a supplement to it in the contexts of what Edmund Burke terms "the dissidence of dissent." The church and the heretics, it has been observed, form a far more vital union than either one will admit. Above all, then, the religious significance of heresy is what needs to be grasped and understood. But before examining this significance in Babbitt, it is best to earmark the major traits of a great heretic in these words of the Swiss theologian Walter Georg Nigg: "He is the extreme antithesis of the indifferentist. . . . He courageously accepts the consequences of his actions. His fervor can teach us the meaning of loyalty to truth. We may even say that the heretic embodies the religious spirit in concentrated form."[12]

Nigg goes on to say that the heretic typifies a repressed interpretation of religion; that unresolved problems come to life in a heretic; that a heretic seeks to advance an overlooked or misunderstood religious concept, so that religious values previously unknown are discovered. "Only great men have brought forth heresies," Saint Augustine tells us. The heretic often resembles the saint; the piety of the latter contrasts with the rebellion of the former to underscore a mission on the part of one who is simultaneously a witness, an outlaw, and even a martyr. It should be remembered that the term heresy is a transliteration of the Greek *hairesis*, meaning an act of choosing, a course of action or thought, and finally the philosophical principles of one who professes them. At its most destructive stage, heresy destroys unity and induces spiritual alienation; at its most constructive, in the words of Leopold Ziegler, heresy is "necessary for the tradition, so that it will remain in flux and not congeal into rigidity."

No less than the Blaise Pascal of the *Lettres Provinciales*, whom Unamuno termed "an orthodox heretic," Babbitt could also say, "I stand alone," as he sought to uphold the sovereignty of conscience to the point of heresy. Pascal, a religious visionary who both attracted and repelled Babbitt, was long the subject of one of his Harvard courses and much discussed in his writings. The spiritual core of Pascal's personality appealed to Babbitt, whose own religio-humanistic position is epitomized in Fragment 378 of the *Pensées*: "To leave the mean is to abandon humanity. The greatness of the human soul consists in knowing how to preserve the mean. So far from greatness consisting in leaving it, it consists in not leaving it." Babbitt, who distrusted "the Jansenist emphasis on thunderclaps and visible upsets of grace," admired the Pascal who differentiated the man of faith from the naturalist, the traditional disciplines from pure naturalism, true faith from "the horrible flux of all things," faith from worldliness. It is the Pascal who finally exclaims, "Joy, certainty, peace," whom Babbitt embraces and whom he equates with the "peace, poise, [and] centrality" he especially admires in Buddhism. Babbitt's admiration of Pascal shows sympathy not with the ascetical and the mystical, with what he speaks of as the Pascalian "expressions of the theological terror," but rather with the conviction and strength that resist the morbid and discouraging.

Spiritual strenuousness remained Babbitt's major tenet of faith: "Work out your own salvation with diligence." Buddha's words dramatize Babbitt's religious orientation, one which clearly disavowed "dogmatic or revealed religion" and the doctrine of grace. G. K. Chesterton, in opposing Superhumanism to Humanism, regarded the latter as one of those "spiritual experiments outside the central spiritual tradition." "Humanism may try to pick up the pieces; but can it stick them together?" Chesterton asks. "Where is the *cement* which made religion corporate and popular, which can prevent it falling to pieces in a débris of individualistic tastes and degrees?"[13]

Babbitt's qualified acceptance of Pascal is indicative of his discernment of institutional religion and its fundamental ideas. His endorsements were selective and limiting. In the religious realm, as in the educational, Babbitt was motivated by a positive critical spirit informed by his absolute rejection of any romantic tendency culminating in man's "expansive conceit" that produces ignorance and blindness. His religious views have a decidedly generalist cast and belong to what should be called the universal moral order. In contemporary religious parlance, Babbitt could be termed an "ecumenist," though this word would be apt to imply nonselective and nondefined religious elements that Babbitt would find antipathetic. Babbitt's religious search goes beyond the frontiers of historical Christianity and is more inclusive in its figures, goals, and essences, as he makes clear when he writes: ". . . if there is such a thing as the wisdom of the ages, a central core of normal human experience, this wisdom is, on the religious level, found in Buddha and Christ and, on the humanistic level, in Confucius and Aristotle. These teachers may be regarded both in themselves and in their influence as the four outstanding figures in the spiritual history of mankind."

This statement identifies the comprehensive features of Babbitt's religious quest, even as it points to its heterodox features. Yet to insist on Babbitt's religious deviationism does him a disservice. Any fair consideration of his thought will corroborate Professor Louis J.- A. Mercier's contention that, for Babbitt, man is a rational animal in whom there is felt "the presence of a higher will ultimately divine." Indeed, in one of his later essays, "Humanism: An Essay at Definition," Babbitt affirms Pascal's belief that the humanist must finally take part in the debate between naturalists and supernaturalists. Babbitt proceeds to state a principle of belief that elucidates the religious character of his humanism: "For my own part, I range myself unhesitatingly on the side of the supernaturalists. Though I see no evidence that humanism is necessarily ineffective apart from dogmatic and revealed religion, there is, as it seems to me, evidence that it gains immensely in effectiveness when it has a background of religious insight."

In their thrust and ramification Babbitt's religious ideas and acceptances are cautious. Any excess of rarefied religious sentiment or spirituality is checked. One cannot, he iterates, pass from the human to the religious level too quickly; the world would be better if men "made

sure that they were human before setting out to be superhuman."
There are priorities to be observed, levels of growth to be attained,
particular paths to be followed, and adjustments to be made if humanism and religion are to have a gainful encounter. At the same time, as
Babbitt avers, "humanistic mediation that has the support of meditation may correctly be said to have a religious background. Mediation
and meditation are after all only different stages in the same ascending
'path' and should not be arbitrarily separated."

Humanism can work in harmony with religion in opposition to
what Babbitt sees as a common foe when he writes: "The chief enemies
of the humanist are the pragmatists and other philosophers of the flux
who simplify this problem for themselves by dismissing the One,
which is a living intuition, as a metaphysical abstraction." "Humanism: An Essay at Definition" occupies a high place in an understanding
of Babbitt's religious views. Its chief value is corrective. Babbitt was
keenly aware of the misunderstanding and misrepresentation of his attitude toward religion. His statements in this essay have a concentrated
purpose, not only in definition but also in clarification. He is painstak-
ing in formulating his religious views. "It is an error to hold that humanism can take the place of religion," he emphasizes. "Religion indeed may more readily dispense with humanism than humanism with
religion." Here Babbitt is speaking to critical friends, to the Paul Elmer
More who asks in trepidation: "Will not the humanist, unless he adds
to his creed the faith and the hope of religion, find himself at the last,
despite his protests, dragged back into the camp of the naturalist? If we
perish like beasts, shall we not live like beasts?"[14]

These are defiant, even embarrassing, questions which Babbitt answered with the patience and dignity of the great teacher that he was.
So much more was demanded of Babbitt than of others, perhaps because he, more than others, meditated on first causes and ultimate ends.
If anything, Babbitt's orientation was one of opportunities and striv-
ings. Between humanism and the Christian communions Babbitt
sought for a basis of cooperation in a united struggle against "the humanitarian programme." "The weakness of humanitarianism from
both the humanistic and the religious point[s] of view," he declared,
"is that it holds out the hope of securing certain spiritual benefits . . .
without any ascent from the naturalistic level." What is constant in
Babbitt's religious thought is his stress on man's need for a morality of

ascent, the ultimate standard of spiritual effort and life. That man needs to submit his ordinary self to some higher will is, for Babbitt, a central religious tenet. In this submission there reside the elements of awe and humility and the ultimate attainment of peace. It is the ethical dimension of religion that he advances. As he remarks: "The final reply to all the doubts that torment the human heart is not some theory of conduct, however perfect, but the man of character." Though Babbitt repeatedly warns of the perils of intellectual unrestraint, he is critical of the Christian tendency to get rid of the intellect in order to get rid of the pride of the intellect. Unfailingly Babbitt keeps his eye on the universal center, on the middle path. As a true Aristotelian, he writes: "To use the intellect to the utmost and at the same time to keep it in its proper subordinate place is a task that seems thus far to have been beyond the capacity of Occidental man."

Not so much an historical, and sacramental, but a critical Christianity is what Babbitt addresses himself to. What he most sympathizes with in Christianity are its elements of joy and illumination; what he most opposes is a "romantic religiosity" mired in "the web of illusion" and "metaphysical despair." Particularly in the Catholic Church did Babbitt find aspects to admire, or what he singled out as its "discipline and the definite standards that could protect society against the individual." On the other hand, he felt that the Protestant churches were turning more and more to the doctrine of social service and thus were "substituting for the truths of the inner life various causes and movements and reforms and crusades."

For Babbitt there was an overarching religious problem that he saw confronting modern man. It went back to Rousseau. That religious problem, Babbitt said, involves a major judgmental choice "between a dualism that affirms a struggle between good and evil in the heart of the individual and the dualism which, like that of Rousseau, transfers the struggle to society." Insofar as the Rousseauistic attitude has prevailed in the modern world, according to Babbitt, spiritual disorder has become ascendant. He was concerned with an existential as opposed to a theological evil, with those forms of evil that embody an evasion of moral responsibility, so that they result in what he termed spiritual indolence. To resist this form of breakdown he prescribes the humanistic virtues—moderation, common sense, and common decency. He viewed these virtues in the context of "a positive and critical humanism" in which there is an emphasis on the educative function: man "must be trained in the appropriate habits almost from infancy." "We need," he says, "to restore to human nature in some critical and experimental fashion the 'old Adam' that the idealists have been so busy eliminating." As necessary as they are, the theological virtues of faith, hope, and charity are subsequent to the humanistic as an ultimate developmental stage in the morality of ascent and in "the paths of Truth."

It bears repeating that Babbitt's attitude toward revealed religion was essentially one of "suspended judgment." He perceived humanism as a common ground upon which dualists, Christians and non-Christians, could meet. No less than the "humanistic Goethe" (as revealed in the *Conversations* with Eckermann and in the critical judgments uttered in his later years), Babbitt "would have us cease theorizing about the absolute and learn to recognize it in its actual manifestations." Man, Babbitt would say, needs to learn the lessons of renunciation, but the renunciation of temperament and impulses must be "the natural outgrowth of this life and not, as so often in religion, the violent contradiction of it." Of Babbitt, as of Goethe, it could be said that he avoided confusing the planes of being. "No inconsiderable part of wisdom," writes Babbitt, "consists in just this: not to allow the mind to dwell on questions that are unprofitable in themselves or else entirely beyond its grasp." In the Goethe who expressed the humanistic virtues Babbitt found a mirror of himself that enabled him to trace the anatomy of his own religious identity. What was finally disclosed was Babbitt's stress on what he calls "instinct for a sound spiritual hygiene" and on the need to turn away from grace to works. "The right use of grace and similar doctrines," Babbitt states, "is to make us humble and not to make us morbid or discouraged." Speculations about the "insoluble mysteries" are basically unrewarding; like Goethe, Babbitt refused "to enter into the metaphysical maze of either the dogmatic supernaturalist or the dogmatic naturalist."

For Babbitt, "sham spirituality" signifies the death of faith. Throughout his writings he provides a diagnostic examination of what he judges to be religious illusions and errors emerging from a monistic naturalism. Babbitt locates standards of what he calls "true spirituality," the truths of humility and of the inner life, in the Orient, especially in the religion and personality of Buddha. In Buddhism, Babbitt applauds a comparative freedom from casuistry, obscurantism, and intolerance. The most significant religious statement that Babbitt makes on the subject is his long introductory essay "Buddha and the Occident," found in his translation of the ancient Pāli classic of Buddhist wisdom, *The Dhammapada*, published in 1936. This essay is Babbitt's spiritual testament, his final witness. No understanding of his religious ethos is possible without a judicious estimation of this essay. A lifelong student of Buddhism, Babbitt was much in sympathy with the Primitive (Hinayāna) Buddhism of Ceylon, Burma, and Siam. Austin Warren believes that Babbitt was in fact a Buddhist and was "motivated . . . by the desire to restate 'genuine Buddhism' in modern terms, as a religion acceptable to those who, like himself, found metaphysics, theology, and ecclesiasticism harmful rather than salutary to the devout life."[15] And Paul Elmer More simply states as a fact that Babbitt "was much closer to Buddhism than would appear from his public utterances."[16] In an essay-review, "Interpreting India to the West," Babbitt crystallizes his concept of a Buddhism that may be used to supplement and support our Western wisdom when he writes, or rather testifies, his own faith:

> Buddha deals with the law of control, the special law of human nature, in a spirit as positive and dispassionate as that in which a Newton deals with the law of gravitation. If a man wishes peace and brotherhood, he must pay the price—he must rise above the naturalistic level; and this he can do only by overcoming his moral indolence, only by applying the inner check to temperamental impulse. "All salutary conditions (*dhamma*)," says Buddha, "have their root in strenuousness."[17]

The experience of the Far East, Babbitt believed, completes and confirms that of the Occident. "We can scarcely afford to neglect it if we hope to work out a truly ecumenical wisdom to oppose to the sinister one-sidedness of our current naturalism," he observes. The historical Buddha, Babbitt believed, was a "critical and experimental supernaturalist," a dualist and individualist who did not rest his belief on those "tremendous affirmations" of dogmatic and revealed religion that revolved around a personal God and personal immortality. Buddha can be defined as a "religious empiricist" to whom the real meaning of faith is "faith to act." Self-mastery is the most eminent aspect of this faith as meaning and as action, that is, as inner action. "Self is the lord of self. Who else can be the lord?" Buddha declares. "By oneself the evil is done, by oneself one is defiled. Purity and impurity belong to oneself, no one can purify another." What ennobles Buddhism, in Babbitt's eyes, is an emphasis on earnestness and on continual spiritual effort to subordinate the evil forces within one to an indwelling law of righteousness. Babbitt especially endorses the words that Buddha uttered at the end of his life: "Therefore, O Ananda, be ye lamps unto yourselves. Be ye refuges unto yourselves. Look to no outer refuge. Hold fast as a refuge unto the Law (*Dhamma*)." Buddhism is not a philosophical system but a "path"; one who follows this path ultimately gains insight that is marked by an increasing awareness, which precedes "right meditation" and "is at the opposite pole from the diffuse reverie that has been so encouraged by our modern return to nature." Wisdom is measured by the degree to which man has been awakened from "the dream of sense."

In Buddhism, Babbitt perceived a religion rooted in a "psychology of desire." "Immediate peace," not "immediate pleasure," is for Buddha a paramount goal. This peace is the "rest that comes through striving." It is a calm that is "without the slightest trace of languor," a "meditative tranquillity" that arises when, as Buddha says, one "has reached the other shore in two states (tranquillity and insight)." For Babbitt a saint, whether Buddhist or Christian, "is rightly meditative and in proportion to the rightness of his meditation is the depth of his peace." If Christianity was originally more emotional and nostalgic in temper than Buddhism, Babbitt states, "it is at one in its final emphasis with the older religion. In both faiths this emphasis is on the peace that passeth understanding." If, as Babbitt noted, Buddha was filled with pity, he was also very stern; in Buddha, as in Christ, love and justice are perfectly balanced so as to constitute a single virtue. The Buddhist's insistence on self-love may appear to be selfish and uncharitable, but Babbitt went on to stipulate that the teaching of true self-love accentuates the love of a higher self. This Buddhist teaching, he pointed out, is similar to the Christian concept of dying that one may live. He most admired in Buddha the importance given to the role of the intellect that is keenly discriminating and that of the higher will that is strenuous.

The security and the serenity that are at the heart of "religious comfort" have given way, Babbitt lamented, to an obsessive search for material comfort. In this shifting of emphasis he viewed the glorification of the utilitarian and sentimental facets of the humanitarian movement.

Basic religious precepts are radically altered so as to satisfy this process of ethical and spiritual transvaluation. "A great religion is above all a great example," Babbitt declares; but "the example tends to grow faint in time or even to suffer alteration into something very different." More than other religious teachers, Buddha, who stands for the idea of meditation, has deep significance for the Occident. This significance is heightened by the fact that Buddha reduces the human problem to a psychology of desire and then deals with desire in terms of conflict and adjustment. Particularly in the passage from the medieval to the modern period, Babbitt contended, the idea of meditation and the transcendent view of life have steadily declined. "Yet it is not certain," Babbitt adds, "that religion itself can survive unless men retain some sense of the wisdom that may, according to Dante, be won by sitting in quiet recollection." In Buddhism, as tested by its fruits, Babbitt saw a striking confirmation of Christianity. Buddha provides spiritual paradigms and humanistic truths that, if accepted, would augment the Christian faith by saving it, as Babbitt hoped, from a Calvinist nightmare or an Arcadian dream. Buddha's relevance to Christianity, he says, is positive and critical in the sense of reinforcing and remobilizing the intrinsic strength in a modern world. These final sentences from Babbitt's essay "Buddha and the Occident" identify the connections that he sought to establish between two great religious movements in a period that has seen the eclipse of the religious sense:

> The meditation of the Buddhist involves like that of the Christian the exercise of transcendent will; this will is not, however, associated, as it normally is in the meditation of the Christian, with that of a personal deity. Persons of positive and critical temper who yet perceive the importance of meditation may incline here as elsewhere to put less emphasis on the doctrinal divergence of Christianity and Buddhism than on their psychological agreement.

Predictably, Babbitt's Christian Platonist friend, Paul Elmer More, and his Anglo-Catholic pupil, T. S. Eliot, had other views of Buddhism. Of the two, More's response to Buddhism was more sympathetic. Unlike Babbitt, More favored Hindu mysticism and the Brahmanic theosophy of the *Upanishads*. By the end of his life he had accepted Christianity as the complement and climax of the Greek tradition. The first essay in his book *The Catholic Faith* (1931) is devoted to "Buddhism and Christianity"; Babbitt himself had gone through the entire book with such "extreme care" as to prompt an extensive revision of that essay. In ways that recall Babbitt, More brought Buddhism into vital relation to Christianity; he saw both religions covering and dividing "the deeper possibilities of faith." In the history of the two religions he found similarities, as he also found in the morality of discipline taught by Buddha and by Christ. More's admiration of the Buddhist's three stages of progress in sanctity—discipline of conduct, discipline of mind, and the higher wisdom and power—is no less than Babbitt's.

But More discerned profound absences in Buddhism: it contains no Creator, no providential Ruler, no Judge, no Savior. Like Babbitt, he considered Buddhism more joyous and even-tempered than Christianity, but, in contrast to the latter, More believed that "the notion of *telos* plays no part in its cosmogony or ethics." That is, in Buddhism there is "no continuity between the end and the means to the end." Though More admitted that Buddha was "the noblest of all religious teachers, saving only one," and that Buddhism, by its reticence about the soul and by its very omission of God, "was preserved from the evils of intolerance and fanaticism and spiritual anguish that have so often darkened the history of Christianity," he also stressed that Buddhism has "missed something of the positive riches of experience that Christianity at its best can bestow." In what can be construed as a magnanimous rebuttal of Babbitt's position, More concludes with these words regarding Buddha:

> . . . it seems to me at times as if that great soul were searching on all the ways of the spirit for the dogma of the Incarnation, and that fact of the historic Jesus, could it have been known to him, might have saved his religion in later ages from floundering helplessly. . . . Buddhism, I think, may be accepted as a preface to the Gospel . . . and as the most convincing argument withal that truth to be clearly known waits upon revelation.

Far less magnanimous is Eliot's critique of Babbitt's Buddhism. It leaves the distinct impression that Eliot, once and for all, is dismissing a heretic who dismisses the doctrine of revelation. This critique constitutes a long introductory essay written by Eliot for a collection entitled *Revelation*, edited by John Baillie and Hugh Martin, and published in 1937. Eliot categorically declares that "the division between those who accept, and those who deny, Christian revelation I take to be the most profound division between human beings." Throughout, his critical perspective is tough and unsparing. In Babbitt he sees "the most remarkable, the most ambitious attempt to erect a secular philosophy of life in our time." He terms Babbitt a "disbeliever," unique because "he attacked the foundations of secularism more deeply and more comprehensively than any other writer of our time."

Eliot concentrates on the essay "Buddha and the Occident" in order to show how Babbitt sought "to evade Christian conclusions at any cost." The Buddhism of Babbitt, he concludes, instances a kind of "psychological mysticism." "This is the mysticism which seeks contact with the sources of supernatural power," writes Eliot, "divorced from religion and theology; the mysticism which must always be suspect, and which sometimes springs up in cults whose aims are not far removed from those of magic." Especially interesting in Eliot's essay is his coupling of Babbitt and D. H. Lawrence: "The point is that the will to get out from Christianity into a religion of one's own operated in Lawrence as it operated in Babbitt." Eliot ends his discussion of "the literature of secularism" by remarking that the religious sentiment, which can be satisfied only by the message of revelation, "is simply suffering from a condition of repression painful for those in whom it is repressed, who yearn for the fulfillment of belief, although too ashamed of that yearning to allow it to come to consciousness."

That Eliot is doubtlessly aware of his arbitrary yoking of Babbitt and Lawrence in their "will against Christianity" is suggested by the tone in which he distinguishes Babbitt ("by nature an educated man, as well as a highly well-informed one") from Lawrence ("a medicine man" and "a researcher into religious emotion"). But his indictment of both men as examples of "individualistic misdirections of will" is uncompromising insofar as both men, he claims, teach and affirm secular philosophies and are examples of "titanism," "the attempt to build a purely human world without reliance upon grace."

Eliot's case against Lawrence's "religion of power and magic" has been largely answered by F. R. Leavis. The case against Babbitt, however, remains curiously unanswered, perhaps because of the paradoxical alliance between Babbitt's Christian friends and his liberal enemies, who propagate Eliot's thesis for their special purposes. The fact remains that Babbitt's humanist beliefs cannot be understood without the background of his religious thinking. He was not an orthodox Christian, but he gave his spiritual witness in the very character of his writing and teaching. He had integrity. He had humility, the humility that Eliot tells us is endless. And he had standards. These qualities never failed to compass his work and thought: his judgments, which he conveyed resolutely and directly. "There appears to be evidence," he says, "that religion has existed without the accompaniment of morality." Such a statement again reminds us that, for Babbitt, the validity of religion lies in psychology rather than in history, and makes even more emphatic Babbitt's reverence for the Buddha who declares in his message of joyful deliverance: "Only one thing I announce today, as always, Sorrow and its Extinction."

To connect and unify the inner life and the outer life constituted for Babbitt a paramount spiritual need. Those who face up to the moral requisites of this need, he believed, "face unflinchingly the facts of life and these facts do not encourage a thoughtless elation." Thus Babbitt esteemed Saint Francis de Sales because this Doctor of the Church had worked out a synthesis between the demands of "this-worldliness" and those of "other-worldliness." By the same token, Babbitt frowned upon Byzantine sacred art, obviously detecting in the ikons of the Eastern Church an obscure, even passive, soteriological quality that he equated with excessive melancholy and with the loss of "one's self in a shoreless sea of revery."

In respect to sacred music, too, Babbitt had clear-cut views. He stressed the need to distinguish between the genuine "devotional music" of Christian plainsong, which inspires prayer and peace, and the "insurrectional music" of *The Requiem Mass* of Hector Berlioz, which Babbitt equated with "emotional unrestraint" and with sheer "noise and sensationalism." Spiritual romanticism, for Babbitt, was no less harmful than the romanticism that subverts the aesthetic criteria of "dignity, centrality, repose." In particular he distrusted what he termed "the expansion of infinite indeterminate desire" that he related to the neo-Platonic side of Christianity, though he was careful to praise that aspect of the Christian faith that "has dealt sternly and veraciously with the facts of human nature. It has perceived clearly how a man may move towards happiness and how on the other hand he tends to sink into despair; or what amounts to the same thing, it has seen the supreme importance of spiritual effort and the supreme danger of spiritual sloth." It is almost unnecessary to theorize how Babbitt would view the current vogue of "liberation theology," which revolves so loosely and sentimentally around a messianic materialism and the whirl of "the secular city." Such a theology of unilateral desanctification, Babbitt would say, is another blatant example of "eleutheromania," or as he writes in *The New Laokoon*: "Everybody is becoming tinged with eleutheromania, taken up with his rights rather than with his duties, more and more unwilling to accept limitations."

We must not judge Babbitt according to a systematic or dogmatic theology; his was not a concern with what Paul Tillich designates as the theology that "is the methodical explanation of the contents of the Christian faith." First and last Babbitt was a moral critic and comparatist, who saw "connections that no other mind would have perceived," as Eliot says. Babbitt practiced the wisdom of Confucius' admonition that "the man who does not take far views will have near troubles." On the first page of *Democracy and Leadership* (1924) he writes: "When studied with any degree of thoroughness, the economic problem will be found to run into the political problem, the political problem in turn into the philosophical problem, and the philosophical problem itself to be almost indissolubly bound up at last with the religious problem." These noble words help to identify Babbitt's achievement in its value and "constant aspiration toward the central unity of life." Nor must we forget that he was a teacher, a *didaskalos*, "an enlightener and enlarger." Hence to assess his religious significance in terms of a theological orthodoxy is to violate the intrinsic spiritual strength of his thought. He was not a religionist, nor a philosopher of religion, nor a teacher of theology. He was quintessentially a spiritual man, indeed, a spiritual genius, "to whom reality was the spiritual life," to recall Warren's words. He revered the interior life, as well as the ethical and moral life. He possessed an informing religious sense, not one that was vague and numinous, but analytical and judgmental. He sought for a "sense of the absolute," for the absolute of an Emerson or a Tennyson, which Babbitt defined as "a purely spiritual perception of the light beyond reason, entirely disassociated from the faith in creeds and formulas."

There is some truth in R. P. Blackmur's symptomatic complaint that Babbitt was a preacher,[18] if by preacher one means a humanistic and religious realist who traces causes and effects and who distinguishes between the law of the spirit and the law of the members, between the "law for man" and the "law for thing." Such a realist finds a common good in morality and affirms the meaning of the moral real and the meaning of all existence within the universal moral real. The religious sense diminishes, as Babbitt averred, when moral struggle and deliberation and choice are minimized. He vividly imaged this reductionist process in his contrast "between the spiritual athlete and the cosmic loafer, between a Saint Paul . . . and a Walt Whitman." "The greater a man's moral seriousness," he reminds us, "the more he will be concerned with doing rather than dreaming." Babbitt clearly indicated that he had no aversion to a humanist who, seeking support in something higher than reason, turns to Christian theology. "I hold that at the heart of genuine Christianity," he declares, "are certain truths which have already once saved Western civilization and, judiciously employed, may save it again." But he also claimed that for one to be fully positive and critical in the modern world, one has to deal with life more psychologically than metaphysically. He thought it possible, perhaps necessary, to conceive of a humanistic or even a religious psychology that transcends both the dictates of a naturalistic psychology and the symbolic view of the world.

Indeed, Babbitt saw a close affinity between the elimination of the teleological element from modern life and the decline of traditional religion and the older religious controls. He nevertheless believed that, from a humanistic point of view, to restore this teleological element it is more advantageous to start with psychological observation, as in early Buddhism, rather than with theological affirmations. Warning against "dogmatic exclusiveness," he says that one could eclectically acquire humanistic and religious purpose without indulging in ultimates and absolutes. "The good life," he writes, "is not primarily something to be *known* but something to be *willed*." And when "willed" the life-problem of avoiding the "indolence of extremes" is mitigated.

Irving Babbitt chose to speak out not as an orthodox Christian but simply as "a psychological observer" and a "complete positivist." In this capacity he judged "the modern movement," the social benefits of which he found largely illusory and the spiritual offshoots of which made "neither for humanistic poise nor again for the peace of religion." He discriminated practically and concretely between true and false religion, as he discriminated rigorously between "the moral imagination" and "the idyllic imagination." His standards were clear and unshakable in demarcating and avoiding "a confusion of categories." Any softening of standards, he never ceased to state, has a commensurate impact on spiritual life. A dire threat to religious, and humanistic, standards, Babbitt said, is man's consuming "interest in origins rather than in ends." In this connection, he especially esteemed Aristotle's dictum, "*To proton ou sperma estin alla to teleion*"—"The first thing is not seed but the perfect being."[19] These words, it should be remembered, closely follow Aristotle's other emphatic declaration, in his *Metaphysics*, that "life belongs to God." The critical centrality of his religious views must be fully comprehended if Babbitt's moral and spiritual vision is to be saved from both the tests of religious orthodoxy and the incubus of heresy. When this reparative task has been finally accomplished, then what Boswell said of Dr. Johnson will be said of Babbitt—that he is, incontestably, a "majestic teacher of moral and religious wisdom."

3

Irving Babbitt and Simone Weil

The abridgement of the heroic spirit is as common to the modern age as is what Thomas Hardy called "the abridgement of hope." We live in a world in which exhaustion is the most unconditional human condition. We have fallen so deep into a collective crisis-situation that human destiny is no longer regarded with fear and trembling. Our moral confusion transposes into moral desuetude. That prophecy of despair announced in the concluding section of Dostoevsky's *Crime and Punishment* (1866) becomes increasingly a bleak reality of world-fact. That apocalypse of the abyss, as warned steadily by existentialists since the "Armistice" of 1918, seems irreversible. The disappearance, the eclipse, the death of God, as variously described, reveal a waste land in its inner depths and outer reaches. It is hardly necessary even to remark on the moribundity of the Judaeo-Christian concepts of man and the universe. Post-historical man has reached an impasse. Indeed, is it possible that, with the demise of Kafka's Joseph K., murdered "like a dog," the humanistic world hears its death-knell? But this song of lamentation needs no further, oppressive elaboration. T. S. Eliot captures the modern predicament in words that return us to lost beginnings and broken endings when he writes:

> Son of man,
> You cannot say, or guess, for you know only
> A heap of broken images, where the sun beats,
> And the dead tree gives no shelter, the
> cricket no relief,
> And the dry stone no sound of water.

Eliot reminds us of poets as prophets contemplating the human scene. We are also reminded that, whatever the extent and depth of man's failure of nerve or his spiritual homelessness, the creative impulse and the heroic spirit can advance in a reciprocal visionary process, manifesting the modern equivalent of a miracle and a mystery. D. H. Lawrence captures the life-saving quality of this process when he declares: "Brave men [and women] are for ever born, and nothing else is worth having." As long as each of us can point to the enduring worth of Lawrence's words by being able to designate its particular exemplars—whether as great poets or novelists, or as great critics or teachers—then what appears as futile in the changing aspects of the historical situation is not final. Belief in the life of value has continuing worth. The creative principle redeems human possibility. We are *not* as fully defeated as Samuel Beckett would have us think when he points to "the absolute absence of the absolute."

That we do possess first principles; that we can locate a center of values, however frightening modern man's inner and outer turmoil and the cruel swiftness of changes wrought by an even crueller history: it is in the insistence on these axiomatic truths that Irving Babbitt, who died in 1933, and Simone Weil, who died ten years later, come together as teachers and critics exemplifying the meaning of Lawrence's statement. Ultimately, too, their critical comparability has a spiritual element that helps to relate the American-Aristotelian New Humanist and the French-Jewish Christian Platonist.

Both viewed with alarm the rise of the naturalistic and relativistic ethos of the modern age. Both were engaged in resisting what Simone Weil saw as the menace of the "Great Beast" of atheism, materialism, and totalitarianism. Both were preoccupied with the eternal struggle between good and evil in the individuating contexts of what Simone Weil imaged as "gravity and grace" and of what Babbitt tested in the categorizing terms of two discrete and irreconcilable laws, the law for man and the law for thing. Both insisted on the ethical, moral character of ascendance and on recalling the ever-informing substance of the venerable words, in their intrinsic contrasts of value, that our "sociological dreamers and reformers," as Babbitt called them, have debased: virtue, nobility, honor, honesty, generosity, decorum, reverence, discipline. Both were profoundly concerned with the spiritual idea of value and, consequently, with the burden of moral responsibility. Both stressed the necessity for the defining discernment of standards on all levels of life and specifically that operative standard which revolves around some absolute spiritual principle of unity measuring mere manifoldness and change. Babbitt chose to connect this standard of stan-

dards with what he conceived of as "the wisdom of the ages." Simone
Weil was no less adamant in her view of an absolute criterion of transcendence, that which embodies "submission of those parts which
have had no contact with God to the one which has."

The critical affinities between Irving Babbitt and Simone Weil go
much deeper than their grounding in the French literary thought of the
seventeenth century, or in their reverence for the classical tradition, or
in their admiration of Oriental religious and philosophical thought.
One must see them as critics scrupulously examining what Babbitt indicted as "the progressive decline of standards" and the "inordinate
self-confidence of modern man." Their critiques of society are both diagnostic and prescriptive, particularly aiming to warn man not to give
his first and final allegiance to the God of Whirl, nor to the religion of
a cheap contemporaneousness, with its lusts for sensation, knowledge,
and power, and with its new gospel that, in Simone Weil's words, asserts that "matter is a machine for manufacturing the good."

As critics of their time, which remains our own in its steady rhythm
of disintegration, they saw their roles in the implicitly moral terms of
a critical mission. Each accepted the painful consequences that are a
part of any mission that taunts man with the message that in perilous
times he has an ever more perilous need of moral transcendence and
transfiguration. Each undertook a role that was supremely critical, didactic, and moral. Each demanded, and expected, of his contemporaries perhaps more than they were willing or able to give. A spiritual
renovation of mankind or a renewal of individual man is often better
arranged in theoretical contexts than in actual and discriminating fact.
Babbitt undoubtedly had this in mind when he said that modern man's
chief need was to be not less but more positive and critical in scrutiniz-
ing life-experience and life-value. Even to ask the right questions, he
said, is no small distinction. Babbitt's words, as they portend moral
action, help us to recall these words of Simone Weil: "If, as is only too
possible, we are to perish, let us see to it that we do not perish without
having existed."

What preeminently connects Irving Babbitt and Simone Weil in
their view of the world is an unceasing concern with the meaning of
man and with the destiny of mankind. The ultimate question of evil is
for both inescapable. To seek to avoid confronting "the wickedness of

human nature," as Aristotle puts it, constitutes a betrayal of man's moral responsibility. It is a decision to remain, as Simone Weil would sum it up, in a state of physical gravity, which pulls us away from God and makes us captives of the outer life with all its false idols. The struggle between good and evil is a constant of human existence, or as Babbitt expresses it: "Poets and reformers need not waste time speculating about the *origin* of evil, but they surely cannot be blind to the *fact* of evil." No less hesitantly Simone Weil avers, concerning the "civil war in the cave," that "we cannot contemplate without terror the extent of the evil which man can do and endure."

Man's encounter with evil demands careful discrimination between moral progress and material progress. For Babbitt this discrimination specially compels vigilance against "the temperamental view of life." The life of value is tied to the required standard of vital, of ethical and rational, control. It culminates in "a rest that comes through striving." "Men cannot come together in a common sympathy," he insists, "but only in a common discipline." To be sure, Babbitt's attitude towards evil was moral and humanistic, whereas Simone Weil's was moral and sacramental. Babbitt's attitude belongs to the category of religious empiricism, Simone Weil's to that of religious mysticism. The difference is obviously crucial. Babbitt believed in the imperative of moral discipline, which he saw as a defense against the dominance over modern man being steadily exerted by the power-centers of utilitarianism, empiricism, positivism, and liberalism. Evil not only can be detected but also must be faced in the maleficent shifting of standards, in the inclination, as Babbitt phrased it, "to eliminate the will to refrain and the inner effort it involves in favor of a mere outer working."

It is true that Simone Weil believed that life is filled with impossibility and absurdity and that man must aim for a higher purifying process of "decreation," of disincarnation. But it is also essential to recognize her firm grasp of social reality and necessity. "The world is the closed door. It is a barrier. And at the same time it is the way through," she maintains. Her reflections on and insights into social reality and necessity are as rigorous and unsentimental, as concentrated and analytical as any of Irving Babbitt's. To view Simone Weil as one curiously suffering from the vertigo of the absolute is to misunderstand and misrepresent her intuitive awareness of the ever destructive mechanisms of what she calls "the empire of might." Nothing better illustrates the depth of her view of a social order in disequilibrium, nor, indeed, better interrelates Irving Babbitt and Simone Weil as critics of modern society, than these words from her essay "Reflections on Quantum Theory":

> Everything is oriented towards utility, which nobody thinks of defining: public opinion reigns supreme, in the village of scientists as in the great nations. It is as though we had returned to the age of Protagoras and the Sophists, the age when the art of persuasion—whose modern equivalent is advertising slogans, publicity, propaganda meetings, the press, the cinema, and radio—took the place of thought and controlled the fate of cities and accomplished *coups d'état*.

Neither Babbitt's nor Simone Weil's social-political judgments have as yet found an audience. Today, as in the 1920s and 1930s, it remains fashionable to dismiss Babbitt's views as a mere sanction of New England and Republican prejudices. Simone Weil has not fared much better. Even if her life has intrigued the American intelligentsia, her religious and philosophical thought is often bifurcated or else subordinated to what critics label the "passions of the 'Red Virgin' " or "the mystery of Simone Weil"—the "passions" and "mystery" here undoubtedly connoting neuroticism or anomaly. Babbitt continues to be dogged by the nemesis of Edmund Wilson's celebrated, and calculated, remark that "the writings of the humanist[s] strike us with a chill even more mortal than that of reason." Simone Weil's nemesis has a more seignorial authority of tone and rejection in the person of none other than General Charles de Gaulle: "She's out of her mind," he said. Today's literary politicians of revolution reject Babbitt's critical achievement as the epitome of the "administrative" attitude toward life and thought. The continuing endorsement of the abusers of Babbitt's thought is, at the very least, symptomatic of the breakdown of standards in our civilization, the causes of which Babbitt himself mercilessly delineated. Reaction to Simone Weil's social and political writings underlines a now all-too-predictable conditioned reflex: they are condescendingly associated with her primarily spiritual message, and anything that is tinged with the word "spirit" is immediately suspect and expendable. "Dean Inge, one fancies, would approve of her metaphysics"—so we are told, the words, in tone and accent, containing a blanket reduction of Simone Weil's significance as a thinker whose belief in "the need for roots" presupposes exacting moral standards.

II

Not prophets of salvation, but prophets of utopian revolution (and resexualization), with their promises of an ecstatic entrance through the "gates of Eden," are today our real cultural heroes. The criteria of wisdom and the paths of meditation implicit in the sapiential criticism of Babbitt and Simone Weil are what the "imperial self" of our techno-logico-Benthamite society treats as luxury or nonsense. "The belief in moral responsibility," Babbitt declares, "must be based on a belief in the possibility of an inner working of some kind with reference to standards. The utilitarian . . . has put his main emphasis on outer working. The consequence of this emphasis, coinciding as it has with the multiplication of machines, has been the substitution of standardization for standards." Babbitt's words, or better his demand for moral austerity and intellectual seriousness, help to explain why he is the enemy in the eyes of those "geometricians in regard to matter" (to use Simone Weil's phrase), who, following a John Dewey or a Herbert Marcuse, promulgate the tenets of "organized intelligence," of "scientific method," of "technological application." It is precisely in their opposition to the modern theories of evolutionism, progressivism, and material secularism, in their uncompromising commitment to the "permanent things," and, hence, in their quest for a basic spiritual orientation in the human realm, that Babbitt and Simone Weil become allies. Such an alliance, always vulnerable despite its possession of the assurance of first principles, must inevitably confront the collected power of a solipsistic titanism, in short, that "permanent force of the world," to quote Eliot, "against which the spirit must always struggle."

Nowhere is this collision better seen than in two books that confront the permanent power of the world and that illuminate the human corollaries and moral consequences of such a struggle, Babbitt's *Democracy and Leadership* and Simone Weil's *The Need for Roots*. Both books belong to what Eliot calls "that prolegomena to politics which politicians seldom read, and which most of them would be unlikely to understand or to know how to apply." *Democracy and Leadership*, which was published in 1924, has behind it the lessons of the tragic happenings of the Great War: "An age [Babbitt states] that thought it was progressing towards Armageddon, suffered, one cannot help surmising, from some fundamental confusion in its notion of progress."

Democracy and Leadership is perhaps Babbitt's most vigorous, completing, and configurating synthesis of his thought; its dialectical integrity and relevance are incontrovertible. It asks fundamental questions that remain peculiarly unanswered by our "cosmic loafers," as he dubbed them. And it contains an unflinching indictment of the Baconian, Rousseauistic, and Machiavellian, that is the utilitarian, sentimental, and imperialistic, doctrines that have contributed to the most nagging modern problem—the absence of leaders with standards. The consequences and concomitants of this absence, he stresses, are disastrously identifiable in the drifting that characterizes ethics and politics; in the softness that is not civilization; in the expansive emotion that does not constitute the inner life. And what, in effect, is even worse than a resultant lack of vision is the prevalence of "sham vision"; pinpointing what remains one of the most shocking sanctimonies of our narcissist society, Babbitt observes: "Otherwise stated, what is disquieting about the time is not so much its open and avowed materialism as what it takes to be its spirituality." We have here a prophetic truth, the continuing applicability of which our contemporary "apostles of modernity," ever zealous in attaining the final "demystification of authority," would be pleased *not* to deny.

In *Democracy and Leadership* he pays close attention to what he calls "imperialism" not only in the social-political but also in the psychological sense. In this imperialism he sees man's centrifugal push for more power, whether in terms of Machiavelli's political naturalism, or of Hobbes's violent materialism, or of Bergson's creative evolutionism. The clear and present dangers of such a push—reliance on naked force, disregard of humility and wisdom, absence of inner discipline and of reverence for some ethical center or principle of oneness—stress for Babbitt the crisis of leadership and the impasse of democracy. Rousseau's "idyllic imagination," rather than Burke's "moral imagination," dictates the expansionist tendencies of modern society, and the law of the average becomes the divinity of the average. "One should . . . in the interests of democracy itself," Babbitt advises, "seek to substitute the doctrine of the right man for the doctrine of the rights of man." Civilization, he maintains, like the good life, is the process of something that must be deliberately willed, even as, so far as man is anything at all, it is the result of self-discipline.

Babbitt's diagnostic judgment concerning the very nature of leadership is undeniable: Lawmakers who themselves have no standards can hardly impose standards on others, and as he goes on to say: "The final reply to all doubts that torment the human heart is not some theory of conduct, however perfect, but the man of character." If for Babbitt there is a greater moral awareness to be gained from the "immediate data of consciousness," for others any intrinsic awareness that "life is an act of faith" has signified "nothing but negative behavior." Babbitt, we hear R. P. Blackmur grumbling, "struck down too much for discrimination, and he ignored too much for judgment." It is almost unnecessary to comment on the perverseness of this statement except to say that, for too long, it has gone unchallenged.

Simone Weil in *The Need for Roots* lays bare the foundations of modern secularism. No less than Babbitt, she believes that there can be neither the assigning of values except in terms of ends, nor a discovery of universal ultimate values except in terms of universal ultimate ends. And no less than Babbitt she insists that "of all the needs of the soul none is more vital than the Past,"—that Past which is the image "of eternal supernatural reality." Simone Weil completed *The Need for Roots* shortly before her death in 1943, while she was working for the Free French in London. Though conceived as a manual for the postwar renovation of France, it is concerned with the fate of Western society and specifically with the most pronounced sickness of that society: uprootedness, or deracination. Her most mature synthesis of her social-political and religious views, *The Need for Roots* singles out four obstacles separating modern man from a form of civilization that has organic worth: the false conception of greatness; the degradation of the sentiment of justice; the idolization of money; and the lack of religious inspiration. Above all it indicts the theory of evolutionism and the philosophy of progressivism, denouncing, on the one hand, the materialistic conception of a present that moves into the future and, on the other hand, affirming man's moral destiny as a transit from time into eternity. "Progress toward a lesser imperfection," she declares, "is not produced by the desire for a lesser imperfection. Only the desire for perfection has the virtue of being able to destroy in the soul some part of the evil that defiles it."

The Need for Roots proposes a code of obligations. In the very first sentence, we read: "The notion of obligations comes before that of rights, which is subordinate and relative to the former." These obliga-

tions, she shows, remain independent of conditions, transcend the
world, are eternal insofar as they are co-extensive with the eternal destiny of human beings. The list of obligations towards human beings as
such corresponds to the list of human needs analogous to hunger. The
soul, like the body, has needs that, when lacking, leave it in a famished
state. Among these needs Simone Weil lists *Order* as the first, noting
that in modern life, especially since 1789, incompatibility exists between obligations. She writes: "Whoever acts in such a way as to diminish it is an agent of order. Whoever, so as to simplify problems,
denies the existence of certain obligations has, in his heart, made a
compact with crime." Among other needs of the soul she includes
Duty, Obedience, Honor, and Hierarchy (that is, "the scale of responsibilities").

One must not theorize that in her social-political views Simone Weil
falls into a compassion that turns into "murderous pity." No one is
more aware that "force is sovereign here below" or that barbarism is
a permanent and universal phenomenon: "We are [she states] always
barbarous towards the weak unless we make an effort of generosity
which is as rare as genius." A study not only of *The Need for Roots* but
of her earlier social-political essays collected in the volume entitled *Oppression and Liberty* (1958), as well as of her most famous essay, the first
to appear in English, "*The Iliad*, Poem of Might" (1945), will confirm
the depth of her attempt "to discredit empty abstractions and analyse
concrete problems . . . in every domain of political and social life."
The thrust of her thought is contained in the last complete paragraph
that she ever wrote, found in her essay "Is There a Marxist Doctrine?"
There she applauds Marx's deep concern for human misery and his
conjoining belief that weakness can be a social mechanism for "produc-
ing paradise." Yet she also sees the final absurdity of his position when
she writes: "Marx accepted this contradiction of strength in weakness,
without accepting the supernatural which alone renders the contradiction valid."

Politically, Irving Babbitt and Simone Weil are obviously not in
vogue, and their political views are dismissed as being conservative and
illiberal. Babbitt is written off as a fascist. Simone Weil is categorized
as a non-political and even an anti-political eccentric. The liberal intellectual establishment promotes and maintains this political ostracism.
Any serious thinker who reminds us of moral obligations and duties is

seen as a threat to the secular city of the world. Any doctrine with rooted metaphysical principles pre-dating Marx's dialectical materialism or Freud's sexual materialism is scorned as antediluvian. Any emphasis on humanistic or on religious discipline, and particularly as this discipline condemns the proliferating obscenities of the contemporary life-style, is derided. The ideas of Irving Babbitt and of Simone Weil, hence, insofar as they present a potential threat to a reigning orthodoxy of enlightenment, are downgraded at every opportunity. Their insistence on the idea of human limitation is, in the end, what both brings them together and what also ignites the most hostile opposition. For Babbitt this emphasis on limitation, and on what he called "the inner check," revolves around his profound suspicion of the impulses of expansionism that create the Rousseauistic illusion of unchecked progress and perfectibility in the human realm. Ultimately, he believes, this makes for arrogance at every level of human thought and activity. For Simone Weil this emphasis on limitation revolves around her indictment of a secular, materialistic ethos that abrogates the idea of the Divine. Only God, she maintains, is perfect and it is for man to pursue the higher spiritual forms of perfection. Babbitt and Simone Weil affirm a priority and a standard of belief, a transcendent moral purpose, hard and uncompromising, that tests social and political life in the contexts of "permanent things."

Essentially, their political views are absolutist in the best and highest sense of the word. That is, the politics of each is rooted in metaphysical criteria, in ultimates that transcend the immediate and the expedient, the relativistic, the empirical. Babbitt's constitutes a politics of ethical vision. He demands strict adherence to a value-system informed by scrupulosity and insistent on an ongoing moral effort that challenges naturalism, impressionism, subjectivism, experimentation: in short that which resists the centrifugal constituents of modern political liberalism. His political attitude is, in this respect, old-fashioned and simple insofar as, first, last, and always, he views the value of all political thought in direct proportion to its adequacy in dealing with the problem of leadership. Political thought and political action must be judged in their inextricability. At the center of each there is to be identified either a positive, virtuous force or a negative, evil one. In this belief Babbitt sought to embrace and maintain a concentric standard of political thought and action. Politics was for him not so much a euphemistic art of the possible but rather a practicing discipline centered in the power of discriminating. In the political realm standards of discrimination attained their beginnings and their endings, as well as their definition and their universality, in unconditional moral contexts, nowhere better defined or summarized by Babbitt than in these words found in the concluding paragraphs of *Democracy and Leadership*: "The unit to which all things must finally be referred is not the State or humanity or any other abstraction, but the man of character. Compared with this ultimate reality, every other reality is only a shadow in the mist."

Babbitt's political emphasis is on an individual and not on a collective orientation. Politics cannot be absolved from the truths of the inner life. A political orientation that emerges through the abstraction from moral distinctions, Babbitt never tires of stressing, must lead to moral obtuseness on all levels of thought and action. It leads, that is, to an orientation, in reality a disorientation, that negates the causal nexus. For Babbitt a positive political orientation is one that affirms an abiding unity; a negative political orientation asserts flux and relativity. The politics of naturalism is perhaps another way of depicting this latter process. Babbitt could neither accept nor endorse the opinion of so many modern political theorists that since there are no permanent problems there are also no permanent alternatives. He judged the political realm, as he did the entire human realm, in relation to the opposition it offers between the principle of control and the expansive desires. The political problem which he confronted, and which he saw as the most serious confronting modern man, was one that he associated with the phenomenon of material efficiency concomitant with ethical inefficiency. In his view of modern politics Babbitt never failed to see and make connections, to take, in short, the far view. "When studied with any degree of thoroughness," he says, "the economic problem will be found to run into the political problem, the political problem in turn into the philosophical problem, and the philosophical problem itself to be almost indissolubly bound up at last with the religious problem."

Simone Weil's judgmental response to social organization is always that of a political moralist; she is particularly severe in her rejection of the uncritically accepted myth of revolution and of material progress. Inevitably she casts a cold eye not only on the mechanics of society but also on the exercise of political power, as one can see, respectively, in those two interrelated political tracts that, in their sustained development, meaning, and wholeness, have earned her a permanent place of importance among political theorists: "Reflections Concerning the Causes of Liberty and Social Oppression" (1934), the long essay now included in the volume entitled *Oppression and Liberty*, and *The Need for Roots*. (She considered her long essay as her "testament"; Albert Camus, who later served as a devoted editor of her posthumous works, praised it as being unequaled, since Marx's writings, in its social, political, and economic insights.)

In both these tracts the approach, the tone, the criteria of judgment disclose an impelling austerity and honesty—a critical disinterestedness "of the first magnitude," as Alain, Simone Weil's famous teacher, said—that are, in fact, crystallized in Spinoza's words of advice to a philosopher that she quotes as an epigraph to "Reflections Concerning the Causes of Liberty and Social Oppression": "With regard to human affairs, not to laugh, not to cry, not to become indignant, but to understand." With special reference to Marx, who, she felt, "arrived at a morality which placed the social category to which he belonged—that of professional revolutionaries—above sin," she goes on to stress that the phenomenon of revolution, like the phenomenon of power, is generally destructive. The former, emancipating not men but productive forces (as in Soviet Russia), leads to "religion of productive forces." And the latter phenomenon ultimately signals "the race for power [that] enslaves everybody, strong and weak alike." Together these two phenomena create "the mechanism of oppression," one of the primary and ineradicable "conditions of existence."

Simone Weil saw the social machine as leading to greater centralization and ultimately to a "blind collectivity." She especially decried the paradox of the process by which judgment of values is increasingly entrusted to material objects, to the power-machine. For within the automatisms of the social-political process she saw the invasion of modern civilization by an ever-increasing disorder. And for her this contributed to a "destructive disequilibrium." Her social and moral sensitivity was, in these crucial matters, particularly keen: "Human existence is so fragile a thing and exposed to such dangers that I cannot love without trembling." Modern technological society, she contends, accepts material progress too easily and complacently, ignoring the conditions at the cost of which it occurs.

Her assessment of the whole of modern thought, since the Renaissance, is tough and unsentimental in exposing what she terms "vague aspirations towards a utopian civilization." Diagnostic insight characterizes her penetration into what has become increasingly the thought—the great liberal illusion—behind the belief in the triumph of mechanisms of matter. This belief, she insists, reduces life to mere instrumentality. Now, as we are nearing the end of the second millennium, what Simone Weil says in the following words has a validity that is incontrovertible in its relevance of meaning as a counter-prophecy to Marx's millennial vision: "The very being of man is nothing else but a perpetual straining after an unknown good. And the materialist is a man. That is why he cannot prevent himself from ultimately regarding matter as a machine for manufacturing the good."

III

It will be said that Babbitt would have disapproved of Simone Weil on the same intellectual basis that he disapproved of "the tremendous spiritual romanticism" of Saint Augustine. It will be said also that he would have been sharply critical of the mystical essence of her thought, viewing it as an excess of "metaphysical illusion" or a form of postponement and procrastination. Her eschatological concepts of "gravity and grace," of "waiting for God," of "the love of God and affliction" would have seemed unduly ascetical, even morbid, to one who believed in the complete moral responsibility and effort of the individual. Undoubtedly, too, in some aspects of her life he would have detected signs of effusive self-expression—her early left-wing activities like picketing and refusing to eat more than did French workers on relief; her experiences as a factory worker and as a farmhand; her brief service as a member of an anarchist training unit in the Spanish Civil War.

For Babbitt, in whom, as Paul Elmer More remarked, "the immobility of his central ideas" was a monolithic characteristic, Simone Weil would have revealed a mode of sensibility that tended to separate his humanism as much from her Platonic sensibility as from emotional romanticism. Even in their study of Oriental religious thought their antithetical preferences are telling: Babbitt preferred the Pāli language and the Buddhist sacred texts stressing adherence to the laws. This choice is crystallized in these words from the *Dhammapada*, Buddha's Sermon on the Mount, which Babbitt embraced and honored: "Work our your own salvation with diligence."

Simone Weil preferred the Sanskrit language and the *Upanishads*, with their speculative and mystical thought, which, she said, when linked to the thought of Hellenism, of Stoicism, of Christianity, contributed to one identifying truth. It is her recognition of this overarching spiritual truth that inspires this entry in one of her notebooks: "There is no attitude of greater humility than to wait in silence and patience. . . . It is the patience which transmutes time into eternity. Total obedience to time obliges God to grant eternity."

In any case, it will be asserted that Babbitt would have found in Simone Weil some of the ambivalences that he perceived in George Sand. In particular, Simone Weil's obedience to the promptings of the soul would have been to him as excessive as George Sand's to the promptings of the heart. This reference to George Sand is at the same time helpful in establishing a positive connection between Babbitt and Simone Weil. For in George Sand, Babbitt did finally find cause for hope. He noted that towards the end of her career she was able to rescue the principle of belief from false ideals and to have a faith that outlived shocks of disillusion. In an age of great enlightenment and little light, Babbitt noted with satisfaction, George Sand managed to sustain "the contemplative sense wherein resides invincible faith." The same kind of interiorizing virtue he would have finally saluted in Simone Weil, who, dying at the age of thirty-four, never had the advantages of George Sand's longevity.

Babbitt would have seen in Simone Weil a commitment to the discipline of ideas, as well as an intellectual honesty and a moral realism, that he believed to be indispensable to one who addresses oneself to the problems of the modern world. "The man who is spiritually strenuous," Babbitt writes in *Rousseau and Romanticism* (1919), "has entered upon the 'path'. . . . Progress on the path may be known by its fruits— negatively by the extinction of the expansive desires . . . , positively by an increase in peace, poise, centrality." Simone Weil's possession of the contemplative sense and her example of spiritual strenuousness would have earned her a revered place among Babbitt's "masters of modern French criticism." In her he would have discovered a defeat of Rousseauistic enthusiasm, an indictment of the variable and impres-

sionistic element in literature and thought, a critical check against the
centrifugal elements of originality and genius, and, above all, a defense
of the belief that individualism starts not from rights but from obligations.

The Need for Roots is both a vindication and an updating of Democracy
and Leadership. The false values that Simone Weil focuses on in history,
in politics, in art, in religion, and in science are those that Babbitt
warned against. The spirit of truth that Simone Weil finds absent from
the whole of human thought is of a piece with that false intellectual
pride that Babbitt saw displacing the order of moral character. For
him, as later for Simone Weil, the historical actualities of this displacement impel reflection, or as he writes: "A consideration of man's ignorance and blindness as they are revealed on a vast scale in the facts of
history gives a positive basis to humility." No two books could be
more in agreement with respect to the cumulative effects unleashed
upon man and society through the union of material efficiency and ethical and moral unrestraint. No two critics of modern society could be
more in agreement with respect to the scientism that, subjecting man
and verifying values according to the "law of thing," inspires divine
discontent and romantic rootlessness, and delivers man into the hands
of a blind collectivity.

Modern scientific materialism, which Babbitt connected with "the
whole fatal circle of naturalism," has become identified with diminish-
ing spiritual effort and increasing spiritual sloth. This form of science,
which indicates for Simone Weil a dislodgement of religious contemplation, is for Babbitt an arrogant imperialism. It leads to what Babbitt
calls "the efficient megalomaniac" and to that use of science which, in
Burke's phrase, seeks to "improve the mystery of murder." It was to
lead, Simone Weil concluded, directly to Hitler, in whom some of our
own features are enlarged. Both concluded that what we build, in the
long run, is an impregnable social machine. In effect, collective
thought, collective measures, collective actions, collective mediocrity
underline the dispossession of mind and body in the modern world.
"The powerful means are oppressive," says Simone Weil, "the non-
powerful remain inoperative."

In their critical opinions Babbitt and Simone Weil disclose a moral
centrality uncompromising in formulation and application. First principles and, equally, principles of order were, for both, transcendent

principles of discovered truth: and ultimate criteria of judgment. Neither one could ever separate the creative imagination from the moral imagination. "I believe in the responsibility of the writers of recent years for the disaster of our time," Simone Weil declares—a declaration that conveys the intrinsic tone of moral severity in her critical responses. Indeed, she was consistently unsparing in her criticism of men of letters who "introduce into literature a Messianic afflatus wholly detrimental to its artistic purity." Like Babbitt she denounced the romantic attitude that has invaded and captured so much of the province of the modern literary imagination.

"Everybody is becoming tinged with eleutheromania," writes Babbitt in *The New Laokoon* (1910), "taken up with his rights rather than with his duties, more and more unwilling to accept limitations." His words here anticipate in a remarkable way the moral-critical standards that Simone Weil held to with astonishing tenacity. Babbitt in his time and Simone Weil in hers—and both were quintessentially of their time—subscribed to the moral view of the literary imagination as being successful according to the degree in which it affirms the "law of units, measure, purpose." For both, the excrescence of the romantic outlook and temper, impressionism and expressionism, for example, sabotaged the idea of value. Romanticism constituted, in short, a debauch, a crippling lapse of discipline, whether as a discipline of "humane concentration," in Babbitt's critical vein, or of an "absolute attention," in Simone Weil's.

In their critical determinations Babbitt and Simone Weil returned to the *exemplaria graeca* for the paradigms of what the New Humanist calls "vital unity, vital measure, vital purpose." The ancient Greeks, he maintained, possessed humane standards, held flexibly, and effected mediation between the One and the Many. To be sure, Greek civilization, Babbitt admitted, disclosed the same problem of unrestraint that he believed was pervasive in modern society and that he described as the "barbaric violation of the law of measure." But he also revered in Hellenism the power to triumph over this problem through a combination of "exquisite measure" with "perfect spontaneity." Through such a combination man was at once "thoroughly disciplined and inspired."

Babbitt and Simone Weil were to condemn artists who promote the cult of personality, who usurp the function of spiritual guidance, gen-

erate easy morals, and tolerate baseness. In the end such artists violate
the literary-critical catechesis that Simone Weil underlines in one of her
finest essays, "Beyond Personalism": "The man for whom the development of personality is all that counts has totally lost all sense of the
sacred. . . . So far from its being his person, what is sacred in a human
being is the impersonal in him." Going even beyond Babbitt, she
viewed the Gospels as the last and finest expression of Greek genius, as
the *Iliad* is its first. In such a modern literature she, like Babbitt, saw a
diminution of "strength of soul" and capitulation to self-deception.
And, like Babbitt, she refused to exempt literature from the categories
of good and evil. Both thus emphasized a transcending sapiential order
of art, whether as "the responsibility of writers" or as "morality and
literature." Babbitt believed that "the problem of beauty is inseparable
from the ethical problem." Simone Weil believed that art should give
insight into moral world-order and resist the seductive pathologies of
the modern age.

These two critics of twentieth-century culture and society remind us
of moral and critical standards. One of the extraordinary qualities that
they share, and one found only in the greatest thinkers, is the ability to
reflect the whole of their work in each of its parts. Babbitt examined
"mind in the modern world" dialectically, from within a university
purview. Simone Weil, also a teacher—and, like Babbitt, no doubt a
great and fearless teacher—chose to examine the soul of the world,
choosing to enter at every available opportunity the cockpit of strife.
Her choice was hastened and heightened by the advancing crises of civilization that Babbitt detected as early as 1908, with the publication of
his first book, *Literature and the American College*. Theirs was not so much
a search for general principles of order as it was a demanding confirmation of these. Moral toughness permeates their life and thought. Stuart
Sherman's complaint that "the path Babbitt asks us to tread is only
wide enough for one" is echoed in the complaints against Simone Weil.

Her contention that "real genius is nothing else but the supernatural
virtue of humility in the domain of thought," recalls for us a theory of
literature that Babbitt relentlessly asserted in the totality of his writings. Her message that "the glossy surface of our civilization hides a
real intellectual decadence" is Babbitt's. Her statement that "in every
sphere, we seem to have lost the elements of intelligence: the ideas of
limit, measure, proportion, relation, compassion, contingency, inter-

dependence, interrelations of means and ends," epitomizes the impelling meaning of the critical mission of Irving Babbitt. Her insistence that "nothing concerns human life so essentially, for every man at every moment, as good and evil. When literature becomes deliberately indifferent to the opposition of good and evil, it betrays its function and forfeits all claim to excellence," is that insistence for which Babbitt has long been condemned by the philistines who continue to view him as a "suzerain of an elite-university literature department." Her charge that "culture . . . is an instrument manipulated by professors for manufacturing more professors, who in turn, will manufacture still more professors" is precisely Babbitt's indictment of that specialization that he equated with overemphasis and with a loss of a sense of proportion.

Babbitt has been called a "New England Saint" and Simone Weil a "Saint of the Churchless." In their perception of the world and in their conception of the meaning of life there is much to be found that endorses these honoring designations. Yet there is still another path of sympathy that they travelled. It marks a still higher ideational parallelism, and one that instances the highest point of the convergence of their thought. It relates to a definitive ethos, with its complex of civilized ideas and habits, its embodied moral beliefs and certitudes, its reverent apprehension of a spiritual unity and discipline of order, as well as an order of reality with a standard of value. Babbitt and Simone Weil labored to save this ethos from a modern world that, in its Promethean secularism, proclaims "the end of the modern world." Babbitt's moral centrality was born of earnestness, Simone Weil's, of grace—surely compatible and complementary centralities. Each spoke out bravely regarding the modern experience of affliction and shipwreck.

Men, Babbitt declares, "tend to come together in proportion to their intuitions of the One. . . . We *ascend* to meet." And Simone Weil insists: "Faith is above all the conviction that the good is one." As critics they refined their world view in the face of the active hostility of the times in which they lived—the hostility that, then and now, characterizes *la trahison des clercs*. Irving Babbitt and Simone Weil resisted and challenged the vaunting powers of betrayal and disbelief with a conviction and a vigor arising from the affirmation of a moral and spiritual ethos that achieves permanence among impermanent things. Their example, both as presentation and as interpretation, testifies to a double mission: the critical pursuit of truth and the search for salvation.

II

Epistolary Encounters

The letters of an imaginative artist can help to explain the birth and the growth of his artistic consciousness. They can reveal the undisguised workings of his mind, the reaches of his intellectual comprehension, the interior realm of his psyche. Letters can communicate the elemental immediacy of an artist's thought and art. They can help in discovering a writer's impelling pattern of thinking and working; in providing hints, that is to say, as to the ways in which his vision first manifests itself and progresses. Letters of men of genius give clues, record reactions, clarify and amplify the process of vision. They also disclose a writer's critical process, which plays no small part in the maturation of his creative vision. The force of insight, the intuitive perception of human meaning and truths, the enduring formative power of overwhelming impressions, the discriminations of a fertile mind and a creative imagination: these intrinsic facets, indispensable to a writer's rendered vision of man and his world, can be identified, even in their rawest forms and fragments of enunciation, in his letters. A writer's letters thus contain a running commentary with regard to his immediate personal situation, whereby he comments existentially and, above all, spontaneously on his world, on his time, on himself and others, on his public and most private concerns. Such letters contain the infinite reverberations of internal dialogue.

4

Henry James and Paradigms of Character

I

Reading the letters of Henry James is always a civilizing experience. One is the better for such an experience as one comes variously and gratefully into contact with the virtues of reverence, loyalty, courage, kindness. James discloses these virtues in relation to others, to his time, to his view of the world, and for us they become standards, paradigms, of character by which to measure and judge our own approximation of civilized life. Indeed, in James's disclosure of these virtues, and in one's response to them, even to their *données*, there is ignited a communion of sensibility, a rare and delicious process.

In the letters written in 1883–1895, James's "middle years," one watches, with amazement and awe, a genius of observation, discretion, and taste in his double pursuit of art and public life.[1] Refinement and dignity never fail him; critical intelligence is ever at his command; and the deep spiritual and human essentials that impel and shape vision are, in short, never absent from James's artistic existence, from his "magic spring," as Joseph Conrad imaged his friend's achievement. All these virtues, all these strengths and abundances of commitment and purpose, thrive in James's letters. Magnanimous and vivifying in the feelings they inspire and the lessons they impart, his letters illustrate quality of character as moral impulse and consciousness. Where other great letter writers communicate harshness and discord, as in the case of Thomas Carlyle ("the prince of letter writers," James called him), or tension and impatient passion, as in the case of D. H. Lawrence, James communicates order and control, proportion and perspective; humaneness, above all.

In reading these letters, each detailing impressions, observations, emotions, griefs, loyalties, and each chronicling the days, events and persons illuminating, crowding, and pressing a writer's life, one is astonished by the energy with which James fulfills his commitments in the daily business of his work and interpersonal relations. This prodigious, and meticulous, energy belies the ponderous and sacerdotal presence, the portentous massiveness, that one usually associates with the famous portrait of James by John Singer Sargent or with the caricature by Max Beerbohm. The seriousness and importance with which James meets his obligations, personal and professional, exhibit *le trait juste* of one who is concerned not with the job of "getting on" in the world—that most philistine of human habits—but with celebrating (in F. R. Leavis' apt phrase) "the living principle." To all his life-concerns and life-relations James was to give of himself completely. Neither opportunist nor shirker he exemplifies by his words and actions, sensitively and discriminatingly, the truth of what Josiah Royce defines in these memorable words: ". . . all those duties which we have learned to recognize as the fundamental duties that every man owes to every man, are to be rightly interpreted as special instances of loyalty to loyalty."[2]

That for James loyalty meant remaining true to responsibility exemplifies a virtue upon which life rests. "Yours faithfully and constantly" were words with which he often, and characteristically, closed his letters. However favorable or unfavorable the circumstances of life and fate, James's grasp and affirmation of the virtues as forms of moral life never wavered. In his letters it is the voice of "the civilized man" that one hears and comprehends—and admires. No recipient of a letter, regardless of position in life, is ever slighted, and on each James bestows his greatest intentness and most generous interpretation, the very qualities that gave to his genius and work a perfect distinctness of vision. No letter capitulates to the ugly or the devious or the dishonest. A judging intellect and a delicate investigative understanding pervade and permeate James's letters, satisfying, too, that moral criterion to which he responded, and possessed, in his unfailing belief that "One has to be *equal* to things."

The letters reveal cumulatively the measure of James as man and writer, and that measure is ultimately a virtuous one. The ancient Greeks singled out excellence and nobility of character with the word *aristeia*, which connotes both heroic and moral value. This *aristeia* glows in the beauty and symmetry of James's own person. "Character—character is what he has!," words that he applied to Robert Louis Stevenson, can be applied to James himself.[3] The classical and not the sentimental temper prompts such an encomium. That is, the Hellenic, more specifically the Sophoclean, quality of character, of poetic vision and critical insight, of instinct for what is good, is what inheres in and stamps James's presence in the letters. One comes to revere James in the same way that the ancients came to revere their greatest tragedian. For no less than Sophocles, Athenian gentleman of the fifth century B.C., James, civilized man of the modern age, transmits a note of human sympathy and comprehension that, incidentally, makes H. G. Wells—the Wells who claimed that James was a novelist of "nothingness," a "leviathan retrieving pebbles,"—appear the vulgar "satyr-cupid" of Fabian socialism that he was.[4] (Wells correctly consigned his worth when, in 1938, he wrote his own epitaph: "He was clever but was not clever enough.")[5]

Clearly, in his personal life and relations James left a large impression of majesty, beauty, and greatness. "He is beyond words. I cannot speak about him," the novelist Hugh Walpole said of his friend and encourager.[6] "The only thing is to be there," we hear James pleading, "to wait, to sympathise, to help if necessary."[7] His words (spoken to a young friend, A. C. Benson) could serve as the epigraph to all his letters. Even in the midst of the most unpromising or distressing situations James sustains his courage of faith by a steady commitment to what he thinks he has to do: "I have plenty of work, thank heaven, in view—I say thank heaven because I don't on the whole tire of it, but find it the indispensable movement that keeps up vital heat."

During this period of "vital heat," James wrote such major novels as *The Bostonians* (1886), *Princess Casamassima* (1886), *The Tragic Muse* (1890), as well as an assortment of tales. But it was also a period of profound disappointments for James. Financial matters triggered some of these disappointments. Though James was prolific and though his writings were always published, he was never in his lifetime a popular and critically acclaimed writer and his books had "depressingly small" sales. (From the *Bostonians* and the *Princess*, he confessed to William Dean Howells, he "expected so much and derived so little.") Insofar as he had to make his living as a writer he had to depend on his royalties; he had no private fortune, it should be remembered, having turned over to his invalid sister, Alice, the income from his legacy. One will detect in the letters that, beneath his persistence and confidence, James was often anxious as to how to reconcile the demands of economic necessity and artistic excellence. Still, his life-style, as instanced by an active social life, recurrent travels on the Continent, the fashionable London flats in which he lived, and the other material comforts generally associated at the time with a man of his station and reputation, was not too adversely affected by financial importunities. His ordered bachelor life no doubt worked in his favor in this respect. In any case the severe financial deprivations that one sees stalking a Dostoevsky, a Conrad, or a Lawrence do not loom large in James's life.

In all things he remained a master of control and form—and phrase. (Even when close to death itself, in the first days of his last illness, James said, describing an attack of angina pectoris: " 'So it's come at last'—I said to myself—'the distinguished thing!' ") Possibly one could even theorize that James's attention to finances was a way of covering up—artists, he declared, are "well-advised to cover their tracks"—the deep hurt to his authorial pride resulting from his awareness of the absence of public and critical recognition of his achievement. The "serious writer," he nevertheless claimed, should not be bothered by "the imbecility of babyish critics," "should move in a diviner air." But the deeper psychological import of these strictures is made much clearer when read in the light of an author, of "an old and honourable reputation," having to confront "the hostile majority" as Ortega y Gasset has termed it, that found James's writings not only unpopular but also anti-popular. The line of descent, as we know to our horror, from "the awkward age" to the age of the rabble is irreversible.

James's concern with the craft of fiction, with the principles of writing and the critical function as a whole, radiates with integrity in his letters. His advice to Vernon Lee, "Cool first—write afterwards. Morality is hot—but art is icy!" epitomizes a major Jamesian literary judgment. Moral concern, he stresses with an ascetic purity, should not be confused with moral passion: exaggerations, overstatements, tactless insistences should be restrained. Life for the novelist should mean moral and intellectual and spiritual life, "not the everlasting vulgar chapters of accidents, the dead rattle and rumble, which rise from the mere surface of things." Though much admiring Stevenson's novel *Catriona* (that "so reeks and hums with genius that there is no refuge for the desperate reader but in straightforward prostration"), he goes on to observe with critical acuteness, even starkness, "The one thing I miss in the book is the note of *visibility*—it subjects my visual sense, my *seeing* imagination, to an almost painful underfeeding." Elsewhere, and no doubt having in mind the newspaper reviewers of his day, he remarks with prophetic relevance, "To tell the truth, I can't help thinking that we already talk too much about the novel, about and around it, in proportion to the quantity of it having any importance that we produce."

Characteristically, when invited by a London newspaper, the *Pall Mall Gazette*, to send his list of the hundred best books, James (along with Matthew Arnold), refused to do so: "I have but few convictions on this subject—and they may indeed be resolved into a single one, which however may not decently be reproduced in the columns of a newspaper and which for reasons apart from its intrinsic value (be that great or small) I do not desire to see made public. It is simply that the reading of the newspaper is *the* pernicious habit, and the father of all idleness and laxity." Characteristically, too, he shunned literary gamesmanship; declining Edmund Gosse's invitation to attend the funeral of Walter Pater, James wrote: "But I was deterred by considerations—that of my very limited acquaintance with Pater, my non-communication with him for so long, and above all by (what I suppose would be) the compact Oxfordism of it all; in which I seem to feel myself to have no place."

The years 1890–1895 brought further disappointment—"the humiliations and vulgarities and disgust, all the dishonour and chronic insult incurred"—as he devoted slavish efforts to the writing of plays. "My books don't sell," he wrote to Stevenson, "and it looks as if my plays might. . . . I feel as I had at last *found* my form—my real one—that for which pale fiction is an ineffectual substitute." The dramatization in 1891 of his novel, *The American* (1877), in the provinces in England and Ireland had some early successes. But the London production, after lasting seventy nights, failed, "with circumstances of public humiliation," as James remarked. "The papers slated it without mercy, and it was—by several of its interpreters—wretchedly ill-played; also it betrays doubtless the inexperience of its author and suffers damnably from the straight-jacket of the unscenic book." Undoubtedly, even though he denounced the "saw-dust and orange-peel" of the theatre, he was challenged by a need to master the dramatic form itself. "The whole odiousness of the thing lies in the connection between the drama and the theatre. The one is admirable in its interest and difficulty, the other loathsome in its conditions." Yet James innerly knew that, in laying down his "critical pen" and in turning to drama, he was doing so only temporarily, just long enough "to dig out eight or ten rounded masterpieces and make withal enough money to enable me to retire in peace and plenty for the unmolested business of a *little* supreme writing." He wrote a number of plays but only *The American* and *Guy Domville*, which was written in 1893 but not produced until 1895, were seen on the stage. Of this latter play, with its lack of a "happy ending," James was aware of its unsuitability as "theatre-stuff," or as he was to declare in words that bring to mind Ortega's warning, "Whenever the new Muses present themselves, the masses bristle":[8]

> I have a general strong impression of my constitutional inability to (even in spite of intense and really abject effort) *realise* the sort of simplicity that the promiscuous British public finds its interest in—much more, after this indispensable realisation, to *achieve* it. Even when I think I am dropping most diplomatically to the very rudiments and stooping, with a vengeance, to conquer, I am as much "out of it" as ever, and far above their unimaginable heads.

Guy Domville appeared for the first time at the St. James Theatre, London, on January 5, 1895. "Thrown into the arena—like a little white Christian Virgin to the lions and tigers," as James said, the play ran exactly a month—and then vanished, to be replaced by Oscar Wilde's *The Importance of Being Earnest*. In the production of this play James worked "with unremitting zeal and intensity," with an implicit honesty and habit of discrimination, which "the roughs" in the gallery, as James wrote in "disappointment and depression" to his brother William, rewarded with "hoots and jeers and catcalls" and the "papers," for the most part, with "ill-natured and densely stupid and vulgar" notices. The entire spectacle, "one of the most detestable incidents of my life," filled James "with horror for the abysmal vulgarity and brutality of the theatre and its regular public." "The stupid public is the big public and the perceptive one the small, and the small doesn't suffice to keep a thing afloat."

But neither "the shipwreck of *Guy Domville*" nor the "roars . . . of the howling mob," phenomena that made James terribly aware of "evil days," robbed him of his great resources of "courage and patience." A new resolution and a reaffirmation of his vocation as a poet-novelist— *The Awkward Age* (1899), *The Sacred Fount* (1901), *The Wings of the*

Dove (1902), *The Ambassadors* (1903), *The Golden Bowl* (1904) remained, after all, to be written—stirred his imagination and strengthened his determination not to surrender to the *ressentiment* of the masses or to fall into "traps, abysses and heart-break." To his notebooks, then, James confided: "I take up my *own* pen again—the pen of all my old unforgettable efforts and sacred struggles. To myself—today—I need say no more. Large and full and high the future still opens. It is now indeed that I may do the work of my life. And I will."[9]

Death is another unflinching enemy of James during these years, and repeated cries of grief, *de profundis*, echo in the letters. The elegiac tone that he strikes (and accentuates in his parabolic tale "The Altar of the Dead" [1895], which, it is claimed, can be thought of with *Lycidas* and *In Memoriam*) is often soul-shaking in its emotional reaches and exquisite in its poetry. He duly records and laments, and yet comments incisively on, the loss of relatives, friends, inspirers, supporters. Sympathy and tenderness coalesce warmly and genuinely in his expressions of sorrow and also mitigate necrolatrous and melancholy elements.

Of the death, in 1883, of his younger brother Garth Wilkinson, James writes: "But it was a dark end for such a gentle, genial, sociable soul for whom the world should have been easy, as he was easy (too easy) for it and for everything." Of his friend James Russell Lowell's death, in 1891, he says: "My soul is grieved indeed for dear old J. R. L. and for the painful, darkened, unhelpable *end*—from which, always, he seemed to me—as I knew him and saw him—personally far." Of the death, in Samoa, in 1894, of Stevenson, he states with unabashed feelings: "What can one think, or utter or dream, save of this ghastly extinction of the beloved R. L. S.? It is too miserable for cold words— it's an absolute desolation. . . . One feels how one cared for him— what a place he took; and as if suddenly *into* that place there had descended a great avalanche of ice. . . . He lighted up a whole side of the globe and was in himself a whole province of one's imagination." Of the death, in Italy, in 1894, of Constance Fenimore Woolson, an American writer with whom he had a close friendship, he reports: "I had known Miss Woolson for many years and was extremely attached to her—she was the gentlest and tenderest of women, and full of intelligence and sympathy. But she was a victim to morbid melancholia, and one's friendship for her was always half anxiety."

James's perceptive solicitude and refinement of delicacy reveal an
unimpeachable sincerity of character and make completely justifiable
Edith Wharton's words of tribute to him: "We who knew him well
know how great he would have been if he had never written a
line."[10]

Of his fictive hero George Stransom, in "The Altar of the Dead,"
James says: "He had perhaps not had more losses than most men, but
he had counted his losses more; he hadn't seen death more closely, but
had in a manner felt it more deeply." These words describe James himself and are crystallized in his letters telling of the death in 1892 of his
gifted but neurasthenic sister Alice. Alice James first joined her brother
in England in 1884, staying in separate lodgings until her death. Increasingly, however, he assumed a responsibility for her welfare, for
which she was to be deeply appreciative as this entry in her remarkable
diary shows: "I have given him endless care and anxiety but notwithstanding this and the fantastic nature of my troubles I have never seen
an impatient look upon his face or heard an unsympathetic or misunderstanding sound cross his lips."[11] (James himself counted his sister's
presence in his life as a great blessing: ". . . she contributed constantly,
infinitely to the interest, the consolation, as it were, in disappointment
and depression, of my own existence.")

There is no more agonizing letter than that in which he gives his
brother William a first-hand account of Alice's death from cancer.
James renders the details of the death-drama—"They were infinitely
pathetic and, to me, most unspeakable hours"—with pathos and consummate artistry, bringing to mind (even in some of the astonishing
similarities) what is perhaps the most vivid scene of death in the modern novel, D. H. Lawrence's description of the mother's death in his
first great novel, *Sons and Lovers* (1913). Epistolary art certainly attains
a dramatic apex in this excerpt from James's letter that portrays Alice's
end:

> Her face then seemed in a strange, dim, touching way, to become clearer.
> I went to the window to let in a little more of the afternoon light upon it
> (it was a bright, soundless Sunday), and when I came back to the bed she
> had drawn the breath that was not succeeded by another. . . . I have sat
> many hours in the still little room in which so many months of her final
> suffering were compressed, and in which she lies as the very perfection of
> the image of what she had longed for years, and at the last with pathetic

intensity, to be. She looks most beautiful and noble—with *all* of the august expression that you can imagine—and with less, than before, of the
ghastly emaciation of those last days.

Taking "the silent roll-call of the Dead" was not, of course, James's
final occupation, or preoccupation. Rather, he addressed himself, with
the same gravity, consistency, and dignity that he admired in Sainte-
Beuve, to forging "some expression of a total view of the world" and
acquiring a comprehensive vision of things through "the wear and tear
of living and talking and observing." His letters amply corroborate
both the ambition and the process of the creative and critical spirit. "I
have my head, thank God, full of visions," he wrote in his notebooks.[12]
His dedication to what he called the exercise of his art was complete
and exceptional. But James learned to have no illusions about his "popularity" as a writer, even as he had no illusions regarding the reconciliation of possibility and fact. "Mr. Henry James, great artist and great
historian, never attempts the impossible," Conrad iterates.[13]

James's dedication to his solitary profession was inviolable: "One
must go one's way and know what one's about and have a general plan
and a private religion. . . . One has always a 'public' enough if one has
an audible vibration—even if it should only come from one's self." He
adhered bravely to standards of art and civilization, and of virtue and
wisdom, ever assaulted by "commonness" and "mediocrity." For him
this adherence, necessitating "Personal renunciations" and "heroic sac-
rifice," constituted "an act of life." "It all takes doing—and I *do*,"[14] he
was to admonish a disillusioned Henry Adams, who had bleakly confessed of his own work that "All I could prove was change."[15] To be
sure, no less than Adams, James was utterly aware of "this terrible hur-
rying age and roaring place" and "the awful doom of general dishu-
manisation." "Criticism is of an object density and puerility—it
doesn't exist—it writes the intellect of our race too low," he wrote of
cultural and intellectual conditions of his, *and* our, time.

To the end he remained a "lover and interpreter of the fine amenities,
of brave decisions and generous loyalties" (to quote words inscribed
on the James memorial tablet in the Chelsea Old Church in London).
He and his work, in their reciprocal totality, contain inexhaustible paradigms of character and remind us of how much we are in need of those
"artists of consumption," as Max Scheler describes them, who can

guide our uncertain taste and define and defend the hierarchy of values
and of men.

II

Between 1895, the year in which his play *Guy Domville* failed in London, precipitating Henry James's feeling that he had fallen upon evil
days and was not "in the least *wanted*, anywhere or by any one," and
1916, the year in which he died, James enacted his own Book of
Changes.[16] He was to purchase a typewriter in 1897, for example, and
start to dictate his writings to a typist: "The use of my hand, always
difficult, has become impossible to me; and since I am reduced to dictation, this form of dictation is best. May its distinctiveness make up for
its indirectness," he confided to Grace Norton. He was to leave London
and to move into Lamb House, Rye, Sussex, in 1898:

> I marked it [Lamb House] for my own two years ago at Rye—so perfectly
> did it [he writes to Mrs. William James], the first instant I beheld it, offer
> the solution of my long unassuaged desire for a calm retreat. . . . It is the
> very calmest and yet cheerfulist that I could have dreamed—in the little
> old, cobble-stoned, grass-grown, red-roofed town, on the summit of its
> mildly pyramidal hill and close to its noble old church—the chimes of
> which will sound sweet in my goodly old red-walled garden.

He was, in the spring of 1900, to shave off his beard, which he had
worn since the Civil War. As he announced to his brother William: "I
have totally shaved off my beard, unable to bear any longer the in-
creased hoariness of its growth." He was to begin a series of intimate
friendships with gifted young men like Hendrik C. Andersen, Rupert
Hart-Davis, Jocelyn Persse, and Hugh Walpole: "I not only love him—
I *love* to love him," he said of Persse. He was to return to the United
States in 1904–1905, traveling widely and becoming the "restless analyst" of the "American scene." "Out of the midst of *this* unalterable or
incalculable Democracy," he writes, "I don't, I confess, at all ardently
democratise! The U.S.A. are prodigious, interesting, appalling."

During the first year of the Great War of 1914–1918 James was to
assist the war effort by working with Belgian Relief, visiting the
wounded in hospitals and supporting the American Volunteer Ambu-
lance Brigade: "Horrors encompass us, I mean above all in the limitless
loss of all our most splendid young life, the England of the future; but

one seems to make head against them a little in any definite deed done in mitigation of the actual woe," he writes on June 17, 1915. He was to become a British subject on July 26, 1915: "Your good letter makes me feel that you will be interested to know that since 4:30 this afternoon I have been able to say *Civis Britannicus sum!*" he writes to Edmund Gosse. And during his final illness he was to be awarded the Order of Merit by King George V on New Year's Day, 1916. After Lord Bryce brought the insignia of this order to his bedside, James said to his housemaid, "Turn off the light so as to spare my blushes."

James's Book of Changes was to include, then, what he himself termed his "afternoon of life," that is, the twilight phase. The visionary genius, the moral confidence, the personal generosity that identify James's paradigms of character remain, in his last years, untarnished. But one detects in the elegiac mood and tone of the letters written during his last years a distinct troubledness, an underlying nervousness, an anxious solitariness and insecurity as James contemplates old age creeping up on him, undergoes serious and even mysterious illnesses, suffering them with "the last acuteness," duly receives and mourns "the bulletins of the dead," and grimly resigns himself to his lack of popular or critical success. "I remain at my age . . . ," James laments in 1915, "and after my long career, utterly, insurmountably, unsaleable." But these anxieties do not finally defeat James the "passionate pilgrim"; do not fix him, bleakly and pitiably, to "the bench of desolation." In their own inimitable way his anxieties make him all the more aware of the need to preserve the order of civilization in all of its human drama: its sacred history, its great traditions, its spiritual glories, which he reveres and celebrates till the end when, inevitably, as James writes in the very last words of his last letter, "the pen drops from my hand."

The virtue of determination, ever a sturdy and steadfast quality in James's life and work, gives him, in the afternoon of life, the will to press on with his creative purposes and personal loyalties. Even in the midst of severe sickness, his periodic bouts "with the black devils of Nervousness, direst, damnedest demons, that ride me so cruelly and that I have perpetually to reckon with," James selflessly gives of himself not only to his literary commitments but also to his family and to his friends. His admirers are unsparing in their praise of the "Master": for Hugh Walpole, James is "by far the greatest man I have ever met"; for Joseph Conrad, "the most civilized of modern writers"; for A. C.

Benson, a man of "majesty, beauty, and greatness." Doubtlessly such praise could easily be equated with the expected hyperbole of catechumens who enter what James describes as "a temple of the old persuasion." In this connection Sir Almeric Fitzroy reminds us of the Jamesian mystique possibly contributing to the language of praise: "Henry James, anchorite and novelist, who has a hermitage at Rye, and there nurses in spacious reverie his spiritual enchantments, not seldom the fruit of sheer loneliness of soul."

But whatever the mystique or even the myth surrounding the great "anchorite and novelist," James discloses in his letters a deep concern for life outside of his own operative center, his so-called hermitage. Self-centeredness is for him a violation of being, or as he writes: "It takes at the best, I think, a great deal of courage and patience to live—but one must do everything to invent, to force open, that door of exit from mere immersion in one's own states." No less than the moral imagination, the moral virtues—truthfulness, gratitude, disinterestedness, understanding, unselfishness—elicit his highest allegiance. His lifelong commitment to standards of discrimination, however fierce and uncompromising it was, never diminished either his acts of magnanimity or his gestures of encouragement, which he gave with generosity. Nowhere are his words more heartfelt than when he writes to Joseph Conrad concerning the latter's *Mirror of the Sea* (1906):

> I read you as I listen to rare music—with deepest depths of surrender, and out of those depths I emerge slowly and reluctantly again, to acknowledge that I return to life. . . . You stir me in fine to amazement and you touch me to tears, and I thank the powers who so mysteriously let you loose with such sensibilities, into such an undiscovered country—*for* sensibility.

Throughout James's letters there is a presiding magnificence of concern and of understanding at its most sensitive, even clairvoyant level. This element in James remains inviolable, despite the wear and tear of life's struggles and changes, and despite, too, the exactitude and the exaction of the creative process. Principles of control and order inform not only James's craft of fiction, but also his interior life, that deeper part of one's being in which mind and soul discourse and render final decisions affecting the meaning and destiny of one's life. James's letters vividly, almost transparently, depict this ongoing tensive dialogue and judgmental process. In this binary process one can observe dramatically a pattern of magnificence. And this magnificence is all the more remarkable when one keeps in mind the full extent of what James himself was experiencing in his own life and in the history of his time. It should especially be remembered that he lived on long enough to witness, "disillusioned and horror-ridden," the coming of the Great War of 1914–1918, which in the European psyche has always held a place of epochal importance. The "modern age," as we know and live it, begins with the happenings in the summer of 1914—a "moment of shipwreck" as Karl Jaspers has imaged it. In a letter to one of his oldest friends, the novelist Rhoda Broughton, James responds to the events leading to England's declaration of war on Germany on August 4, 1914. The following words evoke the ruin of order that James associated with the Great War and that would never allow England to recover:

> Black and hideous to me is the tragedy that gathers, and I'm sick beyond cure to have lived on to see it. You and I, the ornaments of our generation, should have been spared this wreck of our belief that through the long years we had seen civilization grow and the worst become impossible. The tide that bore us along was then all the while moving to *this* as its grand Niagara—yet what a blessing we didn't know it. It seems to me to *undo* everything, everything that was ours, in the most horrible retroactive way—but I avert my face from the monstrous scene!—you can hate it and blush for it without my help; we can each do enough of that by ourselves.

James's afternoon of life coincides, then, with "the world in the crucible," in short, with the epochal events that were sparked by the Great War and that have become a part of what can be termed the crisis of modernity. Indeed, his letters end, as Virginia Woolf somewhere observes, in the heart of darkness. (James's own death on February 28, 1916, preceded by only a few months the Battle of the Somme with casualties on both sides of a million men.) The "monstrous horror" that had broken into the world ushered in an era of "broken lights," as Nietzsche calls modern times. Clearly, the civilization to which James pays tribute in his letter to Rhoda Broughton was to come to an end on August 4, 1914, even as it brought to its real end the nineteenth century, in which there reigned, as Basil Willey has reminded us, "the unquestioning sense that life has a momentous meaning." The shock of the war, as the letters confirm, fell heavily upon James: "[A]lmost everyone of anything less than my age is, or is preparing to be, in the imminent deadly breach," he writes in one of his most eloquent war letters on November 21, 1914. Certainly the European world of the nineteenth century, as James loved it, and loved its civilization, ended in "the utter extinction of everything that mattered"; and that which was for him "toned and seasoned and civilized," in Percy Lubbock's words, became raw and crude and ugly.

In their moral character and attitude, James's war letters reveal him to be "England's chief conservative critic" (to use F. W. Dupee's phrase): a great conservator of the humane graces and beauties of a civilization that he saw a-dying in the year and a half preceding his own death. "No writer was more conscious that he was at the end of a period, at the end of the society he knew,"[17] Graham Greene perceptively writes of James. The war was for James, in all of its electrifying drama of moral anarchy, a supreme historical instance of the corruptive process, which is also at the center of his "principal tragedy," *The Wings of the Dove*, in which the "darkest James," with his sense of "the black and marvellous things" and with what he also calls "a sense of the insecurity of life," can be seen. It is this "darkest James" who can also be viewed in the war letters—a witness in terror of the catastrophe that he sees occurring around him and that envelops the civilization and tradition that James treasures and sanctifies. For James the Great War epitomized "a huge horror of blackness," when "nothing exists but the huge enormity."

The death from blood-poisoning of the soldier-poet Rupert Brooke, on a French hospital ship in the Aegean Sea on April 23, 1915, en route to the campaign in Gallipoli, dramatized for James "the limitless loss of all our most splendid young life, the England of the future." Brooke, whom he had met in 1909, was, James writes, one "on whom the gods had smiled their brightest." Upon receiving news of Brooke's death, James wrote almost immediately and plaintively to Edward Marsh, the young poet's patron and friend; for James, Brooke not only symbolized Youth, but also, as Leon Edel observes, remained "a bright vision of another time—another century":

> This is too horrible and heart-breaking [James writes to Marsh]. If there was a stupid and hideous disfigurement of life and outrage to beauty left for our awful conditions to perpetrate, those things have been now su-

premely achieved, and no other brutal blow in the private sphere can better them for making one just stare through one's tears.

The elegiac mood that one finds in the reaction to Brooke's death also appears on a deeply personal level in the summer of 1910, with the death of William James in Chocorua, New Hampshire, on August 26. The death of his older brother filled Henry with "abject weakness of grief and even terror." "I sit heavily stricken and in darkness—for from far back in dimmest childhood he had been my ideal Elder brother," James writes on September 2, 1910, to his long-time friend Thomas Sergeant Perry, "and I still, through all the years, saw him, even as a small timorous boy yet, my protector, my backer, my authority and my pride. His extinction changes the face of life for me—besides the mere missing of his inexhaustible company and personality, originality, the whole unspeakably vivid and beautiful presence of him." In a letter to the philosopher Josiah Royce warmly thanking him for giving an address on William's work and influence, Henry was to write nearly a year later: "Strange how with Death and recession a man of genius becomes a *figure*—a representative of two or three stateable things, or things that have to be made *stateable*—to the public at large; save for the few who knew him best and saw the whole complexity, always."

Death, whether the death of loved ones and friends, or the death of civilization, or the death of some promise or possibility, had a prominent place in James's last years. "But the trouble is we are all gone or going—dead or dying," he cries at one point. The death of a tubercular Stephen Crane, not yet thirty years of age, brings this cry of loss from James: "What a brutal, needless extinction—what an unmitigated unredeemed catastrophe! I think of him with such a sense of possibilities and powers." The thought of death as finality, as the inconsolable *telos*, James often also sees in the context of what he calls the "idea of *Too Late*"—the idea, that is to say, that "the wasting of life is the implication of death." In the journey between life and death, James views human "terminations" with a sympathetic but realistic acceptance. No one, as T. S. Eliot says of James, "has ever been more aware—or with more benignity, or less bitterness—of the disparity between possibility and fact." Eliot's statement is confirmed in the voice of James himself in this passage, radiating as it does felicities of phrase and brave realities:

I *am* face to face with it, as one is face to face, at my age, with every succes-
sive lost opportunity . . . and with the steady, swift movement of the ebb
of the great tide—the great tide of which one will never see the turn. The
grey years gather, the arid spaces lengthen, damn them—or at any rate
don't shorten; and what doesn't come doesn't, and what goes *does*.

John Cowper Powys once declared that "James has the most reverence of all the great novelists." And certainly James's reverence for the
past, for the discipline of continuity, as it shapes both personal and social history, informs the spirit of his letters, as it does autobiographic
writings like *A Small Boy and Others* (1913) and *Notes of a Son and
Brother* (1914). In the new age that he saw coming, James detected "the
abatements and changes and modernisms and vulgarities" that he repeatedly condemns in his letters. "There is no happiness in this horrible
world," he writes to Leslie Stephen, "but the happiness we have *had*—
the very present is ever in the jaws of fate." To a nephew, Edward Hol-
ton James, he writes: "We live in a frightfully vulgar age; the twaddle
and chatter are much imposed upon us. Suspect them—detest them—
despise them." And to Hendrik Andersen, the young sculptor, he
sends this warning: ". . . I would beseech you to return, to sound and
sane Reality, to recover the proportion of things and to dread as the
hugest evil of all the dark danger of Megalomania." In the letters, in
style and tenor, there appears a Virgilian stress on piety and courage in
the face of adversity and social decay. Thus, in a letter to Edmund
Gosse, dated October 15, 1914, James affirms man's need to speak for
life and growth in midst of deaths in belief. But such an affirmation is
not easy when a society scorns the law of measure and murders the idea
of order and value of life:

I myself [James tells Gosse] find concentration of an extreme difficulty:
the proportions of things have so changed and one's poor old "values"
received such a shock. I say to myself that this is all the more reason why
one should recover as many of them as possible and keep hold of them in
the very interest of civilization and of the honour of the race; as to which
I am certainly right—but it takes some doing!

Characteristically, James's letters disclose a sacramental act in which
the mystery of existence is ultimately evoked in relation not only to
spirit of place but also to the nature of man. "Everything is treated sac-
ramentally," Powys says of James's approach to life and art. The letters
written between 1895 and 1916 flesh out James's increasing apprehen-

sions of the desanctification of the idea of man. This process ordains an inorganic conception of man and the universe and dramatizes the crisis of modernity as it infiltrates and assaults all levels of human consciousness and systems of value. Two major casualties of this reductionist process are the symbolic imagination and intelligence that, for James (as for Hawthorne and Melville), are sacrosanct ontological entities, especially as he treats them in later "metaphysical" novels like *The Wings of the Dove* and *The Golden Bowl*. Austin Warren, who sees the major theme of the latter novel as "the discovery that evil exists in the forms most disruptive to civilization: in disloyalty and treason," rightly warns that we must not ignore "the inner James who never leaves the sanctuary, where are the altars of literature, the dead, and the Good."

The sacramental constituents of James's art obviously irritated socialists like H. G. Wells and Bernard Shaw. Thus an irascible, piping Wells, in a savage parody in *Boon*, compares James's fiction to

> a church lit but without a congregation to distract you, with every light and line focused on the high altar. And on the altar, very reverently placed, intensely there, is a dead kitten, an egg-shell, a bit of string. . . . And the elaborate, copious emptiness of the whole Henry James exploit is only redeemed and made endurable by the elaborate, copious wit.[18]

After reading Wells's attack—"it has naturally not filled me with a fond elation," he confesses—James firmly and dignifiedly protested against his "bad manners" and defended his conception of life and literature against Wells's sociological predilections and utilitarianism: "It is art that *makes* life, makes interest, makes importance, for our consideration and application of those things, and I know of no substitute for the force and beauty of its process."

This remonstrance to Wells crystallizes James's long and unyielding adherence to the moral vision. It also shows that in "questions of art and truth and sincerity" one must seek as a "critical critic" to go beyond "the mere twaddle of graciousness," and at the same time maintain indifference to "Academics and Associations, Bodies and Boards . . . really caring . . . for nothing in the world but lonely patient virtue, which doesn't seek that company." Though he sees "the faculty of attention" much diminished in a world in which "newspaperism and professionalism [have] gone mad," he also insists that, "in our condition, doing anything decent is pure disinterested, unsupported, unrewarded heroism; but that's in a day's work." Against a Shaw who believed that art should be didactic, James defended not only an "adventurous and speculative imagination," but also works of art that "are capable of saying more things to man about himself than any other 'works' whatever are capable of doing." To Wells, whose "rude talent" he admired but whose "anarchic" view of literature he unconditionally rejected, he writes: "No talent, no imagination, no application of art . . . is able not to make much less for anarchy than for continuity and coherency much bigger than any disintegration." The imperatives of order, James maintained, must not be ignored, not even by creative geniuses like Tolstoy, about whom James writes in protest: "He doesn't *do* to read over, and that exactly is the answer to those who idiotically proclaim the impunity of such formless shape, such flopping looseness and such a denial of composition, selection and style. He has a mighty fund of life, but the *waste*, and the ugliness and vice of waste, the vice of a not finer *doing*, are sickening."

For James, as it has been noted, "the esthetic pattern *is* the moral pattern," and in this pattern form has a quintessential function both as an esthetic value and a life value emerging from reality: "Form alone *takes*, and holds and preserves, substance—saves it from the welter of helpless verbiage that we swim in as in a sea of tasteless tepid pudding, and that makes one ashamed of an art capable of such degradations." James's devotion to the sanctities of "dignity and memory and measure," of "conscience and proportion and taste," and his belief that "the moral sense and the artistic sense lie very close together," never waned. He had absolute confidence in the integrity of his craft even when he had to face his brother's caustic criticisms of *The Golden Bowl*. "Why don't you, just to please Brother," pleaded William, "sit down and write a new book, with no twilight or mustiness in the plot, with great vigor and decisiveness in action, no fencing in the dialogue, or psychological commentaries, and absolute straightness in style." Henry's reply rings with the courage that Nietzsche equates with "anchorite and eagle courage":

> I mean . . . to try to produce some uncanny form of thing, in fiction, that will gratify you, as Brother—but let me say, dear William, that I shall greatly be humiliated if you *do* like it, and thereby lump it, in your affection, with things of the current age, that I have heard you express ad-

miration for and that I would sooner descend to a dishonoured grave than
have written.

The formlessness that James decried in art he also decried in the
United States. He returned in 1905, "a restored absentee," after an absence of more than twenty years to find "the immense incoherence of
American things." In the course of his travels to New England, the
South, the Middle West, the whole Pacific coast, he discerned an "unat-
tempted, impossible maturity." He was homesick for his "tight an-
chorage . . . in the ancient world—a secret consciousness that I chink
in my pocket as if it were a fortune in a handful of silver." During a
stay in Chicago he writes that he feels "rather spent and weary, weary
of motion and chatter, and oh, of such an unimagined dreariness of
ugliness. New York City convinced him that "to make so much money
that you won't, that you don't, 'mind,' don't mind anything, is absolutely the American formula." During his visit to Washington, D.C.,
James attended a "quite pompous function" at the White House, and
along with the sculptor Augustus Saint-Gaudens, he sat next to President Theodore Roosevelt, whom he found "a really extraordinary
creature for native intensity, veracity and *bonhomie*—he plays his part
with the best will in the world and I recognize his amusing likeability."
But James's intuitive and probing insight into men of power and political influence was never wanting. "Theodore Rex," he writes to Edith
Wharton, also impressed him as "being, verily, a wonderful little machine: destined to be overstrained perhaps, but not as yet, truly, be-
traying the least creak. It functions astoundingly, and is quite exciting
to see. But it's really *like* something behind a great plate-glass window
'on' Broadway." Washington and the "American scene" as a whole left
him cold and unimpressed: "There is no 'fascination' *whatever*, in anything or anyone: that is exactly what there *isn't*. It is a quality that belongs to another order altogether."

Perhaps the best way to recall Henry James in his Book of Changes
is to study John Singer Sargent's famous portrait of him, commis-
sioned by James's friends for his seventieth birthday, April 15, 1913,
and now in the National Portrait Gallery, London. James had known
Sargent since 1884 and had found him "civilized to his finger-tips." He
had also written on his "exquisite" productions and had used him as a
model for painter-figures in some of his later stories. Of Sargent's
"high talent" James says: ". . . [he] sees deep into his subject, becomes

patient with it, and almost reverent, and, in short, elevates and human-
izes the technical problem." These general qualities are very much
there in Sargent's portrait. Solidity of body and authority of bearing
join in this portrait to convey a wonderfully vital and vigorous projec-
tion of the Master who had "domiciled uninterruptedly in England for
forty years" but had never surrendered his "New England conscience."
The slightly closed eyes with their penetrating gaze, the delicately pro-
portioned nose, the firm mouth, the lips as if ready to speak, the hand-
some, essentially unlined fleshiness of the large domed head accentuate
power of vision, not a mystical or prophetic vision, but one that has
the substance of reality; a humanistic vision with an "emotional center"
ever in contact with the living world.

Sargent's portrait registers an intrinsic, unerring honesty. It communicates a powerfully humane presence and a civilized sensibility protesting mightily against "all sorts of petty tyrannies and petty coercions
at close range," as Ezra Pound once wrote of the novelist. It depicts an
"ancient contemplative man," as James described himself, in search of
guiding moral principles. It commemorates the dignity of a "Lordly
man" in an age "of prose, of machinery, of wholesale production, of
coarse and hasty processes."

D. H. Lawrence:
The Hero-Poet as Letter Writer

I

Of D. H. Lawrence's letters it can be said, as Lionel Trilling once said of John Keats's letters, that they give a picture of a certain kind of man: a hero. There are, of course, different kinds of heroes and different gradations of heroism. In Keats, according to Trilling, we discern a heroic version of the tragic life and the tragic salvation, "the soul accepting the fate that defines it."[1] Lawrence's conception of heroism is far more passional than tragic, or as he himself wrote in the Preface to his play *Touch and Go* (1922): "Tragedy is the working out of some immediate passional problem within the soul of man."[2] In his Introduction to Giovanni Verga's *Mastro-don Gesualdo*, Lawrence laments the absence of heroic awareness, and hope, and insists on the primacy of heroic effort, "that instinctive fighting for more life to come into being."

For Lawrence modern man's tendency to make the hero self-conscious and introspective reduces the possibility of splendor and self-enhancement. "Life," he declares, "without the heroic effort, and without *belief* in the subtle, life-long validity of the heroic impulse, is just stale, flat and unprofitable."[3] In his own life heroic effort characterized Lawrence's struggle "for more life to come into being." Even when one reads his death-poems, written at the end of his life, it is the heroic impulse that remains evident. This heroism, at once personal and critical, is at the heart of Lawrence's letter indicting Aldous Huxley's *Point Counter Point* (1928):

> I have read *Point Counter Point* with a heart sinking through my boot-soles and a rising admiration. I do think you've shown the truth, perhaps the last truth, about you and your generation, with really fine courage. It seems to me it would take ten times the courage to write *P. Counter P.* that it took to write *Lady C.*: and if the public knew *what* it was reading, it would throw a hundred stones at you, to one at me. I do think that art

has to reveal the palpitating moment or the state of man as it is. And I think you do that, terribly. But what a moment! and what a state! if you can only palpitate to murder, suicide, and rape, in their various degrees—and you state plainly that it is so—caro, however are we going to live through the days? Preparing still another murder, suicide, and rape? But it becomes of a phantasmal boredom and produces ultimately inertia, inertia, inertia and final atrophy of the feelings. Till, I suppose, comes a final super-war, and murder, suicide, rape sweeps away the vast bulk of mankind. It is as you say—intellectual appreciation does not amount to so much, it's what you thrill to. And if murder, suicide, rape is what you thrill to, and nothing else, then it's your destiny—and you can't change it *mentally*. You live by what you thrill to, and there's the end of it. Still for all that it's a perverse courage which makes the man accept the slow suicide of inertia and sterility: the perverseness of a perverse child.[4]

We see crystallized in this passage Lawrence's heroic impulse, personal and prophetic, as well as literary and cultural, or what F. R. Leavis sums up as "the life-courage in the product of his creativity." Lawrence's heroism, as it expresses and defines itself in his letters with astonishing consistency and sincerity, and as such expresses and defines his deepest self, is not to be seen on a grand scale or in some majestic framework, for in this aspect, too, he maintained strong and direct control: that of a controlling intelligence always in touch with reality. Any careful re-reading of Lawrence's indictment of *Point Counter Point* should confirm an interweaving critical intelligence and a humanistic concern that give his words their tone and authority, their integrity—their humility.

Lawrence's heroism does not produce ecstatic flight, it does not fall into illusion, it does not induce reverie; it is neither a martial heroism nor a romantic heroism, but rather substantive, active, and humane heroism, sensitive to limits and respectful of the differences between appearance and reality. It is, in short, a living and discriminating heroism. In its critical honesty, too, there reside its sympathy and generosity. Its openness—the attempt of the writer to give of himself as authentically as he can, without any attitudinizing or moralizing, without the sham of mechanical or politic pieties—is exactly that openness that Lawrence, in a letter to Catherine Carswell, associates with the writing of poetry itself (in a passage later praised by T. S. Eliot): "The essence of poetry with us in this age of stark and unlovely actualities is a stark directness, without a shadow of a lie, or a shadow of deflection anywhere. Everything can go, but this stark, bare, rocky directness of statement, this alone makes poetry today."[5] Lawrence as a letter writer speaks that language of honesty and courage which he demands not only of poetry but also of one's spiritual being. In the face of the persistent attempts of critical revisionists to submerge Lawrence in the "river of dissolution," it needs insisting that his letters underscore an innately religious vision and search, conveyed and conducted with that endemic moral strength that Lawrence discloses in this sentence: "For me, it is better to die than to do something which is utterly a violation to my soul."[6]

One ultimately reads Lawrence's letters, in their totality and spiritual unity, as *explications d'héroïsme*. An unfailing and undoubting consistency informs the letters from beginning to end. No matter what the degree of adversity or the pull of despair his letters accentuate a note of final affirmation: "Life *can* be great—quite godlike. It *can* be so."[7] Early on in his letters, Lawrence casts the heroic element in the form of rebirth. Writing to A. D. McLeod, Lawrence declares: "I hate England and its hopelessness. I hate [Arnold] Bennett's resignation. Tragedy ought really to be a great kick at misery. But *Anna of the Five Towns* seems like an acceptance—so does all the modern stuff since Flaubert. I hate it. I want to wash again quickly, wash off England, the oldness and grubbiness and despair."[8] Shortly after, this time in a letter to Joseph Conrad's (and Lawrence's) generous friend and helper, Edward Garnett, he has this to say on the great novelist: "But why this giving in before you start, that pervades all Conrad and such folks—the Writers among the Ruins. I can't forgive Conrad for being so sad and for giving in."[9]

Lawrence's own decision to be his own man as an artist was nothing less than heroic: "They want me to have form: that means, they want me to have *their* pernicious ossiferous skin-and-grief form, and I won't."[10] A mixture of confidence and arrogance often characterizes his statements: "Read my novel [*Sons and Lovers*]," he advises Garnett. "It's a great novel. If *you* can't see the development—which is slow, like growth—I can."[11] His faith in his genius, and in his destiny as a man and his mission as an artist, had an impelling resoluteness of purpose. "I shall change the world for the next thousand years," he declares. It is as a catechumen that Lawrence speaks in this extraordinary passage in an early letter to Ernest Collings: "I often think one ought to be able to pray, before one works—and then leave it to the Lord. Isn't it hard, hard work to come to real grips with one's imagination— throw everything overboard? I always feel as if I stood naked for the fire of Almighty God to go through me—and it's rather an awful feeling. One has to be so terribly religious, to be an artist."[12]

These words remind us of a presiding reverence in Lawrence's life and art. Reverence embodies a disciplined fusion of passion and principle, the two most active energies that, for Lawrence, create a delicate equilibrium and that belong to and embody the life of virtue and the idea of value. The possession of this quality of reverence is for Lawrence a precondition to the religious search for meaning and to one's need to attain a fuller relationship between one's self and the universe and between one's self and one's fellow man and woman. "We have to know how to go out and meet one another, upon the third ground, the holy ground," we find Lawrence writing to Rolf Gardiner in 1926, his words containing the biblical pulsebeat that one hears in some of his most inspired prose fiction.[13]

Spiritual heroism, in the contexts of "the courage to be," radiates in Lawrence's letters. A metaphysic of virtue and value, however, remains dangerously one-dimensional, incomplete, and unconsummated without due attention to what Lawrence called "the phallic consciousness." His adjectival emphasis here undoubtedly troubled even some of his most ardent supporters as his experiment with the language of emotions became increasingly radical, to judge especially by late writings like *Lady Chatterley's Lover* (1928) and *The Man Who Died* (1931). But critical irritability should not be allowed to distort Lawrence's heroic vision, anchored as it is in concern and commitment. His art is his heroic vision insofar as Lawrence also creates there his phallic conception of heroism and visibilizes heroic qualities appropriate to the modern age. Lawrence's is a heroism of possibility; eventually it is even an apocalyptic heroism, to be viewed against the background of the great crisis of civilization that announced itself with the Great War of 1914-1918. If Lawrence was aware of the need for virtue and value in relation to what Simone Weil terms "the need for roots," he was also aware of a need for returning to "the source of all real beauty, and all real gentleness": "And those are the two things, tenderness and beauty, which will save us from horrors."[14]

What impresses one when reading Lawrence's letters is the religious tone of his language, particularly when he discourses on his literary aesthetic. A numinous quality is pervasive, disclosed in a reverent awareness of the idea of the holy, which reminds us of Lawrence's contention that the imagination is at its maximum religious. What perhaps best distinguishes Lawrence's letters, when they are read and judged in their collective thrust and meaning, is the element of transcendence that informs and defines, giving distinction and recognition to, his burden of vision, his view of himself as a novelist-poet. That self-view is heroic in precisely that spiritual sense that Jacob Burckhardt identifies with "greatness of soul," which gives the poet "the power to forgo benefits in the name of morality, in voluntary self-denial, not merely from motives of prudence but from goodness of heart."[15] Strength and greatness of soul, at their depths heroic in the full sense of the word, are at the heart of Lawrence's vision. For what else better identifies what Lawrence terms the "heroic effort" that must be exerted before enacting the kind of self-searching, and self-humility, that appears in this passage of a letter to Edward Garnett: "But primarily I am a passionately religious man, and my novels must be written from the depth of my religious experience. . . . But you should see the religious, earnest, suffering man in me first, and then the flippant or common things after."[16]

Thomas Carlyle recalls for us the great worth of the "Hero-Poet" in whom we hear the voice of genius, "to be heard of all men and times."[17] In Lawrence's letters that voice never wearies; his seriousness of purpose and commitment and his honesty are undeviating and uncompromising. Lawrence's transparency is one of the most exceptional qualities of his heart and mind and soul, in their triadic harmony of relationship. The letters, as an extension of and commentary on his art, possess an equivalent honesty, the language of which, in its thought and expression, discloses a constant attempt to communicate "a complete truth of feeling." Lawrence's letters dramatize his innate concern with providing a language of integrity, enabling him to confront himself in relation to another without recrimination or guilt. His quest is always that of transcending, by defeating and excising, any attitudinal or false language that impedes the emotional and linguistic approximation of a deeper and a purer truth as it emerges from one's tensions of consciousness. Lawrence's letters, in their spontaneity of expression, bring one into contact with an inviolable, innocent self; and that contact is Lawrence's attained version of virtue as a diffracted form of moral life.

"A true virtue," Romano Guardini tells us, "signifies an ability to penetrate with a glance the whole existence of man."[18] In his art Lawrence's "glance" acquires its consummate and universal scope. In his letters, however, it is Lawrence's interior "glance" that stirs one most. Self-examination, *de rigueur*, is the process encountered here, especially in the pre–1918 letters. What Lawrence writes about his second novel, *The Trespasser* (1912), tells us something also about his epistolary process, in its own inner struggle and demands: "But this is a work one can't regard easily—I mean, at one's ease. It is so much oneself, one's naked self. I give myself away so much, and write what is my most palpitant, sensitive self, that I loathe the book, because it will betray me to a parcel of fools."[19]

In the letters prior to the Great War one sees Lawrence the aspiring poet-novelist, unalterably loyal to his commitment to his art. A kind of electrical energy infuses his literary effort to understand and clarify and define his vision; and invariably his letters attest to the seriousness of his purposes as an artist. Moral courage is at the center of his attempt to come to grips with his imaginative genius; fearless exploration of his sensibility brings from him self-revelation of profound significance: "But one sheds one's sicknesses in books—repeats and presents again one's emotions, to be master of them."[20] "I have always tried to get an emotion out in its own course, without altering it. It needs the finest instinct imaginable, much finer than the skill of the craftsmen."[21] "I don't care about physiology of matter—but somehow—that which is physic—non-human, in humanity, is more interesting to me than the old-fashioned human element—which causes one to conceive a character in a certain moral scheme and make him consistent."[22] The early letters abound with statements like the preceding, filled as they are with faith and courage and with enthusiasm and confidence. Lawrence's concern with literary criteria, as these bring him closer to a realization of his genius, shows a tough and persevering critical intelligence. If that concern is self-critical, it is also selfless in the contexts of Lawrence's total involvement in mastering his creative impulse. "It needs a certain purity of spirit to be an artist, of any sort," he has to write in a 1929 essay, "Making Pictures."[23]

II

The Great War was undoubtedly a dire threat to Lawrence's belief in heroic impulse and effort and posed the kind of danger to Lawrence's "societal instinct" ("Myself, I suffer badly from being so cut off") that, analogously, his mother's death in 1910 caused to his personal life. These twin disasters did not in the end defeat Lawrence's heroic apprehension of life, though they did sharpen his sense of the immense difficulties impinging on the possibilities of existence. We find progressively in Lawrence, after 1914, heroic endurance in the face of loss and desolation. We are now in connection with a man who sees himself in a world falling apart and in which possibility gives way to death. "I've got again into one of those horrible sleeps from which I can't wake," we find him writing to Lady Ottoline Morrell. "I can't brush it aside to wake up. You know those horrible sleeps when one is struggling to wake up, and can't."[24] The struggle to awake from "those horrible sleeps" remained his fate until his death in 1930. It is not hard to make a connection between Lawrence's nightmare of war and the conditions that he deplores in his indictment of *Point Counter Point*. Huxley's novel is a verification of Lawrence's prophetic witness and testimony. His suffering during the war years, and its aftermath, was in its unique way prophetic: "The persistent nothingness of the war makes me feel like a paralytic convulsed with rage."[25] But these words of negation are repeatedly assuaged by Lawrence's heroic determination not to surrender to the Negative: "One must speak for life and growth, amid all this mass of destruction and disintegration."[26] Lawrence never abandoned his faith in the redemptive theme, "Look! We have come through!" Paul Tillich's words help us to fathom the condition of Lawrence's interior self and the essence of his heroic outlook: "Courage is the self-affirmation of being in spite of the fact of nonbeing."[27]

The letters of this period are a graph of those sharp tensions of consciousness, of being versus nonbeing, that Lawrence confronted in the years after 1914. Externally, of course, this was a time of perils to humanism, for the war embodied a total crisis of civilization, when "the past, the great past," as Lawrence wrote, "[was] crumbling down, breaking down . . . the past, the past, the falling, perishing, crumbling past, so great, so magnificent."[28] "Hopelessness," "decomposition," "decline," "nothingness," "blasphemy": these words form a leitmotiv in Lawrence's language of nonbeing in relation to his feelings about the teleology of "the outer world." At the same time, Lawrence's inner being had to face even greater menaces, these often becoming in the process painful "wounds to the soul, to the deep emotional self," as his creative genius, with its "heaps of vitality," wrestles with an outer world of nullity; as the power of being, to paraphrase Tillich, struggles to transcend nonbeing with its anxiety of emptiness, meaninglessness, guilt, condemnation. Lawrence invokes a deeper form of courage, religious and spiritual in its roots: an ascetic heroism that brings Saint Paul to mind (and prefigures Tillich's paradigms of "the courage to be") when one considers this passage from one of Lawrence's letters of 1916: "One must forget, only forget, turn one's eyes from the world: that is all. One must live quite apart, forgetting, having another world, a world as yet uncreated. Everything lies in *being*, although the whole world is one colossal madness, falsity, a stupendous assertion of non-being."[29]

Lawrence's frantic search for "another country," for a "new life" to be found there in "the unreal world" and in the "inner soul," now commences and continues until the end, when he finally sails away on his "ship of death" ("for you must take / the longest journey to oblivion. / And die the death, the long and painful death / that lies between the old self and the new.") A ceaseless interior debate rages between the Lawrence of nonbeing and the Lawrence of being; between the Lawrence who cries out, "for I am no more a man, but a walking phenomenon of suspended fury,"[30] and the Lawrence who affirms, "Only the living heart and the creative spirit matters—*nothing else*."[31] In addressing himself to the perennial debate between *pro et contra* Lawrence expresses a power of self-affirmation rooted in courage and transcendence; he expresses, in effect, a heroism of great spiritual magnitude when viewed in these defining contexts of which Tillich writes: "The faith which makes the courage of despair possible is the acceptance of the power of being, even in the grip of nonbeing."[32]

Yet Lawrence's should not be approached as a theology of heroism, for it is too closely shaped by what Huxley once spoke of as his friend's "mystical materialism." That is, Lawrence's heroism, like his art, was the product of his *daemon*, ultimately manifested as a *numen*. Lawrence renders that heroism concretely rather than abstractly. Belonging to the realm of creative thought, it is a heroism of striving and possibility rather than of revelation and grace. "It is necessary to get the germ of a new development *towards the highest*, not a reduction to the lowest," he stresses.[33] Lawrence is not a hero-saint but rather a hero-poet whose articles of faith, in the form of "the living intuitive faculty," give substance to what Leavis terms "the living principle." "Let us be easy and impersonal," Lawrence writes to Katherine Mansfield, "not for ever fingering over our own souls, and the souls of our acquaintances, but trying to create a new life from the roots that are within us. . . . [W]e must grow from our deepest underground roots, out of the *unconsciousness*, not from the conscious concepts which we falsely call ourselves."[34] In the war Lawrence saw the substitution of pseudo-heroism for the integral heroism that is needed to create "a perfectly new *body* of purpose." "But we are not compelled to live," Lawrence wrote in an essay, "The Reality" (1917). "We are compelled to die. . . . We must *choose* life, for life will never compel us."[35]

If, before the war, Lawrence was seeking to find the best means of presenting the courage of his genius ("write what is my most palpitant, sensitive self") and to discipline and refine his vision, without violating that "certain purity of spirit" that he deemed indispensable for an artist, during and after the war he discerned his main task to be one that sought for the survival, and the resurgence, of "the great creative process." "War cannot be thought of, for me, without the utmost repulsion and desecration of one's being," he wrote to Lady Cynthia Asquith.[36] The need of survival no doubt presented serious problems for the Lawrence who suffered the full extent of his "deaths in belief." In his war letters, as they might be called, Lawrence was often to show an ability to withdraw from a "foul world" and to maintain "a separate isolated fate": "Believe me, I am infinitely hurt by being thus torn off from the body of mankind, but so it is, and it is right."[37]

At times, in his furious protestations against the war, Lawrence discloses an indulgent lyrical note and his language becomes infused with tragic grandiloquence, as well as excessively self-righteous pleas and feelings. On these occasions the role of the preacher in Lawrence gets the better of him as missionary zeal and a pontifical style color his reactions: "I think I am almost ready to set out preaching also, now: not only cessation of war, but the beginning of a new world."[38] But these occasions are essentially abbreviated and transitional, another phase in "the voyage of discovery towards the real and eternal and unknown land." In the letters that record these occasions it is Lawrence the moralist rhetor who is speaking, simultaneously revealing the art of reasoning and teaching by similitudes and analogies, as found in this excerpt from a letter to Lady Cynthia Asquith:

> Oh, and *do not think* I blame the Government or howl at it. The fools who howl at the Government make my blood boil. I respect the Prime Minister [Herbert Henry Asquith] because I believe in his real decency and I think Lloyd Georges, etc., are toads. I must here assert again that the war is and continues because of the lust for hate and war, chiefly hate of each other—"hate thy neighbour as thyself"—not hate of Germany at all which is in the hearts of people; and their worship of Ares and Aphrodite—("But a bitter goddess was born of blood and the salt sea foam")—both gods of destruction and burning down. But in many hearts, now, I fully believe that Ares and Aphrodite have ceased to be gods. We want something else: it is fulfilled in us, this Ares-Aphrodite business: let us have something else, let us *make* something else out of our own hearts. Germany, peace terms, etc., don't matter. It is a question of the living heart—that only.[39]

Whatever the rhetorical flourishes in this passage, heroic critical insightfulness also emerges here, stamped by the experience and the truth of history when "we were all drowned in shame." Lawrence did not fight in the Great War, but no doubt he felt some deep inner need to disclose a commensurate heroism. That is, he was to disclose a critical rather than a martial heroism; a prophetic heroism that digs beneath surface experience and meaning. His letters portray a concomitant humanistic concern as Lawrence confronts the creative needs in himself and the social needs outside and around him. Though repeatedly speaking of the need to transform human society, especially after the war, he never fails to acknowledge a humane awareness. His phallic radicalism is invariably moderated by his passional humanism, that is to say, by his inherent reverence for the "living heart." That innate humanism not only saves Lawrence from his phallic extrapolations but also constitutes an inner check that tempers his sometimes exacerbated urgings for the attainment of what he calls "spontaneous-creative fulness of being." Indeed, Lawrence's humanistic sympathy explains his appreciation of the ancient Greek historian Thucydides, whose *History of the Peloponnesian Wars* Lawrence was reading in 1916. "He is a very splendid and noble writer," Lawrence writes of Thucydides, "with the simplicity and the directness of the most complete culture and the widest consciousness. I salute him. More and more I admire the true classic dignity and self-responsibility."[40] In Thucydides' "widest conscious-ness" Lawrence views precisely those humanistic virtues that he be-lieved were being murdered on the Western Front. Indeed, isn't it the destruction of the humanistic world that Lawrence bemoans in his in-dictment of the world of *Point Counter Point*?

III

After 1918 one detects in Lawrence's letters a more reflective, sub-dued, and even at times nostalgic tone. The slaughter of innocence generally associated with the consequences of World War I was for Lawrence and the 1914 generation, "our broken, fragmentary genera-tion," as he describes it, an irreversible fact. No wonder, then, that he was willing to change the title of his war novel, *Women in Love* (1920), to *Day of Wrath*. The "insouciance" that Lawrence always hankered for was hardly obtainable after 1919, a year which was to see the beginning of Lawrence's "savage pilgrimage." In the letters of the post-war years Lawrence saw disenchantment everywhere: "The 'world' has no life to offer. Seeing things doesn't amount to much." A desperate courage identifies his epistolary observations in the early twenties, those years when the survivors were slowly starting to grasp what had gone wrong and what had been lost, even as the map and psyche of European man were irreversibly transformed by epochal events, or as Virginia Woolf observed: "Disorder, sordidity and corruption surround us."

It is a dream-like yearning, yet intuitively cognizant of the infinite pain of change and of death itself—the death of humane civilization—that Lawrence reveals in a letter to Ernest Collings: "I wish there could be a new spring of hope and reality in mankind: I do wish a few people could change, and stand for a fresh and happier world. I suppose it will come, and we shall live through. That is our business, at any rate. We must live through, for the hope of the new summer of the world."[41] Not the "courage to be" but to forbear shapes Lawrence's view of the world during and immediately following the hostilities. Writing to Thomas Seltzer, his publisher, Lawrence has this to say about the life-emptiness of the post-war world and about the terrors that would come again after "the long week-end": "But one feels, the old order has gone—Hohenzollern & Nietzsche & all. And the era of love & peace &

democracy with it. There will be an era of war ahead: some sort of warfare, one knows not what. But Mars is the god before us: the real Mars, not Jesus in arms."[42]

Clearly the early 1920s were for Lawrence a period of trouble and darkness. Any hope that he ever entertained about men meeting one another, "upon the third ground, the holy ground," was now arrested. Lawrence's heroic vision, insofar as it shaped his attitude and thought, was during these years to comprehend the malaise that afflicted the whole of life. The war and its aftermath were to crystallize his estrangement and to intimidate his inherent affirmation of what he called man's "thought-adventure." A severe questioning of the very purposes and possibilities of existence racked Lawrence in the early 1920s: "Will the bird perish, / Shall the bird rise?"[43] This cruel question underlines Lawrence's existential predicament, when his heroism necessarily passes through a stage of dread and despair that comes with the "end of the modern world." Lawrence is to be viewed at this point as a "pilgrim of the apocalypse," when he can be neither a "hero of God" nor a "hero of civilization." He exists in the brackets of nonbeing, abstracted from existence, as seen in the repeated references in the letters regarding his need to flee from the responsibilities of historical being.

Unconsolable alienation was to constrict Lawrence in these years: "I feel a stranger everywhere and nowhere."[44] He found himself forced to summon all of his resources of courage to combat the meaninglessness of an age in which the reifying process accelerated in all spheres of existence. A spiritual homelessness was to signalize his wanderings. Even the pressures that Lawrence felt so intensely in Europe were equally inescapable in the East, as these words in a letter written from Ceylon show: "Well, here we've been for a fortnight—rather lovely to look at, the place—but very hot—and I don't feel at all myself. Don't think I care for the East."[45] Conditions in America were no less oppressive, to judge by these observations in another letter: "Everything in America goes by *will*. A great negative *will* seems to be turned against all spontaneous life—there seems to be no *feeling* at all—no genuine bowels of compassion and sympathy. . . . America is neither free nor brave, but a land of tight, iron-clanking little *wills*, everybody trying to put it over everybody else, and a land of men absolutely devoid of the real courage of trust, trust in life's sacred spontaneity. They can't trust life until they can *control* it."[46]

The last five or six years of Lawrence's life preceding his death in 1930 disclose a metaphysical heroism as Lawrence increasingly contemplates not only the disarray in the world but also the disruption of his soul. This final stage of Lawrence's heroism reveals a deepening spiritual perception of his own and of the human condition. "People who inherit despair," he insisted, "may at last turn it into a greater heroism." A contemplative vision marks his last years. The obsessive anger and disgust of the years directly following the war, though not eradicated, are reduced in intensity, as Lawrence confronts both the world in himself and himself in the world. How does one grapple with the problem of disorientation as it grips man in society? That, for Lawrence, constitutes a major question. The tone of the last letters, like that of the "last poems," is reflective, invocatory, controlled, transcendent, as Lawrence appeals for the re-emergence of "human tender reverence." "What we want is life and *trust*," Lawrence pleads with one correspondent; "men trusting men, and making living a free thing, not a thing to be *earned*. But if men trusted men, we could soon have a new world, and send this one to the devil."[47]

In some of the last letters Lawrence offers specific spiritual guidance; the voice of the moralist preacher in him remained inextinguishable to the end: "The chief thing is to be one's real self, and to be at peace with oneself. Then life comes easily again. While one is in conflict with oneself, life holds back and is difficult all the time."[48] Religious questions also arouse a more responsive and resonant chord as he considers the eternal clash between the sacred and the profane. For Lawrence the "journey through dread" must finally reach "the new unknown." The widespread moral nihilism of the late twenties and early thirties does not overcome him. As one who probed and rendered the possibilities of existence, even when these were under fire, Lawrence instinctively rejected the limit-situation of the Existentialists. The confirmation of possibility was Lawrence's answer to the Heideggerian "possibility of impossibility." "I know there has to be a return to the older vision of life," he writes in a letter dated July 4, 1924. "But not for the sake of unison. And not done from the *will*. It needs some welling up of religious sources that have been shut down in us: a great *yielding*, rather than an act of will: a yielding to the darker, older unknown, and a reconciliation."[49]

Heroism, especially since the Great War, has lacked those archetypal

qualities that one usually associates with the heroic prototype and attitude. Heroism has been increasingly technicalized or collectivized as
uniformity and standardization have taken toll of those opportunities
that validate the heroic temper and *praxis*. A devalued and desanctified
heroism, lacking promise of greatness and assimilating common and
pluralistic habits of mind, fabricates modern forms of the heroic. Heroism has also been robbed of its intrinsically divine element, for the re-
crudescence of which Lawrence is asking when he writes to an American correspondent, the psychologist Dr. Trigant Burrow: "There is a
principle in the universe, towards which man turns religiously—a *life*
of the universe itself. And the hero is he who touches and transmits the
life of the universe."[50] Lawrence's words also remind us that it is a
moral heroism, rooted in individual heroic effort, that he is invoking.
His letters depict a life of perpetual striving in the face of those dehumanizing conditions that debase the "heroic impulse." For one, too,
to see, with Eric Bentley, Lawrence merely in the tradition of Heroic
Vitalism, with its emphasis on the implementation of power (that for
too long led Bertrand Russell and others to connect Lawrence with
protofascism), is to oversimplify Lawrence's understanding of a heroism that he believes must be centered in what he terms the "God-
knowing human consciousness."

More than ever the theme of Lawrence's letters in his last years is
adumbrated by his affirmation of life, his "eroica," as it were: "*My single constancy is love of life!*"[51] His letters preach a loyalty to this article of
faith, and his firmness in adhering to and defending it underlines his
heroic capacity. "I shall live just as blithely," he declares, "unbought
and unsold." In the world in which he lived and created Lawrence saw
a heroism reduced in stature, vitality, dignity; a devalued heroism in
accord with an age of demystification in which a pernicious process of
"living death" triumphed. With "the subordination of every organic
unit to the great mechanical purpose," modern civilization had reached
a point of stasis. "The hero is obsolete," writes Lawrence to Witter By-
nner, "and the leader of men is a back number. After all, at the back of
the hero is the militant ideal, or the ideal militant seems to me also a
cold egg. We're sort of sick of all forms of militarism and militantism,
and *Miles* is a name no more, for a man."[52] Human experience had been
so much altered since 1914, Lawrence believed, that the leader-cum-
follower relationship of earlier times was now inoperative. Life in an

age in which, as Joseph Campbell has reminded us, the old mysteries have lost their force, and in which, therefore, their symbols no longer interest the psyche,[53] requires a new and intuitive heroism, possessing a "curious close intimacy" and "an instinct of beauty" as Lawrence would have it. In his letters Lawrence never ceases to call for an epiphanic heroism, as it might well be described: "And the new relationship will be some sort of tenderness, sensitive, between men and men and men and women, and not the one up one down, lead on I follow, *ich dien* sort of business."[54]

For Lawrence a hero must be a "great-souled man," a man of honor and integrity, fearless and persistent. Heroism needs to be passional and instinctive, expressed individually as well as collectively. In the Mexican people, for example, Lawrence finds his standards of heroism satisfied for the reasons he gives in this extract from one of his letters: "But there is a sort of *basic* childishness about these people, that for me is the only manliness. When I say childishness, I only mean they don't superimpose ideas & ideals, but follow the stream of the blood. A certain innocence, even if sometimes evil. And a certain childlike patience & stoicism.—I like it really, our tough dry, papier-mâché world recedes."[55] The sacred and the heroic are, in Lawrence's contexts, qualitative equivalences insofar as they emerge from a common spiritual center, or noumenon. In a sense, Lawrence's concepts of heroism are both ancient and modern: in his reverence for the idea of the holy, as it moulds the heroic impulse, he clearly reveals an understanding of biblical and sacramental rhythms as these preserve, in the recesses of the human consciousness, a religious value of permanent worth. His increasing respect for Roman Catholicism provides an interesting facet of his religious attitude in the last years of his life: "I think too the Roman Catholic Church, as an institution, granted of course some new adjustments in life, might once more be invaluable for saving Europe: but not as a mere political power."[56]

True heroism for Lawrence is essentially an inner heroism that influences conscience and character and fortifies mind and soul. Sanctity and candor are direct expressions of this process at its highest point of development. It is not the definition but the immanent expression of the heroic that Lawrence advocates. There is nothing schematic about his approach to heroism; its re-mobilization is his main goal. An intrinsically moral form of that heroism appears in this paragraph from one

of Lawrence's letters: "I tried Casanova, but he smells. One can be immoral if one likes, but one must not be a creeping, itching, fingering,
inferior being, led on chiefly by a dirty sniffing kind of curiosity, without pride or clearness of soul. For me, a man must have pride, good
natural inward pride. Without that, cleverness only stinks."[57]

As a hero-poet Lawrence illuminates in his letters the traits of "an
aristocrat of life": "greater being," "a purer manhood," "a more vivid
livingness." His heroism, however, defies absolute categories precisely
because, as André Malraux has observed, "Lawrence has no wish to be
either happy or great, he is only concerned with being." His is a life-
heroism of character, robust and responsible, earthy, and natural, re-
sistant to the abstract gestures that he linked with "disintegrated life-
lessness of soul." The brave man, he believed, is one who, in "the democratic age of cheap clap-trap," seeks for "a new revelation" and "a
living relation in sacredness." "Never yield before the barren," Lawrence stresses, his words here epitomizing a heroism of *living* and *being*,
at the same time adverting to a philosophy of heroism. But that philosophy must not be confused with, say, a Nietzschean non-morality of
the purely natural Will to Power. Lawrence's devotion to the necessity
of tenderness and of "the old blood-warmth of oneness and togeth-
erness" saves him from surrendering to the *Übermensch*. Nietzsche's
heroism of despair—"Oh eternal everywhere, oh eternal nowhere, oh
eternal—in-vain!"—is filled with the vacuity and fatality that negate
any possibility of redemption. "Those who cannot bear the sentence,
'There is no redemption,' *ought* to perish," Nietzsche said.

For Lawrence, to be sure, the crisis of modern life was desperate,
and he wondered whether there would be "a new wave of generosity
or a new wave of death." But as his letters show, he never lacked creative faith, creative understanding, or creative responsibility. He cared
about man, as his creedal statement clearly shows: "One writes out of
one's moral sense for the race, as it were." And he cared about his life's
work: "I care about my books—I want them to stand four-square *there*,
even if they don't sell many."[58] In caring about things that really matter
Lawrence affirmed a restorative heroism, the constituents of which he
sees in this ascending order of redemption: "Patience, tenacity, the
long fight, the long hope, the inevitable victory—that's it."[59]

III

Polemical Forays

The dialectical lures and joys of discontinuity portray the supertemporal directions, if not predispositions, of those in positions of leadership, who contribute to and shape the ethos of modern life. Such leadership often assumes the guise of enlightenment and formulates public policies and programs that encourage progress and growth and in due course lead men and women on the path of a bigger and better society. For those who foment the Zeitgeist of unlimited change and expansion—"pistol-shot transformations," as they have been imaged—discontinuity signifies infinite opportunity, "the wave of the future" that merges with "the wave of new technologies." An inescapable consequence is that in much of modern life a "mastering of the realm of quantities" is accompanied by the disappearance of a sense of purpose and values. Not the principle of unity but the laws of multiplicity are those that are propagated ad infinitum. And everywhere we find unchecked enthusiasms for and the legislation of "the opportunities thrown up by discontinuity," which are hurled in the faces of those who seek to preserve the discipline of continuity as a front-line defense against what Joseph Conrad discerns as "moral anarchies and cynicisms and betrayals."

6

The Liberal Tone

Stephen R. Graubard is a professor of history at Brown University and also the editor of the quarterly magazine *Daedalus*. Both positions obviously give him an authority and an influence of some importance, and what he has to say publicly cannot easily be ignored or underestimated. Thus, in an issue of the *New York Times Book Review* (July 24, 1988), he wrote a lead essay entitled "Western Civ and Its Children," which seeks to answer, by easing, fears "that an earlier sense of community created by a common learning in certain basic texts is being eroded." Drawing from his own teaching experiences going back to 1947, when he assisted in an introductory European history course taught at Harvard University, he attempts to rebut "the arguments of late 20th-century merchants of nostalgia." "It is possible," he observes, "that the post-World War II teaching of someone who remains skeptical of our contemporary academic Cassandras may serve some purpose." The upshot of his essay is that things, after all, are not too bad, that changes in curriculum and text are inevitable, that old pedagogical values cannot remain permanent, that social and intellectual standards necessarily alter in response to the new demands of history and of a civilization in transition. But there is no need to go on paraphrasing Graubard; his own words, as found in the following quotation, summarize his position:

> As for my students' values, while they are clearly not those of Matthew Arnold or T. S. Eliot, it is not apparent that they are as banal or as inferior as certain critics have suggested. The surprising thing is that although their exposure to many great books before their arrival at the university is not all one might wish, in the land of second and third chances it is remarkable what can be accomplished even very late in the day.

Graubard's remarks, with their confident coolness of tone, undoubtedly are designed to silence those of us who continue to believe in the preservation of not only our sacred patrimony but also our sacred texts. He is telling us that our longstanding criticisms of educational conditions are not creditable or warranted and that our view of American society since the end of World War II lacks both substance and reality. There is also an underlying political implication in his commentary: that those who condemn current educational policies and practices perhaps lack sympathy for or any true understanding of our pluralistic society and its great possibilities. These educational critics, he seems to be saying, in rejecting the ongoing need for enlightened change and progress, are to one degree or another backward or even reactionary in their views. Or to put it in contemporary parlance, they simply are not "with it." Reading between the lines, we are to infer that the recalcitrants who "complain vociferously about what they perceive to be the fall in standards in America's colleges and universities" lack compassion, as well as insight. Unlike the professor and editor of a well-known journal, the "detractors" of present-day education are simply blind to the dynamics of the modern world and of the "new era" in which we live. They are persons, in short, who do not have Graubard's understanding of human experience and indeed of *his* own professional experience, or as he finally concludes (with, it seems, an inflated sense of his own self-importance and the superiority of a discerning intellect), "My own experience speaks only of the last 40 years. It tells me that I have no wish to return to 1948."

Actually, what one reads in "Western Civ and Its Children" contributes nothing new to the subject; we have heard it from our liberal and enlightened leaders often enough, *ad nauseam*. At the same time we cannot permit Graubard to go unanswered as he is an honored historian who also edits *Daedalus*, the influential magazine that is published by the American Academy of Arts and Sciences, which was first organized by James Bowdoin and John Adams, among others, in Boston in 1780, with the express purpose "to cultivate every art and science which may tend to advance the interest, honour, dignity, and happiness of a free, independent, and virtuous people." In his *Times* article Graubard speaks for himself and not necessarily for the Academy, but his views, regardless of where they appear and the official sanction they may or may not have, are very revealing as both symptom and portent. They tell us something about the thinking of the leaders of American education, and beyond that about the reigning views of a secularist intelligentsia in general, and how these views are communicated in major newspapers and periodicals, with their large circulations and even larger spheres of influence. These are often the same leaders who define and mold public policy and who shape public opinion and even the destiny of an entire nation and people. And to a large degree they constitute a liberal network that disdains and sometimes punishes "dissidence of dissent."

What particularly stands out in Graubard's essay is its homogeneity of tone—the arched, meretricious, progressivist, supercilious accents that mask the sneering disposition of the liberal character. Sooner or later one who reads and listens discriminatingly will recognize this liberal tone, as it might be called. The liberal pundit, especially, relies on this tone to bully and belittle his opponents in "the stupid party." And this liberal tone is *there* in Graubard's rhetoric as it cleverly conveys the thoughts of an advanced educator-historian-editor, now speaking both in hindsight and in sight of the twenty-first century. And it is all so cleverly presented, complete with the all-too-virtuous voice of modern experience, temperateness, reason, understanding, perception to the point of unnerving even the most skeptical reader and thus precluding any close censorial inspection of Graubard's point of view and all that it represents. It is an imperial and ideologized tone that, in its prepossession and conceit, is not only clever but also slick, exactly because it is centered in moral relativism. Its slickness, once recognized for what it is, cannot hide its own automatic or deliberate attitudinizing, or the insidious attitude it adapts to a reader or a listener. Nor can it hide, in the long run, its unalterable faith in itself alone—the gnostic faith of the chosen. The liberal tone is dissimulating and this quality is invariably to be found in the rhetors who articulate it (further and dangerously refined these days by copying the techniques of the entertainment and electronics media).

Graubard's article also discloses what Richard M. Weaver calls "a melioristic bias," that is, the kind of underlying assumption which characterizes "the rhetoric of social science": "that man and society are improvable." In this respect, too, the article is symptomatic of the tendency for the discipline of history to become, in Jacques Barzun's words, "retrospective sociology." The liberal tone, as it is employed by those who now dominate the academy and high journalism, thus becomes in their language a highly polished and sharpened technique rejecting and supplanting the moral tone that is registered in terms of insight, wisdom, reverence, restraint, order. This liberal tone identifies

a categorical repudiation of any hieratic idea of permanence or transcendence. It is an implicit part of both the larger liberal *Zeitgeist* and
its agents of deception who ultimately betray the sacred values of a civilization rooted in the classical and biblical traditions. And it is especially appropriate to those whom Jacques Ellul singles out as utopists,
geometers, and technicians—and whom Irving Babbitt, earlier on,
placed in the vanguard of "Rousseau and romanticism." Whether in
the written word or in the spoken word the liberal tone proclaims, *ipso
facto*, its sham humanitarianism and absolutisms, "rotten and rotting
others."

As already noted, what especially characterizes the liberal tone is its
implicit contempt for the moral constant and imperative. There are *no*
standards or absolutes or paradigms and those who claim that such verities exist are totally uninformed and unenlightened: That is precisely
what one hears in the liberal tone of voice, as Graubard's article discloses to anyone who scrutinizes what he writes and the way he presents his arguments. Only those who possess it, it seems, are to be believed and followed. Through conveying an aura of tolerance and
understanding, the liberal tone revolves around its own self-assert-
iveness and self-righteousness. There is haughtiness here and a refusal
to accept any other viewpoint than its own presuppositions and predisposition. Scorn, derision, disdain, even hatred, however masked by a
sophisticated articulation, finally guide the liberal tone and its commanding power and influence in all areas of American society and culture. Day in and day out, the humdrum liberal tone is duly registered
and certified in the columns of the great newspapers and magazines, in
the commentaries of television commentators and personalities, in the
books promoted by famous publishing houses, in the decisions of the
rich foundations, in the educational policies formulated in the most
prestigious colleges and universities. Inevitably and inescapably the
liberal tone is pervasive—and destructive.

Destructive is a strong word to use here, but anyone who reflects on
the liberal tone and weighs its consequences will not fail also to see that
the elements of materialism, positivism, and utilitarianism inform the
liberal tone—and the liberal ethos. First principles are necessarily abandoned altogether or subordinated to the relativistic valuations defined
by or associated with the dictates of progress, modernity, change, plu-
rality, innovation, expansionism. In a word, it is the sophistry of the

liberal tone that makes it as suspect and alarming as it was, in a much earlier period, to Plato, who vigorously opposed its moral and metaphysical relativism. What makes the liberal tone so untrustworthy, above all, is the smug and specious manner in which it not only scoffs at the moral standards of existence but also conduces the erosion of a moral code. Deeply embedded in the liberal tone, and style, one thus finds an instinctive antagonism to the moral sense; to the moral view of the universe as a spiritual cosmos rooted in the principle of unity; in short, to the moral view that the late Will Herberg underlines when he writes:

> Unless *some* principle, some standard, *transcending* the particular context or situation, is somehow operative *in* the context or situation, nothing but moral chaos and capriciousness can result. No human ethic is possible that is not itself grounded in a higher law and higher reality beyond human manipulation or control.

Herberg's words are to be found in an essay entitled "What Is the Moral Crisis of Our Time?" which first appeared in the January–March 1968 issue of the *Intercollegiate Review*. This essay should remind any serious reader that moral valuations (no less than the moral virtues) are not obsolete, even if the *Times* and all its liberalizing Graubards systematically choose to discount a moral theory of value and, in effect, to bank on ceaseless decline in "spirituality."

7

The New York Times *and Eric Voegelin*

As a native New Englander who at an early age somehow intuited a peculiar provincialism that characterizes local newspapers of that region of the country, I have been a regular reader of the *New York Times* for nearly four decades. Actually my introduction to that great national newspaper came after my first being introduced by a neighbor—a Communist—to the now defunct *PM*. That newspaper, to the horror of my family, excitingly tainted much of my early social-political thinking in ways that, in time, I myself found blemished and contaminative. Later, after several years of brutal public school teaching, I came to believe that the gospel of the liberal left preached by Ralph Ingersoll's *PM*, and of everything in the liberal persuasion that it reflected and was symptomatic of, was suspect. The *Times*, in any case, was far more even-handed and restrained in its reporting of the news, as I began to find.

If through the years the *Times* has been my daily news educator, I have become more discriminating in my own judgmental responses to its reportorial management of "All the News That's Fit to Print." That is, I have had to learn how to detect in the *Times* those editorial subtleties, those quietly controlled but ever-present biases, that patronizing liberal tone, with its implicit innuendoes, its insidious *divertissements* and *données*, that call for one's intellectual resistance, if not for one's rebuttal, if one is not to be stamped by the *Times*'s editorial ethos (no less than, for a period, I was stamped by the Max Lerners and I. F. Stones of *PM*).

Dutifully I continue to read the *Times* on a regular basis, though increasingly I find substantive reasons to quarrel with its editorial policies and opinions and its overall arrangement and presentation of the news. I have learned, of course, not to expect to gain any spiritual edification from the *Times*, even as I have learned to distrust, or at least to question, the *Times*'s "monopoly of virtue," to use an apt phrase that appears as the title of Russ Braley's concluding chapter in his absorbing book, *Bad News: The Foreign Policy of The New York Times* (1984). (This book confirms some of my own feelings and suspicions as these have been germinating these past forty years.)

I do not intend to go into matters here that Mr. Braley examines with authoritative care and awareness in his book, which I am glad to recommend to those who are concerned with the various ways in which the *Times* influences American foreign and domestic policies. Though I am also concerned with these influences, I am more concerned at this moment with directing readers' attention to the way in which the *Times* chooses to treat the life and achievement of thinkers "whose ideas have consequences." No occasion reminds me more of just how derelict and dismissive the *Times* can be in its treatment of conservative expositors than in its recent notice reporting the death of Eric Voegelin at the age of 84 in California on January 19, 1985. The full text of the obituary notice, as belatedly printed in the *Times*, on January 23, is worth quoting in full if only to catch the perfunctory tenor of the notice and all of its neutralist and abjectly factual elements, those very elements that cumulatively seek to convey an objectivity that, in reality, is informed by ignorance and slight.

One finds in the *Times*'s obituary notice the absolute absence of any kind of sympathetic understanding or illumination of the life and work of a great philosopher and teacher. One will also discover that at the heart of this absence is what Braley calls a "*Times* ideology," that is, a way of seeing and presenting things, defining or expressing a point of view, identifying a particular predisposition, in short, pinpointing what can be perceived as still another example of a journalistic orthodoxy of enlightenment that erases "the faculty of attention" (as Henry James calls it), which should be fully and disinterestedly engaged in the adjudicative critical process. Here, at any rate, is the entire text of the *Times*'s obituary notice of Voegelin's death, found under the caption, "Eric Voegelin, Philosopher, Author, and Professor, Dies":

> Eric Voegelin, a German-born philosopher, author, and professor who fled the Nazis from the University of Vienna during World War II, died last Saturday at his home on the campus of Stanford University in Stanford, Calif. He was 84 years old.
>
> Professor Voegelin, who became a United States citizen in 1944, taught at Harvard, the University of Alabama and Louisiana State University. In 1968, he went to Stanford as a distinguished research scholar.

His works included *The New Science of Politics* [1952] and *Order and History*, a four-volume work on historical philosophy [1956–1974]. He was working on a fifth volume at his death.

He is survived by his wife, Lissy.

Clearly, this obituary notice lacks an appreciative note of friendliness, or sympathy, or comprehension. It simply and expeditiously records the death of *a* philosopher and teacher, as it would that of some business figure, or convicted criminal, or political underling, or pop musician of yesteryear. No recognition of the great stature of Voegelin as man and thinker is indicated anywhere in the report of his death and in the mere listing of his magisterial publications. It would, in fact, be embarrassingly impossible for the *Times* to quote from any of its own views of Voegelin's writings precisely because there has never been a single review of any of Voegelin's books, as can be easily and distressingly verified by examining the *New York Times Index*.

For the *Times*, Voegelin has never existed and his work has never been deemed important. This neglect is a scandalous example of the positivistic proclivity that afflicts the *Times* as much as it afflicts social and intellectual conditions in general in the United States. And it is precisely this proclivity that would find inescapably antipathetic a philosophical thinker who sees history as "a mystery in process of revelation," who insists that "God and man, world and society, form a primordial community of being," and who asserts that "the destiny of man lies not in the future but in eternity." To modern positivists and empiricists such views are held in contempt, to be eliminated in any way possible.

Indeed, when one looks at the listed reviews of Voegelin's major books, what is notoriously evident is that not only the *Times* but also major journals of opinion have more often than not chosen not to take notice. The recognition of a philosophical and spiritual genius, in other words, has not been generously forthcoming, or if it has, it has been negligible and even grudging. In this respect the skimpy obituary notice in the *Times* serves as a representative instance of how Voegelin's achievement has been perceived and treated through the years by academic philosophers and political theorists and scientists, who for Voegelin himself provide "a very good picture of the intellectual corruption and destruction which characterizes the contemporary academic world." That Voegelin, as Ellis Sandoz remarks, remained a philosopher and physician rather than becoming a prophet and healer has additional relevance here: Voegelin rejects the kind of panaceas offered by positivism, Marxism, and Freudianism, and such a rejection entails considerable consequences in a liberal society.

Voegelin had the kind of standards of integrity that preclude popular acceptance and success. In refusing to endear himself either to the powerful Eastern intellectual community or, for that matter, to the *Times*'s ethos, Voegelin refused to play the game that pundits like the Galbraiths and the Schlesingers play so cleverly and rewardingly. None of these influential figures would ever have the temerity to assert, as does Voegelin with absolute conviction and candor, "that the history of philosophy is in the largest part the history of its derailment." Such a defiant, uncompromising assertion directly challenges the climate of opinion as we know it in the academy and all its affiliates. Inevitably those who pose such a disquieting challenge—and here one also thinks of Irving Babbitt in an earlier period and Aleksandr Solzhenitsyn today—become marked men, dissident thinkers consigned to fateful obscurity in the Gorky that obviously extends beyond a Soviet oblast.

The fact remains that in his writings and world view, Voegelin indicts the sacred idols, the *doxai*, of technologico-Benthamite civilization, and that his indictment emerges from a deeply spiritual conception of human existence and an affirmation of the experience of transcendence and of "the permanent things." "The long history of post-classical Western Gnosticism," he declares, "appears in its continuity as the history of Western sectarianism." Surely, pan-*Times* sectaries, and the "libidinous profiteers," as Voegelin calls them, who are everywhere in commanding positions of power and influence, could hardly condone such a declaration. To say, as does Voegelin, that "the destiny of man lies not in the future but in eternity," is to utter an indiscretion in a Sartrean world, East and West, which scornfully rejects the *Logos* (or, for that matter, any consonant logocentric acceptation of life, literature, and thought).

To appeal, too, to the past for paradigms of meaning, or to reflect, for instance, on classical studies, on their purpose and prospects, for apprehension of the order of man's existence, as well as of man's nature, is for Voegelin (as he tells us in his remarkable essay "On Classical Studies" [in the Winter 1973 issue of *Modern Age*]) a sacred noetic task, a living principle of thought and belief. Such reflection requires a greater heroism in a world in which moral virtues have been abridged. Voegelin never lacked moral or intellectual heroism. He steadfastly refused to capitulate to the agents of reductionism who legislate what he calls "the two closely related processes of the fragmentation of science through specialization and the deculturation of Western society." Doubtlessly no amount of paraphrase or of critical commentary can replace Voegelin's diagnosis of the inorganic conception of the world that prevails in modern culture and society. His words, as we read and meditate on them in the following extract from "On Classical Studies," an essay which should be required reading for all teachers and students (but won't be, things being what they are in an educational world in which preside the priests of deconstructionism, the *chic* contemporary version of Jacobinism), hold an urgent message that we can dismiss only at our peril:

> The public interest has shifted from the nature of man to the nature of nature and to the prospects of domination its exploration opened; and the loss of interest even turned to hatred when the nature of man proved to be resistant to the changes dreamed up by intellectuals who want to add the lordship of society and history to the mastery of nature. The alliance of indifference and hatred, both inspired by *libido dominandi*, has created the climate that is not favorable to an institutionalized study of the nature of man. . . . The protagonists of the Western deculturation process are firmly established in our universities.

We choose our intellectual and spiritual heroes elsewhere. Not Eric Voegelin but Herbert Marcuse is the modern philosophical and political thinker that the *Times* honors by the attention it showers upon him. Where the *Times* could assemble only seven sentences to report Voegelin's death, it displayed on August 31, 1979, a long article by Kenneth A. Briggs on the death of Marcuse. He is described as "a guiding figure of many social activitists of the 1960's because of his radical Marxist critique of Western capitalism," especially his Marxist and Freudian "indictment of American society, which he called a 'repressive monolith.'" Reference is made to Marcuse's influence on student radicals, especially his most famous student, Angela Davis, in the civil rights and antiwar movements. Briggs remarks that Marcuse believed that for reason and science to create a "new man" and a "new age," violence was justified. What Marcuse, looking back on the 1960s, later told an interviewer is quoted as follows:

You see the heroic period was that of the hippies and yippies. They did their thing. They did an indispensable job. They were heroes. They probably still are, but we have moved into a different period, a higher period in terms of historical sequence. We are now in the midst of the organized counterrevolution. You cannot have fun with fascism.

Briggs also notes some of the reasons for a decline in Marcuse's influence as the social unrest of the 1960s diminished, stressing at the same time that Marcuse drew passionate criticism from a variety of sources: "He was the object of verbal assaults by, among others, former Vice President Spiro T. Agnew, former California Gov. Ronald Reagan and the American Legion." The obituary article glances at the political perspective of Marcuse's ideas: "in most of his work, the soft-spoken philosopher aimed at an analysis that transcended national boundaries. He saw both the Soviet and American systems as repressive." That, too, Marcuse regarded the "sexual revolution" with disdain and that he saw drugs as a form of enslavement are points stressed by Briggs, who goes on to say: "In flower power, in the language of the hippies and the street people, in their coarse and abusive epithets, Dr. Marcuse found traces of a truly radical ethic."

The preceding synopsis of the *Times*'s obituary of Herbert Marcuse is given here in order to underline the seriousness and the attentiveness with which Marcuse's reputation and influence are invested. It is a commendably full and informative obituary account, exactly what one would naturally expect to find in a distinguished national newspaper. Reinforcing the significance of the obituary account, it should be further noted, is an editorial entitled "The Power of Negative Thinking," which appears in the same issue of the *Times* and which echoes Briggs's own words as it concludes:

> Herbert Marcuse was tolerated, and he caused a great stir. In fact, a dozen of his books are still in print. But the days of violent protest have faded and so has Marcuse's notoriety. Did his fate prove his theory? He may have wondered. Yet it's more likely that his critique, while generally interesting, was too flawed to sustain the excitement.

But such a conclusion, portentous, and cavalier, of the vintage that one has slowly come to expect in the liberal temper and idiom, will not appease those dissidents among us who witnessed and suffered the events of the 1960s as these were inspired by Marcuse's defined goal of the destruction of society and his aversion to any piety for past achievements, for that saving and transcending principle of *humanitas* that George Eliot, more than a century ago, expressed in words that Herbert Marcuse, "nihilist heresiarch" of the modern age, could hardly begin to understand: "The first condition of human goodness is something to love, the second something to reverence." We tend to forget, as does the *Times* editorial writer, that a philosopher's ideas have consequences and that inferior ideas have particularly bad consequences. The things he says and writes and teaches can have enduring impact and, as in the case of Marcuse, inspire acts of rebellion and disorder that make it impossible to counter what Richard M. Weaver terms "perversions of truths and acts of bestiality." To grasp both the legacy of impiety and the full extent of Marcusean excrescences, one cannot rely on the *Times* obituary and editorial. For such an understanding one is well advised to turn to Eliseo Vivas' remarkable scrutiny as found in his book *Contra Marcuse* (1971).

Here the point I want to make is that, in terms of attention and emphasis, the *Times* gives almost a kind of institutional sanction to a radical philosopher that it obviously withholds from a Voegelin. That, to be sure, is an editorial choice, but one that also alerts us to the prevailing attitude when the obituary occasion presents itself. In the end, the notorizing of Marcuse and the disregard of Voegelin are curiously characteristic of the *Times*'s liberalism that, as Braley would say, spells "bad news." If the *Times*, then, chooses to ignore the stature of a thinker like Voegelin, what can one expect from the other newspapers in the country? It mythicizes a man like Marcuse—"He had white hair and spoke in a thick accent and influenced thousands of mostly middle-class white American college students in the Sixties and early Seventies," reads the second sentence in the *Times* editorial—and barely notices a man like Voegelin, what he stands for, the insight and wisdom he conveys, the moral and spiritual principles that he defines and defends and that prompt him to say of the Homeric—and of *this*—world: "the disorder of a society was a disorder in the soul of its component members."

For the *Times*-men and their doctrinaire relativistic faith, Voegelin's statement is no doubt meaningless when viewed against what, for example, Marcuse writes in *One-Dimensional Man* (1964). We are urged, it seems, to sanctify Marcusean "negations" and at the same time to scorn Voegelinian "visions of order." In this disorientation, as it might be described, we discern a prescribed debasement of life as we are led deeper and deeper into a "culture of abundance," as well as a "culture of celebrity." Again Weaver's words are particularly apropos here: "Thus present-day reformers combat dilution by diluting further, dispersion by a more vigorous dispersing." Increasingly and fatally, we choose to dramatize "organized counterrevolution" and frown upon the discipline of character. An unbelieving thinker like Marcuse is for us the center, as the *Times* would lead us to assume.

"*Order and History*," asserts Russell Kirk, "will restore to some modern minds an understanding of transcendence." Clearly the modern age has become a "drama of atheist humanism" relentlessly enacted in the demise of transcendence and the triumph of immanentism. No thinker has better diagnosed the essential conditions that have led to this cruel fate than has Voegelin. No thinker has more boldly or keenly viewed the pendulum motion of order and disorder simultaneously striking in the human psyche and in the cosmos. And no thinker has ventured to express with such uncompromising determination the tensive connections between the life of the soul and the life of the civil polity: ". . . the diagnosis of health and disease in the soul is . . . at the same time a diagnosis of order and disorder in society." Voegelin's words emerge from the ground and truth of his vision; they compel us to recognize the need to return to a consciousness of principles. Surely no contemporary thinker has been more daring in raising central questions that have too often been egregiously ignored. Why, he thus asks in "Remembrance of Things Past," a new first chapter written by Voegelin especially for the American edition of *Anamnesis* (1978 [1966]), "why do important thinkers like Comte or Marx refuse to apperceive what they apperceive quite well? why do they expressly prohibit anybody to ask questions concerning the sectors of reality that they have excluded from their personal horizon? why do they want to imprison themselves in their restricted horizon and to dogmatize their prison reality as the universal truth? and why do they want to lock up all mankind in the prison of their making?"

What is most strikingly symptomatic of the modern period, according to Voegelin, is "the perversion of reason," which he believes "has grown . . . into the murderous grotesque of our time." The special constituents of this process as these have shaped the climate of opinion embody for Voegelin the rhythm of deformation that visibilizes in "the concentration camps of totalitarian regimes and the gas chambers in which the grotesqueness of opinion becomes the murderous reality of action." No words better capture the diagnostic acumen found in Voegelin's achievement. It is alarming, then, that the astonishing nature of his achievement, anchored as it is in history and learning, has been scanted by the *Times* and by those in the intellectual community who prefer to bask in modern Gnostic experiences—progressivism, utopianism, revolutionary activism. Yet, as Voegelin declares in *The New Science of Politics*, ". . . since the life of the spirit is the source of order in man and society, the very success of a Gnostic civilization is the cause of its decline."

No less than Plato, Voegelin apprehended the cardinal facts. What Emerson says of Plato is equally true of Voegelin: "His sense deepens, his merits multiply, with study." In death, as in life, Eric Voegelin remains a *spoudaios*, a mature man; a *sophos*, a sage; and, above all, the *aristos phylax*, the best guardian, of a civilized world of reason, dignity, and order.

8

Metaphors of Violence

"It comes in the context of the changes we've seen in our value systems over the last 15 or 20 years. People are more self-centered, narcissistically oriented. The attitude is, if it feels good, let's do it, my needs come first and if that conflicts with society, that's too bad." These are the words of the chief psychologist of the Los Angeles Police Department with reference to the highway disputes and shootings that recently left some people dead and others injured on the congested freeways of California. Similar incidents occurred on major highways in Connecticut, New York, Illinois. In Connecticut, according to one police official, people were "hitting each other with tire irons and baseball bats." It appears that the immediate cause of the violence, in the words of a highway safety researcher, is that "Our society is very impatient with people who don't move fast. It's an unforgivable sin to get in the way of traffic." And still another analyst sees these phenomena in their societal dimensions: "The freeways are a culture medium for this virulent behavior to grow."

Ultimately the pattern of violence on the nation's roads has far deeper significance than what is immediately related to urban problems, transit conditions, demographic exigencies, environmental concerns, and safety standards. The need to look beneath concrete data and examples, to go to the roots of desperate circumstances and consequences, tends to be neglected in a society in which causes and effects are routinely subordinated to instant analysis at the commentator level and short-range solutions, eluding as these often do moral considerations. Political theory and action are in the end incomplete in their appraisal of and solution to problems affecting the total quality of life. No doubt, the specified highway problems will in time be massively confronted and assuaged and then largely forgotten, for we are, after all, a pragmatic people capable of controlling and finally ordering the mechanics of our modern civilization. Our mastery of technique, we have convinced ourselves, is second to none. There is no material problem that our social engineers cannot lick!

We are famous, it seems, for the plans that our "great simplifiers" endlessly formulate in quest of a great egalitarian state, to the extent that we judge political leaders strictly in relation to their potential success as great technicians of a pluralistic society. That is the main political criterion in the secular realm. Managerial experts and technocrats who can harness the mechanisms of matter and organize the instruments of production are the new masters. Pragmatism and scientism, in concert, thus embody the managerial revolution that James Burnham probed in the early forties, often abstracting social economy from morality. More and more, empirical laws of material causality determine men's choices, with metaphysics, morality, and religion relegated to impassive "superstructures." The liberalism and social action that John Dewey championed continue to hold programmatic sway as we address ourselves to problems of which the events on the nation's highways are such alarming symptoms. It is, then, always revealing to examine reactions to the major problems besetting our society and how these in turn transform into solutions. And invariably both the reactions and the solutions are to be seen in the context of that exclusive process that Simone Weil views as one in which matter is used for the manufacturing of the good.

Thus, for one to look at the remedies for the crisis of modernity is for one to become more aware of remedies that basically lack substantive content precisely because most remedies ignore moral values as the metaphysical matrix of any solution for human problems or the alleviation of the human condition. Who are the authorities who counsel us in meeting the general crisis of disorder that we experience? What are the historical texts to which we turn for a viable instruction that speaks to our condition? What, in short, are our paradigms, not only socially but also morally and spiritually? The answers to these questions should provide us with some understanding of how fully we succeed or fail in confronting the problems of modern existence. For in the choices we make we disclose the deeper nature of our beliefs and also define our basic positions. In the end, the viability of our solutions to the problems we wrestle with reflects the integrity of the authorities and the texts we frequent and the kind of discipline we derive from them.

In this connection we can never escape the need for standards within the larger context of the need for roots. Indeed, even in our perception of standards we need to be vigilant if we are to apply standards that emerge from principles that are at once universal and eternal, rather than from what our neoterists and temporalists devise so as to accommodate "the contemporary forward moving world" in all of its flux and transience. Standards, hence, must not be subordinated to some great modern accommodation in a technologico-Benthamite world. The solution to the violence on the freeways and highways must in the end refer back to norms and standards, to enduring values, which transcend the drifts and shifts of a new morality raised on the shoulders of ideologists who promise a brave new world. Before any social-political solution evolves, a demanding metaphysical reorientation will be necessary, one that stresses standards of public virtue, the idea and hierarchy of value, and a ground of being in the moral life and the ethical life. As we view the great crises that threaten our civilization, we must reject the remedies spawned by a neo-pagan *Zeitgeist*.

Frequently and predictably our mentors today are in the mold of a socialist romanticist like Michael Harrington, who soars joyously on "the left wing of the possible"; or a gnostic mythicizer like Joseph Campbell, who places "libido over credo"; or a behavioral scientist like B. F. Skinner, who contends that "the world needs a technology of behavior 'comparable in power and precision to physical and biological technology.'" The techniques of the scientific empiricists displace covenantal and sacramental precepts in the drive to attain a secular accommodation. Rousseau's conception of the "human machine" continues to predominate in the Western world. We refuse to look into the depths of or to attend to the needs of the human soul. We choose to forget that in the end the conditions of society and culture are determined by the discipline and judgments of the spirit. We choose, therefore, to face each new crisis impervious to the virtues of restraint, order, reverence. The imperative of technique, not responsibility, is what generally finds favor; and the reforms that are often advanced are those that ignore any moral measure or spiritual order. In the educational realm, for instance, there is an ongoing crisis that is fully recognized, but the reforms that are presented are far removed from those high goals that Thomas Jefferson defined: "Education generates habits of application, of order and the love of virtue; and controls, by the force of habit, any innate obliquities in our moral organization."

The acts of violences on the highways serve as an acute metaphor of compulsion and self-abandonment and also remind us that we have urgent need to recognize absolute sovereignty and to accept absolute values in the framework of what Romano Guardini, in his book on *Power and Responsibility* (1961), perceives as "essentials": "There is no greatness which is not grounded deep in self-conquest and self-denial. Man's instincts are not of themselves orderly; they must be put (and kept) in order. Man must master them, not they him. Faith in the so-called goodness of nature is cowardice. It is refusal to face the evil that is there too, along with the good." Today, in much of what we read and hear and see it is rare to find the spiritual wisdom and insight that reside in Guardini's words. To pass beyond the walls of our modernity we shall first have to overcome the logic of solipsism habitually advanced by those in commanding positions of influence.

Even our efforts to show reverence are misguided and misdirected when we stop to think, for example, how in 1987, the tenth anniversary of Elvis Presley's death from drug addiction, thousands of faithful gathered at his shrine in Memphis, Tennessee,—50,000 pilgrims, to be exact, brought together during Elvis International Tribute Week. As one gleeful folklorist was to put it, "Elvis has become an icon." The events and the language and emotion of ritual enacted in "Graceland," the home of the singer in Memphis, are another example of the glorification of secular religion and also the defilement of a sacred word like reverence. "You love your family," a pilgrim rhapsodized, "you love your husband, you love your children, and you love Elvis." The modern disorder-pattern affects, it is clear, not only material existence but also spiritual expression—not only public conduct as witnessed on public roads but also individual experience in terms of the soul's holiness. Perversions of faith and order become canons of a new morality as the soul is pushed to a lower status. This is all the more reason why we need "moral pilots" who can lead us away from the Elvis of *Jailhouse Rock* and *All Shook Up* and help us to "recover what has been lost," as T. S. Eliot wrote, "in a wilderness of mirrors."

Like India, the United States is not a nation but a congress of nations. And no less than India the United States is prone to disorder, the consequences of which can be fatal, as incidents on the California freeways illustrate. For these consequences to be arrested it will be necessary to have the kind of leadership, "men of light and leading" who have the integrity and vision to resolve problems not merely in a political but in a metaphysical sense by isolating that "faith in drifting," as Paul Elmer More calls it. In the modern era we have turned almost exclusively to political action as we have come to believe that the machinery of politics can rectify any problem. In effect, we misread external meanings for the internal ones, and there is no let-up in this inclination, even as by the same token we sneer at the truth of Edmund Burke's dictum that "Society cannot exist unless a controlling power upon will and appetite be placed somewhere, and the less of it there is within, the more there must be without."

Perhaps what best identifies the disorder-pattern of modern society are the increasing number of acts violating the moral order of rule and breaking loose from any measure of restraint or bounds of moderation. Contemporary metaphors of violence graphically remind us of the unusual extent and depth of the disintegration of our time as crystallized in the absence not only of what George Santayana called "that essential trait of rational living: to have a clear sanctioned ultimate aim," but also in what he listed as "the virulent cause of this long fever": subjectivism, egotism, conceit of mind. Certainly two of the most essential virtues that modern man has repudiated to his peril are the moderation of the classical temper and the reverence of the biblical faith. Even cultural conservatives who are troubled by our social disarray, as Professor Stephen J. Tonsor notes, "dither in the halfway house of modernity and offer us technical solutions that touch the symptoms but never deal with the causes of contemporary disorder."[1]

In the meanwhile, violence in all forms spreads on a grand scale. Thus, a gang of youths rampages through Greenwich Village, threatening passers-by with ice picks and razors. Still another gang rampages through a subway station on the Upper West Side of Manhattan, robbing and beating passengers, pushing a man onto the subway tracks, and opening fire with an automatic weapon on horrified bystanders. Endless, too, are the reports of students in inner-city schools who carry knives, meat cleavers, brass knuckles, and guns in their book bags—some doing so for self-protection and yet others for felonious purposes. In a Brooklyn high school, minority students, angered by a history teacher's remarks during a discussion of South Africa, storm out of classes and vandalize the school building and stores in the surrounding area. (The teacher, according to reports, had condemned not only apartheid but also black dictators in African nations who committed atrocities against their people.) And in the great metropolitan centers we now see, almost on a daily basis, organized drug gangs—the "New Vigilantes," the "John Johns," the "Do-Wops"—battling savagely for supremacy. "We sell drugs, and we kill," is their war-cry.

No one is safe from violence, including the elderly in Houston, Texas, where residents in age from 60 to 84 have been murdered during rapes, robberies, or burglaries. "I worry about going out in the day. I never go out at night," one retired woman exclaims fearfully. In Nashville, Tennessee, 1,000 youths surging out of a rap concert panic in a narrow, winding hallway, after hearing gunfire, and trample to death other youths. In Westwood, Massachusetts, an affluent town near Boston, high school students hold such wild parties that extensive damage to private property ensues. The police chief of Westwood sums up what is now a common problem in many communities: "You don't think of teen-age parties as crime, but teen-agers and booze are killing people." On the other hand, the insipid response of the principal of Westwood High School is especially illuminating as to the state of educational leadership in the country: "There are parties here, like everywhere else. The issue gets blown out of proportion. It seems like it just never dies." In a way, this educator's response is no less disturbing—and no less shameful—than the response of one of eight youths arraigned on charges of viciously beating and raping a jogger in Central Park: "It was fun!"

In this tide of violence nothing is sacrosanct. Thus, we increasingly hear of arson and sacrilege committed against synagogues, churches, and religious settings. A fire ignited by a time bomb explodes a nativity scene in one church; and a sparrow and a cow's tongue are nailed to the charred ruin of still another church, along with a sign bearing these words: "How many more fires before you realize God is dead?" Nor is the political scene unscarred by violent impulses. In Chicago, for instance, we view an incredibly bizarre scene when an acting mayor is finally chosen by the City Council following twelve hours of street demonstrations, scuffles, chants, jeers. Of this pandemonium one public official laments: "The rule of law has ended. The mob and the crowd have taken over."

But there is no need to go on with this catalogue of crimes of violence. Enough has been said to make us apprehensive of conditions that menace the general weal. A question that remains to be answered is, How are we to alter the existing situation? Any such altering, however, must transcend the blatantly activist secular perspective which rules in the land. For only when we begin to see our problems in the light of just how faulty are the secular solutions proffered by our reigning naturalists, behaviorists, social scientists, and enlightened intellectuals, will we discern the road we must take if we are to stave off total collapse.

It would be foolish to claim that it is easy to end the process of discivilization of which acts of violence are a containing symbol. The language and practice of the moral virtues have been discarded as irrelevant. Sin is now a word that has been excised from the formation of character and the life of the soul. The religious sense has been deconstructed, as it were, by the secular mind, so much so that human sensibility has coarsened to the point that the recovery of the virtue of piety is remote. Indeed, the expanding secular temper of society is so endemic that impieties flourish without end. Modern life itself becomes a perpetual freeway, with its shoot-outs, murder, rapine, incendiarism—a vaudeville of devils, to recall F. M. Dostoevsky's prophetic image.

Alas, we have yet to realize that the absence of a moral code intensifies the difficulty of finding genuine alternatives. Even a common language of concern and understanding is elusive when eternal values and meaning in the lexicon of life and faith have been abrogated. "Without a spiritual authority, *without someone to command*," Ortega y Gasset warned more than a half century ago, "and in the measure that this lack is felt, chaos prevails." But when chaos in the forms of violence and disorder reaches, as it surely must, its zero hour, the alternatives can be dire, as William F. Rickenbacker reminds us in a recent commentary: "And—the larger question—if this mindlessness goes on too much longer in this country, will we find ourselves, some place down the road, faced with the unhappy choice, that Spain had to face, the choice between anarchy and Franco?"[2] This unsettling question must fill us all the more with fear and trembling.

9

A Failure of Nerve

A continuation of the series of essays in *Concepts of Criticism* (1963) and *Discriminations* (1970), René Wellek's later book, *The Attack on Literature and Other Essays* (1982),[1] displays the erudition that characterizes the contributions of the *doyen* of historians of modern literary criticism. One reads these essays, all of them written in the 1970s, with respect not only for the values they convey, but also for the standards of discrimination they espouse. Throughout Wellek addresses himself to the conditions and problems of modern criticism and to the role of the critic. His diagnosis of the critical situation is sane; his tone is even-tempered and prudent. For one to remain dispassionate at a time when the critical picture is filled with impoverishment and grossness, of which deconstruction is now cruelly symptomatic, is in itself a considerable accomplishment. Keeping a cool head, as Joseph Conrad would say, is no easy matter for the scholar-critic whose purpose and meaning are under attack in a society in which gnostic and nihilistic tendencies harden into programmatic policies.

The Attack on Literature and Other Essays makes one more aware of the problems that confront teacher and critic committed to *humanitas*. Wellek assuages one's task of detecting the elements of disorder, the *malaise*, that pervade criticism. He enables one to identify the misdirections, the imbalances, and the perversities of modern literary culture. His book has the added value and, in effect, the added generalist dimension of examining the literary scene in its international features and its comparative nuances. Particularly in stressing literary theory, Wellek counters provincial and solipsistic habits of mind that stubbornly assail American scholarship and criticism. Any attempt to thwart critical provincialism is praiseworthy. One may argue with the specifics of Wellek's "concepts of criticism," but not with the need to resist the provincialism that assaults literary studies in dehumanizing ways.

What constitutes the office of the critic? What are the responsibilities of the critic? How does one measure the frontiers of criticism? How valid is the critical function in an age in which "we sing sad songs of the death of criticism," as one disappointed commentator has declared? These are some of the questions that Wellek asks. Though he sees much that is disturbing in literary scholarship and criticism, his basic attitude is resilient and even hopeful. At the end of his title essay he writes: "There will still be the voice of men of letters and poets, in verse or prose, who will speak (as they have done since hoary antiquity) for their society and for mankind. Mankind will always need a voice and a record of that voice in writing and print, in literature." This optimistic note inheres in these essays and is even surprising to encounter in the midst of the negativisms that Wellek traces in his appraisal of major attacks on literature in recent decades: for instance, the political attack, which views literature as a reactionary force; the linguistic attack, which focuses on the retreat from the word; and the anti-aesthetic attack, which rejects quality and form in favor of technology or subliterature. In these attacks Wellek underlines one common trait, a refusal to "recognize quality as a criterion of literature; quality that may be either aesthetic or intellectual, but which in either case sets off a specific realm of verbal expression from daily transactions of business."

In his Prefatory Note, Wellek sums up his thinking about literature in these words: "I believe in literary scholarship and criticism as a rational enterprise that aims at a right interpretation of texts, at a systematic theory of literature, and at the recognition of quality and thus of rank among writers." The word "quality" recurs in the essays. "We cannot get around the question of quality, which is the central question of criticism," Wellek maintains. His insistence on quality also serves as his indictment of the spirit of relativism that threatens literature and criticism as a whole and that leads to an anarchy of values, which Wellek identifies with "the new barbarism." If, then, criticism is to have meaning and value, it must be evaluation. "Evaluation grows out of understanding," Wellek declares; "correct evaluation out of correct understanding. . . . Logic, ethics, and, I believe, even aesthetics cry aloud against complete relativism. It would lead to a dehumanization of the arts and a paralysis of criticism." This statement deserves careful thought by teachers and critics who honor the function of criticism in the defining contexts of what T. S. Eliot calls "the common pursuit of true judgment." That pursuit has now reached a point of stasis, or of critical entropy, or has taken strange misdirections culminating in that

dread academic disease, *la trahison des clercs*. Wellek frequently reminds
us of the values of the "common pursuit," reminding us, too, of our
mission as teachers and critics when he writes: "One cannot escape the
problem of criticism in the sense of judging. Discrimination, sensitive
weighing of qualities, a simple recognition of what is art, will always
be the main concern of criticism proper. . . . Criticism will survive as
it meets a human need."

The final essay in this book, "Prospect and Retrospect," belongs to
the genre of intellectual autobiography. Its concluding paragraph,
which reasserts Wellek's creed, deserves to be quoted not only because
it contains his basic premises and affirmations, but also because it describes Wellek's achievement of the last fifty years:

> I may be a Laodicean, but I hope that I have preserved my own integrity
> and a core of convictions: that the aesthetic experience differs from other
> experiences and sets off the realm of art, of fictionality, of *Schein*, from
> life; that the literary work of art, while a linguistic construct, at the same
> time refers to the world outside; that it cannot therefore be described only
> by linguistic means but has a meaning telling of man, society, and nature;
> that all arguments for relativism meet a final barrier; that we are con-
> fronted, as students of literature, with an object, the work of art, out there
> (whatever may be its ultimate ontological status) which challenges us to
> understand and interpret it; that there is thus no complete liberty of inter-
> pretation. Analysis, interpretation, evaluation are interconnected stages
> of a single procedure. Evaluation grows out of understanding. We as crit-
> ics learn to distinguish between art and nonart and should have the cour-
> age of our convictions. The lawyer knows or thinks he knows what is
> right and what is wrong; the scientist knows what is true and what is false;
> the physician knows what is health and what is disease; only the poor hu-
> manist is floundering, uncertain of himself and his calling instead of
> proudly asserting the life of the mind which is the life of reason.

In his literary theory Wellek strives to be explicit and systematic,
carefully identifies its properties, and defines its standards. Literature,
he stresses, gives us knowledge of the quality of life and nature; it suggests the possibilities of life, its essential features, its universals. Seen
in the light of high imaginative fiction, literature is characterized by
"the dominance of the aesthetic function." At the same time, Wellek
insists that "literature is not a structured synchronic totality but an
enormous, historically and locally diversified manifold." What Wellek
writes in his revealing Postscript to Volume IV of *A History of Modern*

Criticism: 1750–1950 (1965) identifies an undeviating principle in *The Attack on Literature and Other Essays*, one that rejects any systems that "ignore or minimize the autonomy of art": ". . . the work of literature is the central subject matter of a theory of literature and not the biography or psychology of the author, or the social background, or the affective response of the reader." This principle occupies a dominant place in Wellek's critical thinking. As he specifies in his Postscript: "Criticism aims at a theory of literature, at a formulation of criteria, and standards of description, classification, interpretation, and finally judgment. It is thus an intellectual discipline, a branch of knowledge, a rational pursuit."

The epistemological base of Wellek's theory of literature must be always kept in mind as he himself shows: "In literary study there is an interplay between the intense contemplation of the object and the desire to organize our experience into a network and even a system of concepts. The individual and the general must be kept in balance." Wellek unfailingly stresses the need to dislodge "extrinsic" approaches to literature, particularly those which imitate the methodology of science and belief in deterministic causality: "We cannot accept realism and naturalism, as they confuse life and art and propound the ideal of art mirroring reality instead of creating a new reality of art. Didacticism, moralism, political ideology . . . will distort the meaning of literature. Classicism . . . will impose a narrow ideal of beauty strongly tinged with moral nobility."

The preceding excerpts from "Prospect and Retrospect" and from the Postscript contain the essential Wellek. In their consistency of position and in their formulative principles, they underline what he sees as a paramount critical need, "an axiology, a science of literary values." In this respect, it is difficult to sanction Elmer Borklund's dismissal of Wellek as the author "of arid books in which there is no sense of living contact with the works of literature which criticism is usually presumed to serve."[2] This is an oversimplification insofar as Wellek himself has demarcated his literary and critical premises and positions and has repeatedly enunciated his plea for "a particular need of theoretical awareness, conceptual clarity and systematic methodology in the English-speaking countries, dominated as they are by the tradition of empiricism." Commentators who dwell on Wellek's lack of appreciation for "extrinsic" critical dimensions need to reflect on his own "Reflections on my *History of Modern Criticism,*" in which he writes: "Literary criticism is related to general history whether political or social, and even economic conditions play their part in shaping the history of criticism." There is no lack of definition of priorities in Wellek's critical speculations. A rational mind is at work, as the following statements from *The Attack on Literature and Other Essays* demonstrate: "Today we are confronted not only with critics who reject the past in order to create and justify the future or rather their own brand of poetry, but we have to face a new nihilism, picking up motifs from Marinetti's futurism and Dada." "Recent criticism . . . has become for many an excuse for self-definition, for a display of one's ingenuity and cleverness in battering the object or, in ambition, a pretext for 'vision,' for the discovery of a supernatural reality."

No, one cannot fault Wellek for any want of critical definitions or preoccupations as these apply to literary study and sensibility. Doubtlessly his theoretical and philosophical ethos irritates some of his critics in an age in which the empirical habit of mind fuses with the nihilistic bent for control. Such irritation bespeaks the increasing provincialism that affects the study of literature and that characterizes the forces, the academic gangs, that appropriate the study of literature, often distorting or corrupting its meaning and value. (The essay "American Criticism of the Sixties" touches, rather too gently, on these problems.) In this connection, Wellek's own commitment to comparative literature is reassuring. Thus, in a valuable essay, "The New Criticism: Pro and Contra," though he finds valid much of what the New Critics have taught, Wellek nevertheless stresses a serious limitation: "They are extremely anglocentric, even provincial." Surely, this remark should also make us see that nowhere has literary provincialism had more corrosive results than in the demise of the requirement of courses in world literature in American colleges and universities. This demise evidences the alarming disregard for the idea of *Weltliteratur* and, concomitantly, the general shifting of values in contemporary American life, of which "TV stupor" and "intolerable music" are, as Aleksandr Solzhenitsyn has declared, ravaging conditions of the "present incorrectness." (Christopher Lasch trenchantly views some of the effects of the malady in terms of "the culture of narcissism.") Hopefully, what Wellek says about the inter- and transdisciplinary advantages of comparative literature will impress American teachers and critics:

Neither English literature nor any other literature can be studied in isolation. . . . I have argued insistently against the narrow conception of Comparative Literature prevalent in France. It must not be an arid, academic exercise in the study of external influences, reputations, migrations of themes and the like, but an investigation of the unity of literature, . . . of its great currents, periods and movements. . . . Ideally, we should simply study literature without linguistic restrictions, . . . have Professors of Literature, rather than English, French, or German literature, as we still have Professors of Philosophy and History. . . . Comparative poetics should draw on literatures which have arisen without contacts with the West.[3]

Yet, if Wellek's new book alerts us to the insidious processes of "the attack on literature," and if its critical adjudications are essentially right, it also impels discriminating attention to those special aspects that in the end make one dissatisfied with Wellek's presentation and argument; that make one conclude that Wellek's testimony is inadequate.

Impressiveness and respect identify one's feelings at an initial stage of reaction to *The Attack on Literature and Other Essays*. But one must demand in serious critical matters as they relate to the state of literary culture more than a feeling of esteem. One begins to ask of the book's signification, is this enough? Is something lacking? Is something more needed to make this book worthy of its title and the challenge and the warning embodied in it? In a period of crisis there is need for a more substantive program of action, the absence of which constitutes the most disquieting deficiency in the book. The peculiar essence of the book, one comes to discover, is that of safeness and complacency. It becomes all too obvious that Wellek tends even to defuse the desperate conditions of modern literary criticism and culture. He perceives problems, but he does not choose to cope with them with the urgency they require. What he presents is a kind of catalogue of problems of literature and criticism. "The attack on literature," in other words, is not met with a counter-attack. Wellek shies away from entering the arena of combat; he thus projects the disheartening image of an intelligent and sensitive scholar-critic who places himself *au-dessus de la mêlée* in order to maintain his scholarly equanimity. Inevitably moral relativism and opportunism are the most damaging consequences of one's adopting such a pose. Literary statesmanship, particularly when it conjoins with literary stewardship, has its price!

These criticisms should come as no surprise to anyone who has perused *Theory of Literature* (1949), which Wellek wrote in collaboration with Austin Warren, that generous man of letters and modern "New England Saint." The case against Wellek and Warren has nowhere been better stated than in Seymour Betsky's review of *Theory of Literature* in *Scrutiny*. To reread it is to be reminded of the endemic inadequacies that persist in *The Attack on Literature and Other Essays*. These are not, Betsky iterates, weaknesses that pertain to critical honesty and commonsense. "It is in its way impressive," Betsky writes of *Theory of Literature*. "Learned, even encyclopaedic, it manages to survey the whole province of literary theory, practice, scholarship, history and pedagogy." The book's critical-academic aspirations are what Betsky questions: "Instead of a clearly conceived sense of direction, instead of rigorous subordination, they [Wellek and Warren] offer only the awareness of countless difficulties. . . ." What is more disturbing is that "the book by Wellek and Warren represents the subtle, rarefied, ineffectual flower unaware of the dung out of which it grows."

Betsky applauds the authors' emphasis on literary evaluation, on "the act of judgment," or as one duly reads in Chapter XVIII of *Theory of Literature* (this is a chapter that Warren wrote): "Men ought to value literature for being what it is; they ought to evaluate it in terms and in degrees of its literary value." But it is not the importance of the evaluative process that Wellek and Warren miss as much as they miss the meaning of "the full critical act." As Betsky observes: "The full critical act begins—whatever the complexity of the intermediate stages—with personal responsiveness, the impact kept alive and organic. So far as one can see, Wellek and Warren seem entirely to have eliminated the only justification for taking literature seriously in the first place—the fact that 'it takes place in the developing consciousness of our lives' (L. C. Knights). They substitute in its place the kind of liveliness which attends the solution of intellectual problems." Betsky's review of *Theory of Literature*, it is interesting to note, appeared under the title "The New Antiquarianism," a phrase found in this portentous sentence: "And the surpassing ingenuity of the new antiquarianism is that it utilizes so well all the existing machinery of the old, with almost imperceptible alterations."[4]

The innocuous aspects of *Theory of Literature*, as these are detected by Betsky, are no less characteristic of *The Attack on Literature and Other*

Essays. Wellek's awareness and concerns, however genuine and pertinent, stop short of the kind of commitment, the kind of engagement, that "the attack on literature" requires. Politic scholarly counsel in the search for the "solution of intellectual problems" discloses merely retreat from confrontation. Often to be found in Wellek's book is a tendency to fuse the good and the bad conditions of criticism to the point of innocuousness: "My critical reservations should not obscure my genuine admiration for the brilliance, subtlety, and ingenuity of much recent American criticism." This fusionism is the way in which Wellek concludes his report on "American Criticism in the Sixties." No statement better demonstrates the vacuity of Wellek's approach.

On the other hand, when he chooses to scorn a critic's work, as he does G. Wilson Knight's *The Wheel of Fire* (1930), Wellek shows a tendentiousness that is embarrassing. He singles out Knight as an allegorizer, as one who extracts from Shakespeare "a philosophy which is neither original, clear, nor complex" and which indiscriminatingly reconciles *eros* and *agapē*. The fact remains that Knight is an interpreter of genius whose illuminations of Shakespeare's tragedies have permanent worth for a student of literature. "See that valuable book, *The Wheel of Fire,*" counsels the severe magistrate of literature F. R. Leavis.[5] Its place in the critical canon transcends, even rebukes, the antiquarian mills that operated in 1930, or "the new antiquarianism" that, according to Seymour Betsky, *Theory of Literature* inaugurated. Wellek says he is concerned with critical choices and responsibility. Any honest or brave implementation of that concern should prompt a teacher of literature to direct a student to *The Wheel of Fire* for enlightenment. That is far more than one can say about encouraging a student to go to *Theory of Literature.* Indeed, Leavis once censured F. W. Bateson for suggesting that a student consult *Theory of Literature* because of its "usefulness" and "general good sense." This suggestion, Leavis asserted, "is an irresponsibility that ought to trouble Mr. Bateson's conscience." These are hard words, but if the critical function is to have any centrality, then the time for candor is unending.

The inadequacy of *The Attack on Literature and Other Essays* also helps to identify a fundamental inadequacy of the academy. Roger Sale, in reviewing Volumes III and IV of Wellek's *A History of Modern Criticism*, gives a clue to the nature of this inadequacy when he writes: "Amidst the great concern to cover and do right by everything, Wellek has not asked the relevant questions about literature and criticism."[6] Those "relevant questions" can hardly be asked as long as moral constituents are absent from a critic's creed, and Wellek makes it quite clear that, though he finds in, say, a Leavis, or in an Irving Babbitt, or in a Paul Elmer More things to admire, he cannot give his allegiance to the moral criteria that these critics embrace. Absolutes, in other words, Wellek (with many other scholars) views as impediments to his critical spectrum and investigation, as well as a threat to the objective quality of his intellectualism. He and his sympathizers separate what might be termed their intellectual principles of criticism from moral principles of the kind that Edmund Burke recognizes as necessities.

Doubtlessly Wellek prizes the moral dimension, but he refuses to subscribe to it perhaps because he fears its restraints or the possibility of its becoming a circumscribing metaphysics of art, so to speak. Critical moderation, he seems to be saying, must be separated from fierce critical commitments. In a sense, Wellek's critical position can thus be seen as centrist: he sanctions neither a centrifugal nor a centripetal didacticism or orientation. Characteristically he staunchly differentiates literary criticism from *Kulturphilosophie*. For example, in discussing Matthew Arnold's critical significance, in Volume IV of *A History of Modern Criticism: 1750–1950*, Wellek reveals a notable gap in his approach when he distinguishes the aims of Arnold as cultural thinker from Arnold as critic: "But for our purposes—confined as always to literary criticism—much of this, however important for the great debate on religion and culture, is irrelevant. We must rather try to define Arnold's contribution to thinking about literature and poetry." In imposing this crippling limitation, Wellek underlines an inadequacy that is indicative of his critical *préciosité* and that inevitably denudes his achievement as a comparatist of its full possibility and promise.

Paradigms of the critical spirit, it can be said, are largely absent from the academic world, in which, to apply Henry James's words, "the confusion of kinds is the inelegance of letters and the stultification of values." The need to correct such a condition, particularly as it weakens the humanities, and ultimately *paideia* itself, remains acute. There are always those who prescribe corrective theories, but these have either the deficiency of Wellek's autotelic approach, or the profaneness of the practitioners of a quantum criticism. The resulting predicament for those who care about the discipline of letters is inescapable. If that discipline is to be both viable and rich in cross-fertilization in the total complex of which the study of literature forms a part, it must have exemplars and not mere expositors. This is especially true at a time when the literary and cultural scenes are barren of principles, and when we need the help of those few who, with reverence and awe, give witness to the critical spirit in its crisis. For such a witness and for the sustenance that that witness provides, one should turn to Irving Babbitt's *Literature and the American College: Essays in Defense of the Humanities.* Though it appeared as far back as 1909, it wrestles precisely with some of those issues that Wellek raises, explicitly or implicitly, in *The Attack on Literature and Other Essays.* And it wrestles with them with the courage of faith and the courage of judgment that today one finds almost extinct in the educational realm. It is a book in which the moralist critic as "Man Thinking" and as Witness boldly speaks for the critical spirit; and it is a book that is an answer to those neutralists in the academic community who refuse to take a stand. ("*Non ragioniam di lor, ma guarda e passa,*" Virgil warns Dante when they have passed through "the gate of mystery.") Babbitt undertakes to interrelate educational and literary dimensions and to show how the "confused conflict of tendencies" in one affects the other. That interrelationship, unfortunately, has been egregiously neglected or ignored in recent years by teachers and critics.

There is no more paradigmatic chapter in Babbitt's first book than that entitled "Literature and the College." What "the attack on literature" signifies in postmodern terms of causes and effects receives here the kind of attention that is desperately needed today; that, morally *and* ethically, goes beyond the confines of Wellek's laudable but limited *donné*, "We want to understand and judge literature; we must know what is good and what is bad and why." Critical lucidity and wisdom shape the meaning of Babbitt's scrutiny. It is his recognition of first principles that shapes his critical response and that saves it from the abject intellectual secularism which now absorbs teachers and critics and makes their theories and remedies peripheral and even trivial. In *Literature and the American College* the humanist critic validates connections between literature, life, and thought. Babbitt's critical concern is a moral concern, that of relating knowledge not only to intellect but also to will and character.

To many minds in the academy can be applied Babbitt's words, "But one may shine as a productive scholar, and yet have little or nothing of that humane insight and reflection that can alone give meaning to all subjects. . . ." One regrets not finding in *The Attack on Literature and Other Essays* a comparable sense of a higher critical and pedagogical purpose. Despite its diagnostic truths and its insights, Wellek's book does not radiate the toughness, the centeredness, the clearcut acceptances and affirmations, and the unswerving loyalties needed to resist the "enemies of the permanent things," to use a phrase of Russell Kirk's. For these strengths one must turn to a book like *Literature and the American College,* there to find those critical principles of order and faith that inform representative discriminations like the following:

> We have invented laboratory sociology, and live in a nightmare of statistics. Language interests us, not for the absolute human values it expresses, but only in so far as it is a collection of facts and relates itself to nature. With the invasion of this hard literalness, the humanities themselves have ceased to be humane.

> Certain teachers of literature . . . aspire to be nothing more than graceful purveyors of aesthetic solace, and arbiters of the rhetorical niceties of speech.

"All scholars," writes Paul Elmer More in his essay on "Criticism," "whether they deal with history or sociology or philosophy or language, or, in the narrower sense of the word, literature, are servants of the critical spirit, in so far as they transmit and mould the sum of experience from man to man and from generation to generation."[7] He goes on to emphasize that "at a certain point criticism becomes almost identical with education." Wellek's concept of the critical spirit ultimately lacks the moral centrality that More, with Babbitt, views as a necessity. Wellek's voice is too often that of the academy, and that voice is too often a philistine voice. When one has finished reading Wellek's book, one realizes that here is still another influential teacher-critic who has not spoken out as vigorously as he should, has not voiced his condemnation as uncompromisingly as he should, has not gotten away from abstraction as fully as he should in order to confront the crisis of the humanities resulting from "the attack on literature." That crisis is total in the sense that Babbitt indicated in the early twenties: "When studied with any degree of thoroughness, the economic problem will be found to run into the political problem, the political problem in turn into the philosophical problem, and the philosophical problem itself to be almost indissolubly bound up at last with the religious problem." These are brave and principled words, without a shadow of deflection or a trace of hesitation, that one rarely hears in "dark times." These are words, too, that tell us that criticism is no mere intellectual exercise or prepossession; no mere elaboration of literary theories, trends, or quarrels; no mere demonstration of cleverness or virtuosity. Any concern for standards of living presumes concern for standards in arts and letters.

René Wellek's *The Attack on Literature and Other Essays*, even if one is to react to the implied challenge of combat in its title, ultimately discloses a failure of nerve precisely at a stage when commitment should transform into action and words into deeds. It is Albert Camus, in some memorable words, who tells us about the price which must be paid if that transformation is to be assured: "For a value or a virtue to take root in a society, there must be no lying about it; in other words, we must pay for it every time we can."[8]

Thoughts of a Dissident Critic

I

Readers of *Modern Age: A Quarterly Review*, since its inception in 1957, have been made continuously aware of the crisis of American culture and literature, and, more specifically, of what can be described as the binary crisis of a crass contemporaneousness and an accommodating failure of nerve of our writers, both novelists and critics. This crisis, which is a part of a total crisis of the whole world—religious, moral, social, intellectual, political, economic—intensifies and deepens in scale and consequence. By and large, journals of opinion, general and specialist alike, ignore or even fuel the disordering symptoms of this phenomenon: the abysmal loss of values, the strange and false gods worshipped in the name of escape and fantasy, and the full-scale flight from a commitment to the first principles. Very few journals, or commentators, have disclosed any degree of courage of judgment in diagnosing these symptoms.

Even the belated, heavily endowed and publicized forms of a so-called neoconservative protestation now emanate from borrowers and imitators who will not acknowledge the pioneering efforts of *Modern Age*. Those efforts are an incontrovertible part of the historical record and testify to the permanent and heroic worth of the contribution made by "a conservative review" to American culture and society. From the very beginning, then, *Modern Age* has exemplified what Edmund Burke calls "the dissidence of dissent" by refusing to be indifferent to moral meaning and decision, to choice of character, to counsel of conscience. And, it should be noted, in disclosing and explicating this dissent, "in venturing far out," as Kierkegaard would put it, *Modern Age* has had to find and encourage its own contributors and to make and sustain its own reputation.

Thus to reread Albert Fowler's assessment, in the Fall 1957 issue of the newly founded *Modern Age*, of J. D. Salinger's *The Catcher in the*

Rye (1951), or J. M. Lalley's scrutiny of Mary McCarthy's *The Group* (1963) in the Winter 1963-1964 issue, is to be made keenly aware of the kind of dissident valuations that go against the grain of literary opinion in America; that refuse to give the convenient and comforting critical endorsements that remain the staple of a powerful liberal literary and academic establishment. The latter, it might be further noted as a symptomatic illustration, deftly denigrates, either with a scornful silence or an articulated contempt, Irving Babbitt's conception of the *honnête homme* while at the same time it sings the praises of Herbert Marcuse's tawdry vision of "Erotic Man." Clearly a "sham liberalism" has for too long prevailed in the American intelligentsia. To question its "smatterers" or to defy its fiats, the extreme forms of which now appear in a nihilistic deconstructionism, has its perils even for the hardiest critical and academic dissidents. "Modernistic phantasies" and "utopian dreaming," in Eric Voegelin's phraseology, not only multiply but also dominate at all levels of American life and throttle the humane critical spirit and function. The need, then, for a critical dissidence and in turn for a critical corrective to an unrestrained modernity remains as urgent as a willingness to hear the voices "from under the rubble" warning of the spiritual malaise that enfeebles the West.

In his critique of Salinger's novel, Fowler points to the moral deficiencies and relativistic orientation, the dogmatic naturalism and the romantic impressionism that identify the modern imagination and criticism. What Fowler says about Salinger's *The Catcher in the Rye* (and about its young rebel Holden Caulfield, who is supposedly in search of virtue and truth) underlines these standards of selection and judgment that are absent from American criticism and the absence of which, as seen in the modern American adherents of Rousseau in fiction, reinforces the delusion that man is naturally good and society naturally evil: "Salinger's stand for the individual and against the world, for the heaven of inner desire and opposed to the hell of outward circumstance, brings up the question posed by the disciples of naturalism how deep the split is between moral man and immoral society." In this representative, if, to liberal critics, seditious, critical observation Fowler discloses the qualitative judgment that one now seldom finds in American criticism. It is the kind of critical dissidence that, were it minimally practiced or occasionally recognized, even if rarely accepted, would lessen the desiccating effects of "the dehumanization of art." But in lit-

erature and in the academy it is "the triumph of sports and games," as
Ortega y Gasset puts it, that is so painfully dominant.

And it is "sports and games," in their anatomical or histological detail as Lalley shows, that one finds in Mary McCarthy's *The Group*, a
novel which is about the lives of eight Vassar College alumnae of the
class of 1933 and which critics like William Barrett and Granville Hicks
lavishly acclaimed for its understanding and compassion. The weaknesses of this novel are both intrusive and pervasive, for reasons that
Lalley makes devastatingly clear: "As an artistic effort," Lalley writes,
"the novel must be accounted an almost total failure. The reason is that
Mary McCarthy's interest in her fictive classmates does not go much
beyond a sharp eye for what they wear and eat and drink, the sort of
furniture they acquire, and what she imagines to be their behavior in
bathrooms and bedrooms—and, where occasion requires, in church."
The critical stringency in Lalley's review goes counter to the brilliance
and distinction so often ascribed to Mary McCarthy, "our only real
woman of letters," as *Newsweek* anointed her with journalistic aplomb.
An artist often praised for a prose style that possesses "classic fluidity
and precision," her achievement has been much overrated and overre-
warded not only with prizes and grants, but also with several honorary
degrees, including one from the University of Aberdeen, that most
venerable of Scottish educational institutions.

In offering their critical dissent, both Fowler and Lalley honor and
dignify the function and responsibilities of the critic. They also desider-
ate the reciprocal relations in theory and in practice between a moral
criticism and a moral imagination. But as with so much of the things
of value, the moral centrality that one should be able to find and identify and connect with in the twin realms of the imagination and of criticism, has been increasingly abandoned in literary and academic quarters to nihilistic impulses and theorizings, the *doxai* that are certified in
the name of postmodernism and post-structuralism, the new order that
supersedes universal moral order and marks "the end of the modern
world," to use here Romano Guardini's prophetic phrase.

Indeed, the two phenomena which Guardini feared most, "the not-
human man and the not-natural nature," are the foundations upon
which contemporary society and culture are being erected. The nihilistic forms of such a society obviate the moral standards that define and
inform the concepts of *humanitas* and of *humanus religiosus*. It is the in-

cessant distancing from and rejection of these standards and concepts, in their traditional and sacred moorings, that no doubt impel the minority moral perspective that critical dissidents like Fowler and Lalley disclose in their critical pursuit and that shape and sharpen the critical discriminations and criteria of their estimations of contemporary American fiction. In a word, such a critical dissidence is not fashionable in progressivist literary and academic circles, where it is largely treated with contumely. But that is to say, too, that the transcendent "historic sense" which Fowler and Lalley incorporate into the critical function is what also endows it with the clearer faculty of vision that belongs to a morality of ascent. "The higher the ends," Aleksandr Solzhenitsyn writes in *The First Circle* (1968), "the higher must be the means! . . . Morality shouldn't lose its force as it increases its scope."

Critical permanencies, or universals, as they are evoked by Solzhenitsyn, perhaps our greatest living dissident, are what contemporary creators and critics invalidate. In this connection, as Professor Stephen I. Gurney has recently declared, "it will be the thankless task of future literary historians to determine whether it was the repressive tactics of a totalitarian regime or the boneless liberalism of a derelict critical mafia which was most effective in creating the present debased state of letters." In its literary form, the process of invalidation—the invalidation of moral value, theme, distinctions, and meaning—culminates in the movement known as deconstructionism.

In the very first issue of *Modern Age*, in the inaugural essay "Life without Prejudice," Richard M. Weaver anticipated the nihilistic directions of this movement in the course of pointing to the "traditional distinctions, whether economic, moral, social, or aesthetic, [which] are today under assault as found on a prejudice." American critics would be well advised to meditate on that remarkable essay if only to understand what ultimately comprises the burden of the critical practitioner. Paradigms of critical thinking, and in effect of critical prejudices, are what are most needed today. When Weaver stresses, then, "life without prejudice, were it ever to be tried, would soon reveal itself to be a life without principle," he is also drawing attention to a criticism without principle and, in effect, a criticism in crisis: that criticism, for example, that props up a Salinger or a Mary McCarthy in ways that make their insignificance and deficiencies all the more shocking.

In its literary reviewing and articles *Modern Age* has steadfastly adhered to a moral criticism that contemplates ends and affirms the need for roots of order and for what Simone Weil calls "the needs of the soul." For the fact remains that the critical function has been absorbed by the liberal dialectic of the modern world that rejects serious standards of thought and judgment and endorses the general will in all its perversions. Centerless and rootless attitudes gain widespread acceptance as critical authority wanes. Particularly in the realm of education, this disintegrating pluralistic process has had irreparable effects, for if critical authority no longer commands a fundamental role in the disciplining contexts of criteria and sensibility, and of value and significance, how can the educational task itself continue without being crippled? Indeed, education today all too often aborts the humanistic need to "assert itself as a major 'spiritual power,' higher than the press, standing for serenity in the midst of frenzy, for seriousness and the grasp of intellect in the face of frivolity and unashamed stupidity," as Ortega y Gassett declared over fifty years ago in his treatise on higher education, *The Mission of the University*. This posited "spiritual power" has been sacrificed to the dictates of collectivist sensibility, to the requirements of, for example, "group thinking" and "audience response," of polls and trends, and of talk shows, anchormen, bestsellers, and editorial and op-ed pages. Is it any wonder that even an occasionally troubled novelist can complain that he is no longer able to locate a center of values, and that there is no light to guide him? The vacuum, which these writers decry, is the vacuum of the disinherited modern mind; and the moral imagination is its victim.

II

The preceding thoughts are occasioned by the publication of Professor John W. Aldridge's most recent study, *The American Novel and the Way We Live Now*,[1] in which fulfilling the responsibilities of the office of the critic distinguishes the main concern of the author. We are indebted to Aldridge for reminding us of major cultural issues that are ignored or dismissed by so many other critics and academics alike. His book forces us to examine three nagging questions: What is wrong with current cultural conditions? What is wrong with the literary imagination? What is wrong with the critical function? These questions, as they are formulated and treated in the book, are interdependent; Aldridge is continuously aware of how each of these questions ultimately belongs to an inseparable entity. To ask one of these questions inevitably leads to asking the other two. Aldridge's handling of these questions is essentially prescriptive; he does not fall into the esoteric enticements and the solipsistic snares that claim the loyalty of many academic critics writing (and teaching) today. His selective and illustrative discussions are impelled by and addressed to the state of American society as a whole.

Aldridge speaks as a critic who analyzes the particularities of a civilization in disarray and who conveys valuations commensurate with his honesty and sensitive intelligence. He judges and writes as a critical dissident. One reads him with an increasing sense of respect, for one clearly finds in Aldridge's critical discriminations an implicit integrity. Journalistic habits of mind and peripheral academic interests, regnant cheapness and deadening specialisms, as these proliferate in the house of intellect, never get in Aldridge's way. He is intent on penetrating to the heart of matters that affect literary and cultural conditions. Intensity of purpose, of judgment, stamps each paragraph and page of the book. This is the intensity of a determined seriousness that tells us that the critic has thought deeply on what he has read and observed. The critical function, as one discovers in Aldridge's book, has a moral function, which many teachers and critics now reproach as the height of critical dissidence.

The main critical idea that Aldridge posits is that contemporary American novelists disdain a realistic reflection of life. Closely associated with this idea is another one: that the novel has lost its authority as an art form and as a means of reflecting and educating public consciousness. This loss of reality and of authority can now be measured in terms of the imagination's turning to, and concomitantly degenerating into, a search for salvation through escape from the living community. Contemporary novelists not only celebrate romantic fantasies but also surrender whatever vision they have to the secular decrees of demystification and fragmentation. Aldridge goes on to observe that contemporary fiction also underlines the attempt to replace one's membership in an older form of community with group membership subject to spurious standards endlessly formulated by behaviorists and social scientists. In literature as in life, Aldridge emphasizes, the "solipsistic pre-occupations of the imperial self" thrive; an enervating narcissism iden-tifies a devalued and disconnected existence in which transcendental meaning is rejected or subordinated to "life in entropic terms."

Aldridge sees Joseph Heller's novels revolving around a "nihilistic perception" of human existence and destiny, even as he sees William Gaddis dramatizing anarchical attitudes and habits. American fiction inevitably recreates the disorder of "the way we live now": a soulless, mindless state of being. This debasement, as Aldridge also shows in the fiction of Jerzy Kosinski, emerges from the need "to substitute for the moral anarchy of the void the autocracy of personal law, the tyr-anny of the imperious self." The entropic process of chaos finds in Thomas Pynchon a prime example of a novelist who, though he pos-sesses high literary intelligence, is preoccupied with the thermody-namic dissolution of life. An apocalyptic naturalism ultimately deter-mines and undermines Pynchon's conception of the human social order.

In the longest chapter of the book, "The Troubles of Realism," Al-dridge examines the novels of Alison Lurie, James Baldwin, Norman Mailer, and Saul Bellow. Each of these writers, he believes, has at-tempted to grapple, honestly and realistically, with the stuff of con-temporary American society. "And each has experienced frustration," Aldridge adds, "or the need to make some creative adjustment or com-promise in the face of the recalcitrance of those materials." Lurie exhib-its a deficient comprehension of ambiguities in academic life, and Bald-win sentimentalizes his vision of the black experience. Mailer and Bellow, on the other hand, are more successful in their attempts to confront the dominant realities or unrealities of American society. It becomes only too clear in Aldridge's study that the positive strengths found in these attempts hardly outweigh the inadequacies of American fiction: "Our novels have usually lacked what the best of European fic-tion has traditionally possessed in abundance: the power to deal directly with abstract concepts of being and to depict ideas as concrete modes of dramatic action to be experienced with all the force of physical sensa-tions." In arguing that American novelists lapse into "the banality of evil," Aldridge points to William Styron's *Sophie's Choice* (1979) as an example of what contemporary American fiction and life lack most: "a coherent metaphysical view of the moral nature of existence."

Aldridge's charge that the American literary and cultural situation is limited to the specific and particular and dismissive of the universal is not, of course, an original charge, as any reading of the critical writings of Babbitt or Paul Elmer More will reveal. Still, it is bracing to have the views of the New Humanists brought up-to-date; to have re-confirmation of what happens when the imagination has neither an ethical nor a moral center and is subservient to the flux of relativism, culminating in what Babbitt describes as "the outward push of expression" and "the fatality and finality of temperament."

Aldridge's critical arguments enforce the pertinence of Christopher Lasch's observation in *The Culture of Narcissism* (1979): "As for art, it not only fails to create the illusion of reality but suffers from the same crisis of self-consciousness that afflicts the man in the street." Centering on what he calls "the novel as narcissus," Aldridge cites John Barth's fiction as an example of relativistic thinking, as well as of anti-realism. Barth, in *The Floating Opera* (1967), expresses his mechanistic view in the form of these dialectical propositions, which Aldridge quotes: "I. Nothing has intrinsic value. II. The reasons for which people attribute value to things are always ultimately irrational. III. There is, therefore, no ultimate 'reason' for valuing anything. IV. Living is action. There's no final reason for action. V. There's no final reason for living (or for suicide)." No "propositions" could better summarize the bankruptcy of the imagination! And no "propositions" could better crystallize the process of putrefaction that assaults all meaning of life.

In contemporary fiction, for those who can recognize the frightening significance of Aldridge's findings, what we unrelievedly encounter is the diabolism that D. H. Lawrence equates with "impure abstraction, the mechanisms of matter," and that, earlier, William Blake imaged as "the Cities of the Salamandrine men" and "the Empire of Nothing." Aldridge's examination of the modern writer's relation to and conception of society alerts us to the perversity of estrangement and dread: "But if writers feel—as many now seem to do—so completely estranged that they can perceive their society only as a nightmare aberration, a condition of malevolent conspiracy, or a mass of undifferentiated humanoids, then obviously they will not be able to engage it imaginatively with very much vigor or profundity."

"The Empire of Nothing": that is the symbolic definition of modern society as "machination" and the penal colony in which, as Aldridge

reveals to us, the artist now finds himself both as the executioner and
the executed. Aldridge will be faulted for not augmenting his diagnosis
of the writer and society with programmatic and popular solutions.
The critic's task, it should be stressed, is diagnostic, and his purpose
should be that of conserving values and defending standards, out of
which solutions should, ideally, emerge. We are, in matters of life as
in matters of criticism, too deeply immersed in the art of living rather
than in the knowledge of life. That is our curse of pragmatism, and
that curse makes it impossible for us to discern between good and evil,
between that which is above and that which is below, between the sacred and the profane. Overcoming this curse is the lot of the dissident
critic, as Aldridge so impressively shows. To be able to respond to the
voice of one's critical conscience in the contexts of valuing what needs
to be valued marks the beginning of a solution. An F. Scott Fitzgerald
(1896–1940) who can confess, for instance, that "my generation of radicals and breakers-down never found anything to take the place of the
old virtues of work and courage and the old graces of courtesy and po-
liteness," can give us great literature in ways that the contemporary
novelists Aldridge assesses simply cannot.

Though Fitzgerald could say that "life is essentially a cheat and its
conditions those of defeat," he could also remain dedicated to the "fundamental decencies." Those "fundamental decencies" today are being
flouted not only in the republic of arts and letters but also in "Big Dan's
Tavern," in New Bedford, Massachusetts, early in 1983, by those men
who grabbed and dragged a woman to a pool table where she was
raped for a period of at least two hours, to the accompanying cheers of
other men who were watching.[2] Barth and his confrères would doubtlessly view such an atrocity as a perfunctory offshoot of the dialectical
propositions in *The Floating Opera!*

III

I want to conclude by way of a personal note. In 1971 I reviewed
in *Modern Age* Aldridge's volume of social and cultural history, *In the
Country of the Young* (1970), under the title "The Cult of Mediocrity."
In this book he examined the declining state of American civilization
and in particular indicted "the children of affluence and permis-
siveness." Hard-hitting and unsparing, this book gives unpopular

opinions, searingly analyzing, as it does, those manic and diseased conditions in the sixties that identified the plight of American life at all levels and led me to conclude my review with the bleak and symbolic words, "Meta-barbaric man now dances and fornicates in the streets, and the remnant, protesting but 'very small and feeble,' waits to be called." That epitomizing sentence, and my entire review praising Aldridge's intellectual honesty and courage, I recall quite vividly, did not go well with some of my liberal colleagues in the profession. Those who read the review, or heard about it from other sources, reacted with a kind of disdaining silence. It is of the kind that tells you that you have violated some unwritten but powerful code that says that only the liberal ethos is what academe prescribes and protects, any violation of which is an unforgivable act. That liberal attitude, I realized, did not tolerate the very principle of toleration that liberals claim is their exclusive legacy.

Invariably, and very painfully, I was made to feel that any statement critical of the liberal position, an entrenched and self-perpetuating party-line in itself, made one *persona non grata*. Quite clearly I was stamped as a "conservative" teacher and critic, consigned to a small band of cranky traditionalists: those who, in terms of national honors and munificent foundation grants, find doors shut against them. Indeed, even in terms of prestige, it was made clear to me by direct or indirect means, an academic who appeared in, say, the *New Republic* or the *New York Review of Books* had reached a pinnacle of national visibility and power in the profession. In this, too, the liberal sway has always been formidable. Politically and professionally the liberal position has always paid off. A neutralist position, in fact, was far more preferable to the conservative; it was by far the more tame of the two.

When, too, my volume of essays in literary criticism, culture, and society, *The Reverent Discipline*, was published in 1974, the liberal response was completely predictable. To start with, the title of my book was viewed apprehensively, especially when placed alongside a *Negations* (Herbert Marcuse) or a *Soul on Ice* (Eldridge Cleaver), to which books enormous critical space in the review media was shamelessly devoted. One reviewer, in fact, glibly wrote in the *Library Journal*: "These essays rest on a broad base of scholarship and learning, and it's hard to imagine finding more serious writing about literature anywhere. Nevertheless, the unremitting moral earnestness and intellectual conservatism won't be to everyone's taste, especially if a title like *The Reverent Discipline* automatically makes you feel a little irreverent." And one of my own senior colleagues, a liberal especially liberal in his confusion, saw fit one day to accost me in the commons room by condescendingly declaring he had somewhere seen a notice of my book that he believed—derision stressfully etched in his "believed"—identified *The Reverent Discipline* as a kind of religious commentary with Hellenic and humanistic essences, which, with God, he went on for my edification, with a note of final triumph, had *died* long, long ago—no longer fit for or necessary to the modern world. However disturbing and discrediting these aspersions may appear to be, I have learned, with a patience born in isolation, that they cannot be allowed to deter one's devotion to the Idea of Value. What I wrote in *The Reverent Discipline*, in the following passage, remains for me a steadying principle of acceptance and commitment central to the creed and office of the critic as conservator:

> Reverence has hidden depths which conceptual thought cannot reach, but of which it has immense need. Reverence is a paradigm that sanctifies and saves. Reverence connotes other possibilities of response and attention, of knowledge and presence. It is discovery, discovery of another dimension. It is the finest offshoot of the revelation of order.[3]

The liberal attitude, mean and insidious in itself, was crystallized for me, with a bitterness beyond words, during a scholarly conference at a great mid-western university where I was invited to give one of the two main addresses. My subject, I insisted, would be Irving Babbitt and Simone Weil as moralist thinkers, and my insistence, I later found, carried a heavy price in terms of consequences. I shared the platform with a famous luminary who, giving the first paper and in the course of discussing Edmund Wilson, used the occasion to quote Wilson's miscreant views of neohumanism and of Babbitt in particular. The scholarly audience delighted hugely in the invectives against Babbitt, and no doubt expected more of the same from my own paper. That was not forthcoming. As my analytical defense of Babbitt and Simone Weil gained in momentum and, I hope, in sincerity, so too did the displeasure of the luminary sharing the platform with me and that of an amazed and obviously irritated academic audience to whom Babbitt and Simone Weil embodied a dissentient moral force. The irritability of my audience, I sensed, was characterized by a tension and fidgetiness, by utter surprise, and, at the end, by uncivil whispers, which became almost belligerently vocal as I concluded my address.

Interestingly, the moderator of the proceedings, motivated by tact or tactic, but contrary to general policy, dispensed with the usual question period, claiming that my lecture would best be pondered silently by those in the audience—this action for me again being just another clever facet of the conspiracy of silence that liberals practice with considerable success. As we all then proceeded rather uncomfortably from the lecture hall, the luminary who had cleverly ridiculed Babbitt via Wilson was surrounded by laughing and joking academic lackeys. One very distinguished elderly scholar, I now recall, passed by me, not saying anything, but, with downcast eyes and a nodding gesture of his head, discreetly signaled to me a form of approval—as he, too, then went on to join the majority pack ahead, still laughing and gesticulating. Later, too, one kindly lady, a professor of music, I think, asked me whether I was the "religious philosopher" who had dared to disturb some of the academics at the conference.

Still later, one of my friends, a famous septuagenarian man of letters, told me, in *sotto voce*, with a pained tone of paternal concern, that in giving my lecture on Babbitt and Simone Weil and in delineating their moral views (as was reported to him through the academic grapevine) I had been "imprudent." That charge, for me, was perhaps the most cutting of all. For how, I kept asking myself, how can one be incautious with truth? Kierkegaard's announced principle, "severity first— then mildness," has always seemed to me a better part of truth. At any rate, my good friend's admonition made me realize more than ever how pervasive and poisonous the liberal network is in American intellectual life; how much it controls and shapes the ethos of professional life and creates, harms, or destroys professional reputations; how perilous it is for one to defy it and, in defying it, to expect retribution in subtle or, as I also found, unsubtle forms.

I had seen and felt at first hand the liberal clout. It is always there, ready to strike out at those who do not subscribe to its ironclad doctrines and its enlightened and advanced views and tactics; always ready to apportion its ridicule and hostility; always ready to sow its smear tactics. Only yesterday, it seems, on my way to an afternoon class in World Literature, to lecture to some of my undergraduates, I encoun-

tered one of my liberal colleagues who noticed that I was carrying
Irwin Edman's Modern Library edition of Plato's Dialogues. "I see
you are teaching Plato," he said, his eyes fastening on me with hate,
his mouth pursed cruelly. "That fascist!" snarled this self-admiring
spokesman for the "doctrines of the multitude," as I made my way in
the labyrinthine grove of academe, in the meanwhile reflecting on the
insight and wisdom of Socrates' words to Crito: "Then, my friend, we
must not regard what the many say of us; but what he, the one man
who has understanding of just and unjust, will say, and what the truth
will say."

The destructive actions of my academic colleagues are, I know, egre-
gious but by no means unusual; yet they underline characteristic liberal
habits of mind in academe that, in time, become accepted general policy. Nowhere is this policy more evident than in the making of profes-
sorial appointments, especially in the humanistic disciplines. Academics with a conservative and traditionalist bent are either ignored,
punished, or denied a fair hearing when it comes to being considered
for some coveted university chair. The academic democratizers of
standards and society, the quantifiers, the mercenaries, the nihilists are
accorded the greater privileges and honors. The moles of academe perpetuate the *chic* liberal position that has led to the wildest disruptions
and most blasphemous distortions of basic principles and beliefs for
which the present generation of students is paying the demeaning price
of illiteracy as the lowest and commonest standard.

In the educational realm, as in that of the imagination and of criticism, we are reaping the results of what the late Gordon Keith Chalmers once spoke of in the contexts of a "disintegrated liberalism": "The
general object of education has become more and more to condition
the mass attitude toward specific social improvements, and enthusiasm
for these reforms has diverted energy from the ancient and central task
of converting the reason—of converting it from the knowledge and
love of what is mean to the knowledge and love of what is worthy."
These wise words appear in Chalmers' *The Republic and the Person*, a
great book published in 1952 by Henry Regnery, a great "dissident
publisher." What Chalmers emphasizes in this statement, and throughout his book, reminds us that American leaders, educators, critics, and
creators have shunned spiritual greatness.

Since 1952, the disciplining spiritual idea of critical humanism has been fast disappearing from the American social and cultural scene. This disappearance attests to the beleaguering of genuine conservative ideas and to the general distrust of the "conservative mind" as a working constituent of American life. If, politically speaking, there is now present on a national scale a conservative mood, that merely points to a newly gained respectability. But respectability and viability are often no less antipodal than appearance and reality. "In America, the majority raises formidable barriers around the liberty of opinion," Tocqueville wrote. Basically the liberal power-centers remain as intractable and unchanged today as they were back in the time of Whittaker Chambers' "witness" to the "conflicts of faith": Faith in God or Faith in Man? These conflicts have not abated in either their intensity or their terror. The same kind of resistance to Chambers' view of Faith—Faith in God—as constituting "the central problem of this age" persists. Chambers' warning that "communism is what happens when, in the name of Mind, men free themselves from God," is as much disregarded today as it was when it was first conveyed more than thirty years ago. His is truly a dissident's warning that the liberal intelligentsia, ensconced in high places of power, scoffs at with unconscienced gusto.

The liberal *Zeitgeist*, as a dismayed and embattled Chambers found, is powerful, venomous, unforgiving, monolithic. Those who are brave enough to challenge its formulas and dogmatisms, who have the courage to see its decadences, must necessarily choose to exist as dissidents in "a world split apart." This is their marginal fate, but also their power and glory. For if one chooses to be what I term a dissident critic, he is a partisan in the unceasing struggle between moral relativism and moral truth, between the absence and the presence of the moral sense. "If you do away with this struggle," writes T. S. Eliot, "and maintain that by tolerance, benevolence, inoffensiveness and a redistribution or increase of purchasing power, combined with a devotion, on the part of an elite, to Art, the world will be as good as anyone could require, then you must expect human beings to become more and more vaporous."

"The world outside Communism, the world in crisis, lacks a vision and a faith." So writes Chambers in his "Foreword in the Form of a Letter to My Children," in *Witness*. A dissident statement to make back in 1952, it remains equally dissident today. No liberal, no relativist, could utter such words. Only a true spiritual dissident would be selfless enough to make such a statement of indictment that emerges from the very depths of value and meaning. At first glance, Chambers' is a simple statement, ostensibly mild and unthreatening in its significance. But when it is pondered and repeated in a metaphysical sense, and then repeated and pondered in an historical sense, its significance is totally arresting. For it adverts to what is a consuming crisis in a world which "lacks a vision and a faith." Chambers' words, his "witness," his *agon*, seen in their prophetic unity, point to the *Realpolitik* of disorder that so overwhelms Western civilization. It is precisely the absence of faith, in short, of a religious sense, that stultifies the imagination that Aldridge assesses with a frightening accuracy of insight. Without faith, without a moral impulse, the imagination dies. This necrosis precludes not only the full possibility of human existence, but also the value of order and the order of value.

The need for critical dissidence is especially urgent at a time of history when the liberal temper ossifies in an indulgent process of general softness and slovenliness and a disappearance of honest standards. "Liberalism is the refuge favored by intellectual cowardice," Weaver observes, "because the essence of the liberal's position is he has no position." Intellectual cowardice, in time, disintegrates into intellectual hedonism, to gauge by the eclipse of the moral function in criticism and in the imagination, as well as in the socio-political system as a whole. No doubt this disintegration is what Julien Benda had in mind when, back in the 1920s, he condemned modern intellectuals as traitors extolling particular systems of morality and scorning universal morality. That betrayal has hardened into what is now, dialectically and procedurally, defined policy and standard practice.

An orthodoxy of enlightenment, as the cumulative result of the idea of progress through aggression, remains imperious in its power and influence. A critic who dares to disobey its ordinances or to trespass the frontiers of its tyranny registers a moral choice of dissent. His task, seen and affirmed as such, is defiant, dangerous, surveillant, and censorial. "Watch ye, stand fast in faith, quit you like men, be strong." Saint Paul's words help to remind us that, in confronting the malodorous conditions of contemporary civilization, the dissident critic has hardly begun the work of his ministry.

Educational Paths

∾

The disorder of the modern age has been mirrored to an almost savage degree in the disorder of education. And as modern society has more and more been drawn to the new gods of technology, of computers, and even of cybernetics, so too has humane education lost its true purpose and character: the indefectible rules of faith that comprise its creed and that declare its vision of what is needed to educate, and to civilize, and to save man. This loss now affects education at all levels, and it appears in sundry forms—as pragmatism, utilitarianism, relativism, nominalism, gnosticism. It has helped to dislodge the humane principles of education that have their roots in man's moral nature and in the spiritual disciplines that nourish and mould that nature. The mystery and the divinity of man have increasingly been sacrificed to abject scientific facts and to a cruel process of objectification. The moral dimension of education—that which relates to the character and conscience of man, or what might be termed the inner needs of the soul—has now been transformed into the mechanistic dimension of education that stresses the collective thingness of a society whose allegiance is to outer forms of existence, to the inorganic, the functional, the programmatic.

11

Bustin' Loose

The crisis of American education does not abate, as John LeBoutillier clearly shows in his book, *Harvard Hates America* (1978). If small in size and length, it is also a book that is intense and angry in tone, and, above all, filled with significance. In its immediate contexts it is an indictment of Harvard University, where he studied for four years (1972–76) and where he continued his education at the Business School. LeBoutillier's remarks about the Harvard faculty, curriculum, and students are disquieting and should raise questions and doubts not only about educational conditions at Harvard but also about the educational situation on a national level. LeBoutillier is a young man, but he possesses a moral seriousness that many of his contemporaries and teachers lack. A discriminating, judging, mind is much at work in this book, which is essentially a long essay.

It is heartening to see how a student, who can respond to and be impelled by the intrinsic idea of value, scrutinizes educational problems, as well as related social and political issues. The diagnostic dimension of this book is especially pertinent since it forces one to confront matters of urgent importance that are often ignored or not stressed. The plain fact is that LeBoutillier does not have pleasant things to say about his sense of the way things are going. Unlike the contemporary *Kulturträger* or the apostle of a new enlightenment, he does not make any grand promises. When so much that is mindless characterizes so much in American education, and culture, what LeBoutillier observes, in terms of consequences and concomitants, demands diligent attention. It is the central strength of this book, then, to remind us that mindlessness is now a representative quality of life; that we are unable any longer to locate a center of values; that, in the absence of a positive critical and cultural tradition, we seem more and more to be torn between anarchy and nihilism.

That educators and educational leaders themselves are much at fault for the decline of higher learning in America is one of LeBoutillier's implicit charges. Of course, this is hardly an original observation, and any number of eminent commentators can be cited for their prophetic delineation of educational desuetude in the twentieth century, including Irving Babbitt, Gordon Keith Chalmers, Lionel Trilling, Arthur Bestor, Russell Kirk. The fact remains that educational decline has been a steady one since 1918, accelerating with the end of World War II and becoming especially alarming since the 1960s, with the flagrant radicalization of the curriculum, the deterioration of standards, and the further exaggeration of the absolutes of liberty and equality in all sectors of life. What LeBoutillier does in the special contexts of his book is to supply additional, updated confirmation of the disastrous directions of American education. He substantiates, with a timely relevance and with a fearsome concreteness, Chalmers' warning uttered nearly three decades ago in *The Republic and the Person*: "Years ago it hardly seemed to matter that American thinking was sentimental. Now, it is clear that such thinking will throw in jeopardy the world, our self-respect, and our safety. We can no longer afford leaders, thinkers, and voters in any large number who delude themselves or think irresponsibly." LeBoutillier recreates precisely the contemporary forms of the sentimentality that now transforms into delusion and, worse, into an irresponsibility that signifies the total collapse of educational values. Reading LeBoutillier's book reminds one of just how complete and inescapable, how inclusive is the breakdown, and how it finally submerges ethical and moral life.

Harvard Hates America objectifies a process of educational disintegration that, in its portents and symptoms, is even obscene. Nowhere is this obscenity more effectively seen than in LeBoutillier's trenchant recollection of his experiences in his Harvard classrooms. His first and longest chapter, "Enter to Grow in Wisdom," should be required reading for those who cling to the idea that the mission of the university consists mainly of the pursuit of wisdom as the center of humanistic, liberal education. Anyone who reads this chapter, who reads it disinterestedly, should feel the same kind of nausea that LeBoutillier felt, and still feels. The educationalists will refuse to accept what is pictured here, the monster that they, in fact, have helped to create and have allowed to have been created. Cowardice and irresponsibility are far too often habits of mind to educators who join with the barbarians in de-

stroying foundations. It is an alliance of subversion almost too overwhelming to comprehend.

When LeBoutillier recalls some of his teachers and what transpired
in their lectures, the picture that he conveys is almost incredible. Is this,
one asks again and again, what the educational function has come to?
Is it possible to believe that the teaching process, as a discipline of
mind, has deteriorated to such a low point? One would, to be sure,
prefer not to believe that there is such a disintegration in educational
methods and aims. LeBoutillier, however, does not permit the comforts of illusion to prevail; he depicts a teaching situation that, for those
who want to see and understand, and who are willing to forgo the lux-
uries of illusion, is shocking. In higher education obscenity is now in
the very nature of things. We have gone over the edge!

To speak in such apocalyptic language and tones may seem extreme.
LeBoutillier, nonetheless, does paint an extreme picture in his book,
and for those who in any way hold to the humanist values of education
it is an incontrovertible picture. Decorum, to say the least, is nonexistent at all levels of the educational scene. Often one's teacher is no better, perhaps worse, than the student himself. Sloppiness, ever an ad-
versary of discipline, prevails to the degree that LeBoutillier indicates
in his vignette of his history tutor: "He was wearing a long, shaggy
beard which almost hid his face. He was bald on the top of his head,
and what hair he did have was tied into a pony tail with a red Indian
ribbon. He was wearing a light green tee shirt and scruffy, torn blue
jeans. He wore no socks. . . ." LeBoutillier goes on to render physical
details here minutely and graphically, but the abbreviated quotation is
enough to stress the measure of his dismay (*and* ours): "It would not be
the last time I would be amazed about what went on inside the classroom at Harvard," he demurs.

The ugly outer features of educational breakdown serve to mirror
inner chaos: the absence of any integral values; the loss of standards;
the scuttling of absolutes. To be sure, aesthetic refinement or beauty
can sometimes hide an inner diabolism. "Nevsky Prospect," Nikolay
Gogol's memorable story about an artist's worship of a beautiful
woman from afar, followed by his breakdown upon his learning that
she was a St. Petersburg prostitute, is pertinent here, and does occasion
cause for warning and qualification. That is, the aesthetic dimension of

any human or cultural phenomenon is not to be seen as a conclusive or final criterion of judgment; that it can even be faulty.

But there is really no need here to philosophize aesthetic nuances. LeBoutillier shows, clearly and congruously, the quality of sloppiness in appearance *and* in reality. One gets the feeling that LeBoutillier's teachers and classmates delight in smashing the civilizing reticences, the principles of order, of decorum—of controlling excellence. A cheap contemporaneousness, as Babbitt labeled it, is what we now manufacture in the educational world. LeBoutillier's incisive picture, too, of the personal lives and psyches of his generation can hardly resist one's concluding that the university today is a systolic amalgam of an "adventure in learning" (as promised by some college catalogues) by day and an "animal house" by night! Disease and debility become the attendant qualities of mind and character, or better of mind without character. LeBoutillier provides us with the "case history" of this hypostatic phenomenon in American education.

If, in an old and great university, rotting conditions abound, then what is it like in much less affluent colleges and universities, and in the state institutions? One almost dares not to answer such a question for the answer might well be too frightening to contemplate, let alone to enunciate. It will take courage for one to recognize that "the idea of a university" is being dismantled at a rate of speed and change that may even be (one hopes) baffling to some of the radical reformers within the educational ranks. It is one of the additional values of this book to alert us to the consequences of the continuing radical attack on and transformation of what must constitute the basic principles of humane education—the discipline of intelligence and sensibility, in principle and practice.

Yet to speak of, or to invoke, the moral values that form mind and character, as well as self and society, particularly amid the material pressures, the dehumanizing complications, and the proliferating irreverences of the modern world, is bound to leave one with some uneasy reflections. (Solzhenitsyn's public verbalizing of these reflections, it should be recalled, brought down on him the full wrath of the liberal establishment, whether from the editorial writers of the *New York Times* or from an obviously discomfited Walter Cronkite on television.) One must increasingly face the bleak possibility that even the language, no less than the values, of humanism (moral, ethical, or both) is no longer understood by many people, whatever their certified literacy.

The crisis of humanistic values is now so deep and irreversible that it is difficult to address one's self to a solution either diagnostically or prescriptively. What Julien Benda, in the twenties, spoke of as *la trahison des clercs* and José Ortega y Gasset, in the thirties, as *la Rebelión de las Masas* are, in the present extreme circumstances of civilization, mere preludes to a deteriorating situation. It is a situation that may, for all purposes, be called *meta*-modern, *meta*-historical, or *meta*-prophetic, the Greek prepositional prefix *meta* capturing here the full finality of change beyond change. To say that what we are now living consists of an impasse, or a dilemma, or a predicament is to be indulgent. We can take no comfort in any form of existential lyricism. Indeed, it is no longer a matter of delineating the contours of a "waste land" or chasing the shadow of the "outsider."

If, in the first half of the twentieth century, for example, "the experience of literature," as prose or poetry, assuaged the modern human condition, somehow answering human remorse with the hope of some form of redemption, we are now living in an apocalyptic hour, of which pressing symptoms, quantitative and visual, are everywhere to be encountered. LeBoutillier's picture of higher education, under the circumstances, should contain no real surprise for us. He simply defines and deepens even more clearly the surrealistic images of education (and culture) at an ultimate stage, underlining more than ever Ortega y Gasset's contention that in modern "intellectual life, which of its essence requires and presupposes qualification, one can note the progressive triumph of the pseudo-intellectual, unqualified, unqualifiable, and by their very mental texture, disqualified."

Profundity is not the informing aim or trait of this book. What LeBoutillier does is to take the reader on tour of a college campus, there to glance at faculty and students and peek into the classroom. Neither the tour nor the view is a happy one. (The picture of Harvard Square is no less dismaying than that of Hell's Kitchen.) Disenchantment is a major, inevitable note heard as one repeatedly meets a permeating slovenliness of mind and thought and topography in the supposedly sacred realm of education. The critical and creative spirit is seen floundering in an Orwellian situation in which the Big Three—Marx, Mao, Marcuse—are the assigned "major texts." LeBoutillier's history tutor, with Marcuse's *Reason and Revolution* (1941) in hand, cries out to his students, "This is the Bible, man, the Bible . . . this is what it's all about." No more grotesque or sickening picture of a history teacher and his students could be found than in *Harvard Hates America*! Where in the past it has been the relativistic ethos that has been liberally preached, and propagated, it is now one of absolute fragmentation and negation.

What, one must ask with LeBoutillier, has happened to the critical intelligence: to the transmission of culture? to excellence? to the real mission of the university? The symptoms of ailment that one finds here are not at all hopeful, and even terminal in nature: American higher education is now fixed at its zero hour; the conditions of learning are obviously no better than at the University of Heidelberg, or at some of the universities in South America . . . in Turkey . . . in Iran . . . in all those frenzied places where education has turned into a "no man's land." Principles of humane education are now replaced by a tropical underbrush of unprincipled studies (a recent highlight of which was a degree-credit course given at Harvard University under the rubric, "Fundamentals of Multiflex Offense." According to one description, it was a course for men and women in which "football strategy lends itself to scholarship as easily as 'Introduction to Philosophy.' " This course was taught by a Harvard football quarterback, a senior also hoping to enter professional baseball as a pitcher.)

Just how unprincipled things are is revealed in LeBoutillier's final chapter, "Back at Harvard." In this chapter LeBoutillier describes his transition from Harvard College to Harvard Business School. All the previous defects, misdirections, delusions, and illusions now burst forth to crystallize into one fearfully revealing sentence uttered during LeBoutillier's first week at the Business School by one of his class-mates: "There is no such thing as ethics or morality—there's just get-ting what you want." No less than the "Liberal Mentality" dominating Harvard College, LeBoutillier declares, the "Big Business Mentality" at Harvard Business School underlines the phenomenon of an ethically and morally corrupt environment; it is the decadence of not only an educational but also a social-political system that comes into view. Among teachers and learners alike there is one registering ethos: "ev-erybody does it so it's all right."

Here, it seems, the utilitarian absurdity of Charles W. Eliot's educational theory of "training for service and power"—promulgated during his long presidency of Harvard (1869–1909)—reaches a dissimulating apex. Utilitarian educational theory has now come of age: the will to power, *not* the will to service, is what triumphs in the wake of reckless educational expansiveness. "I can't worry about anything but making a profit," another of LeBoutillier's classmates screams, accenting an attitude that defines the psychology of an educational system that has nurtured him and his opportunism. When LeBoutillier observes that "Harvard has moved towards the production of well-trained technocrats long on ability, but woefully short on conscience," he shows that higher education is not supplying the proper correctives.

One cannot expect the majoritarian response to this book, or to one's reflections on this book, to be sympathetic. Jerry Rubin, the co-founder of the Yippee movement in the 1960s, says of *Harvard Hates America*: "I may have mellowed, but not so much as to like *this* book." At the same time, as becomes sadly more evident, one cannot expect much in the form of a discriminating response from the professoriate insofar as, now more than ever, we lack a pedagogy of the university. From even the most thoughtful members of the educational community willing to respond to the issues that LeBoutillier poses, the stress will be generally on a qualifying delineation of unprofitable subtleties. One can easily conjure up the academic tone and pattern of critical discourse, with all of its academic *jeux d'esprit*—blankness: "Yes, it is probably true that we are drifting toward the full secularizing of education. But 'standards' and 'values' have not really passed out of society. No society after all, lives without standards and values, and what has passed away, really, is some special conception of standards and values. Yes, it is also true that our society seems to be rushing towards egalitarianism, but egalitarianism doesn't really mean vulgarization. The fact is that the drift toward relativity of values, or egalitarianism, or secularization entails the loss of certain consciousness and sensibilities." One could go on with our professor's intoning "broad-mindedness," but it is all so predictable, so recognizable, so confused and cowardly. One needs only to read a few chapters in *Harvard Hates America* to identify this politic voice of authority—of enlightenment—and to understand why the discipline of letters has become the game of letters; why higher education has sunk to rock bottom.

The subtitle of LeBoutillier's book, *The Odyssey of a Born-Again*

American, relates to his political evaluations, or revaluations, as these complement or emerge from some of his educational experiences. Continuing with the criticism that he aims against higher learning, he castigates the Republican party (to the higher values, ideals, and traditions of which he ascribes) for failing to separate profits from people. LeBoutillier describes himself as a political conservative, fundamentally compassionate and idealistic—and, it seems, idealistic to the point of being simplistic, to judge by the political theories and reforms that he propounds in these pages. This part of the book is much less impressive, which is perhaps to be explained by the fact that we have come to grow rather tired of and bored by young men's miraculous solutions to national and international problems. The memory of young President Kennedy's plans for exploring "the new frontier" are too recent and too disappointing (whatever rabietic myth-makers like Arthur Meier Schlesinger, Jr., and James MacGregor Burns have to say to us) to convince us that new young men will be any more successful or any more committed than young men of old.

LeBoutillier's political aspirations—for he has, he tells us, his own future political plans (and programs)—as he discloses them are no doubt desirable and obviously sincere. Yet, one wants to cry out at this point: Who will protect us from the "fair deals" and "great societies" that ambitious politicians are endlessly spawning? LeBoutillier's affirmation of qualities of integrity will need to be tested under fire in the political arena. Hence, this theorizing part of his book remains politically tenuous, as well as tedious, though one can at least be hopeful that LeBoutillier will turn out better than so many of the promising young politicians who become hucksters. However caring and concerned LeBoutillier's principles are in relation to his vision of a re-born Republican party, only time will be able to assess. At any rate, he sees himself as a member of a Republican party in search of its soul, for which, in a period of base compromises and disasters, much can be said.

Still, one must not quibble with the substance of LeBoutillier's diagnoses and prescriptions, impelled as these are by an ascetic insistence that "the oral quality of America is a direct reflection of the moral quality of her leaders." We live in an age in which the existence of the moral act is continuously threatened, and moral meaning derided and discredited; the order of humanism is under savage attack. That LeBoutillier is aware of this sad situation is to his credit. His little book thus helps to remind those who are still capable of being reminded of our predicament. Immersed in mediocrity and immured in vulgarity, we are now also immobilized by roguery. LeBoutillier's concern with the health, destiny, and dignity not only of the individual but also of the institutions of higher education is an estimable one. And it is one that, in its ramifications, is conveniently ignored by so many of our higher journalists and commentators, our educators and administrators, our liberation theologians and sociologists, our political theorists and leaders; by the cultural fantasists who rejoice in leading us through Bob Dylan's *Gates of Eden,* inside of which, as he tells us in his famous song, ". . . there are no kings / . . . there are no sins / . . . there are no trials."

LeBoutillier belongs to that minority that refuses to be taken in by promises of a secular Eden. His book sees things as they are, and as they are not seen by our "interleckchuls" (to use Flannery O'Connor's mocking misspelling). Inevitably the educational and the political institutions described in *Harvard Hates America* reflect the collapse and decay of a "botched civilization." The disease of modern life that Ezra Pound identified with that telling phrase does not abate, as the double abdication of responsibility and moral imperative continues to take a heavy toll of our cultural life.

Current happenings verify the symptoms and portents of upheaval that LeBoutillier notices. The blizzard that hit the greater Washington-Baltimore area in late February (1979) is a case in point. Exploiting this natural disaster to the full, bands of looters ravaged, with clockwork-orange precision, stores and shopping centers, now suddenly cut off from police protection. Adults and children could be seen with refrigerators and televisions strapped to their backs, and jewelry and liquor bottles stuffed in their pockets, sometimes advancing *en masse* on a lone officer. (Since then, most of the looters have been let off the hook with a kindly judicial smile!) Asked about his motives, one nineteen-year-old looter replied: "If you can do it, you do it. . . . Everybody's out for himself . . . do what you have to do. . . . That's the way it is, man." Another looter, this one a fourteen-year-old, replied: "Just like the song says, we was 'bustin' loose.' "

Just how extensive is the craze for "bustin' loose" is a question of life or death that goes far beyond the words from the title of the pop song of Chuck Brown and the Soul Searchers. Whether at Harvard Univer-

sity or at the Old Towne Mall, whether in the teaching of John LeBoutillier's Harvard tutor or in the actions of a Baltimore looter, the commanding words of "bustin' loose" are shouted and enacted in ways
that, no matter what opiates our "bureaucrats of culture" offer, should
appall us.

12

Unrecommended Events

The signs of deterioration in the humanities and in American culture and society as a whole refuse to abate as agents of reductionism continue to perpetuate harmful acts in programmatic fashion and fury. Evidence keeps mounting up that conditions in the intellectual community go beyond the crisis stage. To be sure, we are being given a variety of commission reports enumerating reforms needed to re-assert and revitalize the standards and worth of humanistic disciplines. A flurry of efforts can even be seen in attempts, nationwide, to bring about improvements in education after many years of drifting liberalization and radicalization. These efforts, of course, must be commended and encouraged, especially because the cumulative damage that has been done is immense. Just how demanding these efforts must be is perhaps not as readily perceivable as it should be.

As Americans we are irretrievable optimists and there is no problem that we find legitimately insoluble and no trouble pragmatically insurpassable. There is, after all, always some "New Deal" that can be concocted in confronting an especially perplexing issue. We are a tough-minded generation, or so it is claimed. But tough-minded or not, we cannot permit ourselves the luxury of illusion; we cannot rest secure behind the perennial veil of illusion, including the illusion of easily rectifying the social, intellectual, and spiritual malaise that is now deep-rooted and extensive. Even a cursory reading of Richard M. Weaver's *Visions of Order* (1964) should help us to gauge the unusual difficulty of beginning to countermand the "presumptions of modern thought and the nonhuman sterilities of an industrial civilization." These, collectively, now embody the enemy that continues to threaten the reverent uses of order and tradition that help make possible a humane civilization. Not for one moment must we forget the controlling power of this enemy, or the closely associated fact that, in the words of the English poet Philip Larkin, we live in "a time unrecommended by events."

The presumptions and sterilities about which Weaver speaks are as destructive as ever to judge by Professor Arthur Eckstein's paper on "*1984* and George Orwell's Other View of Capitalism," delivered in April 1984 during a conference on "Orwell's *1984*: The Text and Its Transformation and Legacy" held at a midwestern university. (The text of Eckstein's paper subsequently appeared in the Winter 1985 issue of *Modern Age*.) The particular circumstances of Eckstein's presentation of his paper, and all of the after-effects, are a disturbing reminder of the low state of affairs in the academy. The general lesson to be derived from this conference points to one central fact: that some American intellectuals will go to any possible extreme in attacking what they claim to be the oppressive character of government and society in the United States.

Eckstein's "eyewitness account" of what happened at this conference, entitled "An Orwellian Nightmare Fulfilled," appeared in the *Chronicle of Higher Education* (October 17, 1984). To fathom in full both the bizarre aspects and the distressing implications of this conference one must read the complete text of Eckstein's account. Here it is enough, as a way of adverting to "*1984* and George Orwell's Other View of Capitalism," and also voicing a few dissident warnings, to cite the highlights of Eckstein's piece in the *Chronicle of Higher Education*. To start with, the conference sought to bring together a group of Orwell scholars for the purpose of training "instant Orwell experts, that is, ordinary citizens who, after their exposure to *1984* at the conference, would then go out to the communities 'explaining' Orwell to the people." A good part of the money for the conference and also for a handbook containing the twenty-five papers given at the conference was provided by the state government, and specifically by its Humanities Commission and by the National Endowment for the Humanities. This financial fact notwithstanding, the basic theme of most of the papers, as Eckstein states, was that the totalitarian nightmare of Orwell's famous novel, first published in 1949, "has been, or at least is about to be, most fully realized in America."

Eckstein's personal account of the proceedings helps to disclose the character of the academic mind. The disclosures, simultaneously noteworthy and revolting, could almost come out of F. M. Dostoevsky's great political novel, *The Devils* (1871). But what they especially dramatize is that the academic mind often lacks character—lacks the transcendent moral element that shapes and defines character and diminishes centrifugal forces in life that bring chaos and disconnection. Clearly, Orwell himself, a "man of the left," did have character and would, as Eckstein suggests, have been scandalized by the content of most of the papers and responses given at the conference, often by men who possessed high academic credentials. The scenario at this conference has all the ingredients of ideological claptrap and strongly reminds us of why the intellectual climate of American university life finds itself in a sorry state. It also explains to some extent the steady erosion of standards and the spread of an educational wasteland in the United States.

To read Eckstein's recollection of some of the events at the conference is to be reminded of Pierre de Beaumarchais' saying that one will quickly laugh at things for fear of having to cry. What can one say, for example, about one paper that, promising in its title to discuss the Leninist systems which Orwell detested, focused instead on the "oppression" of psychotics in America? And what can one say about another paper that devoted an entire hour to "deconstructing" *1984*—more than 60 minutes of incomprehensible semiotics, expressed in impossibly convoluted sentences without a single active verb? Indeed, what can one say about a respondent to two papers presented during a session who spent his time advocating vegetarianism, castigating American capitalism for not informing people that "when they eat meat, they eat death," and finally reading his own composition, "A Poem to Peace"? One could go on drearily citing other examples of "scholarly discourse" at this conference, but enough is enough, as the phrase goes. Eckstein, in any case, sums up the representative problem lying at the heart of this conference when he concludes that the speakers' "attempts to portray the United States as the fulfillment of the Orwellian nightmare seem clearly to have been motivated by their politics."

Even the *Washington Post*, a newspaper at times curiously friendly to ideas and movements fomenting a society "worm-eaten with Liberalism," to use T. S. Eliot's words, found Eckstein's account of the Orwell conference alarming, especially when one reads Jonathan Yardley's column of October 22, 1984, entitled "*1984*: Academically Abused." The popularity of "'deconstruction' idiocy" and of computer-written microhistory, Yardley laments, "encourages academics to look inward rather than out into the world." Certainly, when one stops to scrutinize the events that transpired at the Orwell conference, one can hardly avoid ignoring some of the perverse features of the American academic life. Those speakers at the conference are the selfsame educators who are influencing and shaping the minds and lives of students in American colleges and universities. As such, the damage they are doing is inestimable—and frightening. What, one must ask, is going on in the classroom? What can one ever expect to have in the way of intellectual honesty from an academic who remarked at one point in the conference, as Eckstein reports, that he simply couldn't understand why an exchange professor from Warsaw was negative toward Marxism? The combination of intellectual mediocrity and political stupidity is now still another dangerous symptom and portent of decline in institutions of higher learning. The text of this combination, not the text of *1984*, is what needs to be assessed in terms of consequences. Indeed, one sees this awful text being written every day in college and university departments of literature and history throughout the country.

With all its aberration, the Orwell conference dramatizes a collective academic entropy; it provides for us a seminal text in contemporary critical theory, materialist dialectics, and ambitions as promulgated and expounded by educators who seem to subscribe to Leon Trotsky's murky contention, as found in his *Literature and Revolution* (1925), that living literature must have a close association with the existing political and social system and must strive for "the development of a new art" and the formation of a "Socialist culture and literature" to replace the "old literature and 'culture' " of the bourgeoisie. Trotsky goes on to emphasize, "This art needs a new self-consciousness." With immitigably doctrinaire self-consciousness, it can be said, the speakers at the Orwell conference, in interpreting *1984* as an attack on bourgeois democracy rather than on the totalitarian state, were affirming Trotsky's goal in its American setting. Is it any wonder, then, that at the end of one session "unchallenged praise" was heaped on David Dellinger, a member of the infamous Chicago 7, for a speech favoring a nuclear arms freeze. Yet, as Eckstein rightly demurs, "Dellinger, who for so long denied the existence of atrocities such as Khmer Rouge genocide in Cambodia, is precisely the sort of apologist that Orwell heartily despised."

These unrecommended events do not stop with what happened at the midwestern university. There is a documented coda to be related, the meaning of which is almost as dreadful as the thesis of Orwell's last book, *1984*. Obviously, Eckstein's published protestations did not sit well with the state agency, or Humanities Commission, that helped fund the conference; and Yardley's article in the *Washington Post* further enraged the officers of this agency. The angered (and embarrassed) Executive Director of the agency sent out an official letter (dated October 26, 1984) defending its process and judgment in funding the conference, as well as attacking Eckstein's "eyewitness account" as a distortion of the true facts, "just another example of academic conference baiting." The letter then goes on to *solicit* attacks against Eckstein from participants in the conference: "We think that the most effective response to Mr. Eckstein's charges would be rebuttal of his allegations by his peers. Consequently, it would be most helpful if you were to write a letter to Mr. Eckstein . . . and send copies to the [State] Commission and . . . [the] National Endowment for the Humanities. . . . We will send copies of the letters we receive along with our own letters to the editors of *The Chronicle* [*of Higher Education*] and *The Washington Post*."

Eckstein himself was not aware of this campaign of vilification until an outraged recipient of the circular sent him a copy. Yet another recipient of the circular replied to the director of the state agency by questioning the propriety of a funding agency's attempt "to churn up intellectual waters as a means of defending itself." "Why not let academic debate flower of its own accord," this recipient wrote in his letter (dated November 1, 1984), "rather than try to provoke a response (through an agency of the state)?" He goes on to complain that the conference, on the planning committee of which he himself served, was somehow geared to be from the beginning more political than literary. Supporting and largely confirming the dissenting issues raised by Eckstein, he then makes this categorical remark: "Most of the speakers that I heard did criticize America rather than the Soviet Union, and I would certainly agree that Orwell's *primary* target was the totalitarian left."

It can be said that what Eckstein encountered is a form of intellectual terrorism. The resulting crisis, relentless and widespread, is one of magnitude, its upheavals and usurpations no less alarming than those committed by the Jacobins in the French Revolution of 1789 and later by the Bolsheviks in the Russian Revolution in 1917. Indeed, when one considers the Orwell conference in its diverse ramifications, one cannot help noticing a prevailing self-conceit and dogmatism, the two roots of the Jacobin intellect that Hippolyte-Adolphe Taine saw as existing in all countries, "underground and indestructible." This species of intellect, which Eckstein has identified in its American version, is inescapably a sign of educational decomposition. Its critical canonicity is not different from what Taine discerned in Jacobin literature: "Pedantic scholasticism set forth with fanatical rant."

In recent years we have been hearing much about educational reform and about reviving the liberal arts. Words like value, piety, virtue, discipline, and vision, hitherto derided and discarded, are now being saluted as qualitatively significant in educational experience. Even some educators who in the 1960s and 1970s fought savagely for the dislodgement of humanistic studies are now among those who are calling for their restoration. Eckstein's description of recent events helps to remind us how hard it will be to attain any real measure of restoration in the face of so much disloyalty, nullity, and deep-rooted habit: The Orwell conference, in effect, gives us a microcosmic view of the "kingdom of enmity."

Overcoming the relentless process of fragmentation in American culture and society will be no simple matter, for once the rhythm of disintegration has set in, it is difficult to correct. Sociological and psychological patterns of thought as they infiltrate and coalesce in the academic world cannot be easily altered. Prescriptive and corrective actions cannot be readily instituted. And far too often the counsel being proffered relies exclusively on technique, the falsity of which Jacques Ellul has warned against repeatedly.

Changing the ways of academic hucksters and political gamesters requires more than legislative force and reform. It is the inner moral condition and the character of education and leadership that remain to be mobilized. This mobilization means returning to first principles, and it means paying attention to spiritual substance. These prerequisites to reform and restitution are hardly in accord with the secular and blasphemous orientation of the modern age. When, therefore, we are told by "experts" that reforms in the educational system are in the offing, we must be at once skeptical and vigilant; the problems of education go far beyond "60 Minutes" and far beyond commercial and journalistic meliorism. We should be grateful to Arthur Eckstein for presenting us with ungarnished facts, for showing us just how debilitating the malaise in the academic world actually is, and, above all, for enabling us to penetrate the perilously deep strata of what C. S. Lewis has cogently termed an "educated infidelity."

13

The Incubus of Deconstruction

"For there is no doubt that in our headlong rush to educate everybody, we are lowering our standards, and more and more abandoning the study of those subjects by which the essentials of our culture—of that part of it which is transmissible by education—are transmitted; destroying our ancient edifices to make ready the ground upon which the barbarian nomads of the future will encamp in their mechanized caravans." These words, found in T. S. Eliot's *Notes Towards the Definition of Culture* (1949), are no longer simply prophetic but visibilized, daily facts of existence. Not a day passes by that self-proclaimed evangels of deconstruction do not contribute to the breakdown of "the essentials of our culture" which Eliot decries. Great "statesman of literature" that he is, Eliot, too, has become increasingly a victim of the deconstructionist process, his poetic achievement often the object of scurrilous attack by radical commentators. Here, Jeane J. Kirkpatrick, who has been harassed when delivering speeches on several campuses, is very much to the point when she protests that "All too many universities today permit the outrages of the fascist left. One historian, in fact, sees a perilous connection between 'thought reform' and 'thought police' in the 'university community.'"

Ideological trends, declares Stephen H. Balch, president of the National Association of Scholars, are inevitably "the expression of politics, working in their varied ways to compromise, even corrupt, the essential mission of the university." Perhaps the most evident result of the trends that now prevail in American higher education is the pervasive relativism that denies that a literary canon exists or that some moral views are superior to others. In this connection, one can recall here Stanford University's leveling of its required "Western Civilization" courses and the imposition of a quota system that specifies how much attention is to be paid to books by "women, minorities and persons of color," and by non-European cultures and issues of "race, gender and class." Trends in the end often transform into rampages, to judge by each new development, and they are difficult to stop. As the American left has solidified its power-base in the academy, the politicization of the curriculum has accelerated dramatically. Thus, in English studies, for instance, literature is valued simply as sociology or as history, and one concomitant question that must surely arise is, "What happened to beauty?"

Literary and critical values have been diminished and uglified in the name not only of "the academic industry," but also of a prescriptive ideology, as defined and applied by New Left dogmatists. One who seeks to criticize these dogmatists, who have amassed considerable power and governance, is almost immediately charged with racism, sexism, homophobism, etc. The role of "literature in revolution"— "the merciless criticism of everything that exists," as Leon Trotsky phrased it back in 1924—has become, since the 1960s and 1970s, a relentless preoccupation and a dominant standard among many teachers and critics. What best identifies the major thrust of the transformation of American education as a whole is its antinomian character, which Professor Edward Shils cogently describes in these words: "The highest ideal of antinomianism is a life of complete self-determination, free of the burden of tradition and conventions, free of the constraints imposed by institutional rules and laws and of the authority operating within the setting of institutions."

The canon is always suspect and always under attack. The modern radical mind abominates everything that the word canon connotes and includes: absolutes, rule, law, order. Canon presupposes the acknowledgment of the religious sense; conscious and unconscious reverence; sacramental community; the covenant of peace and life; order in reality; moral direction; the idea of wisdom. It is a word that identifies, and is identified with sacred principles and "sacred books," even as it occupies a pivotal place among the "permanent things." As such, the canon serves as a deterrent to antinomian tendencies and practices as these ultimately transform into heresies, blasphemies, fanaticisms, schisms. A canon defines, and ordains, and continues catholicity, acceptation, universal value, the order of tradition, a moral constant, a moral law. Residing in a canon, it can be said, is the spirit of eternity itself. Which is to say that canon is anchored in first causes and first principles and that it prescribes a fundamental loyalty to certain inherited and established givens or laws, visible and invisible.

Contemporary examples of antinomian activity are numerous. For instance, a self-described "revolutionary intellectual" who teaches a seminar in Marxist theory in a state university declares that she "practice[s] revolution with others" and that "revolutionary activity is like being a midwife to help the socialist society that exists now be born." For some of the students in her class (on "Education and the Underclass") their protest activity against the system "was part of their involvement in the course." Whether one terms such actions as freewheeling or democratic radicalism, the effects on the idea and mission of the university are inevitably harmful. Higher learning cannot be commensurate with anarchy or chaos—or with any movement or demonstration that subscribes to antinomian practices.

The current push to rid American education of what its critics label a Western and European bias, "Eurocentrism" as it is termed, further intensifies rampant antinomianism in American society and culture. Doubtlessly the debate over Eurocentrism goes dangerously beyond what happened to the core curriculum at Stanford University since it has repercussions on a much larger scale. The chief goal of the critics of Eurocentrism as the embodiment of "The Imperialism of the Mind" is that of destroying the biblical and classical foundations of the Western world, its traditions and metaphysical roots. Thus, in Camden, New Jersey, there is now a group that actively seeks to overhaul the public school curriculum and to stress a more "Afrocentric and Latinocentric" approach. Is this not yet another symptom, one ventures to ask, of the deconstructionist tendency embodied in the centrifugal forms of multiplicity and pluralism? And that tendency is, in the final analysis, antinomian in character and consequence. It reveals in dark and grim ways the idolatries and the mechanistic politicization of education. And it announces, with strident arrogance, that there is no holy law that needs to be preserved, no sense of rededication to be upheld.

A new morality, in effect, is being forged to accommodate the antinomian character of a gnostic modernity. There is no standard of centrality or conviction that is not being undermined, as the unceasing assaults on our logocentric and Eurocentric legacy disclose. The disciplines of continuity, the need for order, the standards of discrimination, hence, are the perceived opponents of the new morality. "In place of judgment," as Paul Elmer More wrote in an essay assessing "the stress and tragedy of modern times" and the "faith in drifting," "we are to regard all mankind with sympathy; a sort of emotional solidarity becomes the one great virtue, in which are included, or rather sunk, all the law and the prophets."

The pitiless dismemberment of *Homo europeensis* in the twilight years of the twentieth century is now much more than the "drift towards disintegration and disease" that More diagnosed. To judge from the accelerating attacks not only on *Humanität* but also on *tempora christiana*, a total deconstructionist effort proceeds to devalue the history and the teachings of Israel, Greece, and Rome. Those who condemn a Eurocentric concern with the Prophets, with Homer, Virgil, Dante, Shakespeare, and Goethe are far too often motivated by pseudo-metaphysics rather than genuine educational concerns. They are also often part of the deconstructionist movement that thrives on unrest and revolution, no less than the "revolutionary intellectual" whose university class, according to one student, "was an exercise in democracy, run by consensus"; and the teacher "was basically one of us . . . [who would] come out with us at night or come over to our place and hang out."

Present-day revolutionary intellectuals and theorists, the inheritors and continuators of the *Sturm und Drang* of the 1970s, are unreliable guides in any attempt to reform education, or to define curricula, or to restructure society. Radical revisionists, as we see them in fervid action in contemporary American society, are "enemies of the permanent things" who detest the idea of value and the virtue of reverence. Indeed one can examine the entire scene of higher learning these days without discovering the existence of an Irving Babbitt who sought to integrate the teachings of Aristotelianism and Christianity with those of Buddhism and Confucianism. But Babbitt's implicit challenge to Eurocentrism is profoundly different from those revolutionary intellectuals like Harry Magdoff, co-editor of the *Monthly Review*, an independent socialist magazine, who claims that "We have to be aware of the way we worship our culture and the way we judge others." The way of insight and wisdom is not the way of a secular ideology, as Babbitt showed. His conception of *Weltliteratur* was paradigmatically planetary and deeply spiritual. Babbitt never gave in to attempts by wild neoterists to destroy the unity of the One and to obliterate moral virtues. He was constantly aware, as so many of today's liberal and radical intellectuals are not, of the universal truth of Goethe's admonition, that "anything that emancipates the spirit without a corresponding growth in self-mastery is pernicious."

The deconstructionist movement, in all its guises, lacks credibility precisely because it refuses to comprehend or respect the meaning found in these sage words of Gerardus van der Leeuw: "We would like the race of the future to be able to look at a center of history." Deconstruction and devaluation are forces of chaos longing to be free, "to have no ancestors, no classical soil." They are forces that are instinctively antagonistic to what Robert M. Hutchins once referred to as "the Civilization of the Dialogue." One can hardly view their ideas and agendas, as these swiftly proliferate and solidify in almost demonic proportions, without a distinct feeling of dread.

Our historical experience of the antinomian attitude in the twentieth century gives us powerful reasons not only to resist deconstructionist manifestoes but also to see them as forms of modern disintegration and debasement. In the early twentieth century, to recall, we had the iconoclasms perpetrated by Futurism in the visual arts, in literature, in drama, and in music. Futurist nihilism disclosed itself variously in attempts to "depoetize" poetry, to express the "tangible miracles" of contemporary life, and to create "the art of noises." And then, between the two wars, there was Surrealism with its diseased obsession with unrestrained experimentation, its unchecked exploration of the unconscious and the fantastic, its glorification of the element of surprise, its demand that humans recognize the internal "sense" of the irrational and the inexplicable—in short, an attitude that, in the language of the surrealist mandarin André Breton, "regards submission to laws of any given perspective as useless," and systematically strives "to put everything out of place" and "to break loose some day from the law of identity."

Ever armed with the gospel of dynamism and revolution, the advocates of deconstruction belong to a modernism which scorns the normative force of moral law. Ultimately they constitute no less an "infection" than that of the infamous sect of "Ranters" in seventeenth-century England who believed themselves to be above all law and insisted that nothing is sin except what man thinks to be so. George Fox, "the first of the Quakers," was to record in his journal how, while he was held as prisoner at Charing-Cross in 1654, "a great company of

Ranters" visited him there, one of them crying, "All is ours," and another boasting, "All is well," as they violently denounced Fox's affirmation of "the light within" and "the things of God." Clearly the incubus of deconstruction has irrefragable historical antecedents and perversities. It behooves us, then, as we go about undoing sacred traditions and "ancient edifices," to recall the lessons of the past and to reflect carefully on present and future consequences of our actions.

14

An Honoring Equivalent

I

A *Festschrift* is a volume of essays offered as homage by colleagues, students, friends, and admirers to a distinguished teacher. Generally the content of each essay, as an example of the writer's own thought and interest, is also intended to illustrate a tangential relationship to the honored man's own work. Generally, too, the discrepancy between intention and achievement becomes all too evident in most such volumes. The fact remains that a *Festschrift* often becomes a sanctuary for fugitive essays. What is offered as an affectionate gesture of respect transforms into still another essay, still another bibliographical item to be duly, academically recorded. Except for occasioning their composition, the teacher being honored is hardly identifiable in such an assortment of essays. What kind of teacher is he? What are his special personal qualities that they should be thus honored and remembered? What are the particular marks of his "sermon"? What, in short, are the required standards of greatness that signal his candidacy for praise and honor?

For the most part the editors of a *Festschrift* avoid confronting these major and possibly embarrassing questions. Celebration, not revelation, is the keynote. Both the preparation and the reading of a *Festschrift* are tantamount to attending a parade or a testimonial; it is the occasion of a parting salute, of a pleasant, nostalgic, and even festive gathering. As such a *Festschrift* constitutes a missed opportunity, the case too often where reverence is subsumed by safeness—scholarly safeness, and dullness. It is a book that fizzles almost as soon as it is published. One could go on citing other negatives, but these are enough to remind us also of what a *Festschrift* should *be*: a collective portrait of the man as well as the teacher, illuminating everything that he is; evoking his concerns, his commitments, his uniqueness, his charisma; and, at the same time, catching his contradictions, his inconsistencies, his uncertainties, even his eccentricities. A *Festschrift* should be a continuing, synthesizing intellectual and spiritual experience of the man and the teacher, of the scholar and the critic. As an honoring equivalent, it should continue his quest for truth.

II

Ideally a *Festschrift* should continue some sort of insightful contact with the scholar as teacher. Indeed, this is precisely the kind of volume in which students' reminiscences of their teacher in the classroom can be of enormous pedagogical guidance in their own teaching careers. There is, or would be, more to learn from a student's own recollection of his experience of a teacher than from all that is so cheaply and functionally peddled in the "training" manuals of the "educationalists." A *Festschrift* should be an enriching learning experience of value, a disciplining and humbling encounter. As a published record, it should enable us to delineate and to reflect upon the marks of great teaching, even as it should afford us the opportunity to examine critically the record of the man who is being honored. And it must have the effect, ultimately, of stressing the serious need for applying and distilling standards of excellence of which the honored man must provide genuine examples and models. It should also serve as an antidote against the conditions that favor mediocrity, popular success, and the back-slapping tendencies that one finds increasingly (and cynically) glorified in the sociology of the academic world.

If a *Festschrift* does not have a critical conscience, it must inevitably fail in satisfying the highest standard of scrutiny. It must finally communicate not the profession but rather the character of a man of letters. In the academic as in the literary "game" today rewards are too easily given to club figures and for club reputations. The conditions for the making of great teachers of humane letters in particular are necessarily subject to the rules of *this* game. Clearly the academic club is hedonistic and self-propagating. It does not always sanction (as it does not recruit or promote) the criticism that applies critical values—moral discriminations, as it were—or the teaching that stimulates and matures. These are additional reasons why a *Festschrift* needs to be as scrupulously pondered as, say, an annual "honors list." As a product of the club spirit it can have stultifying effects, of which, surely, we need fewer than ever.

III

Communicating the value of teaching in its various allied dimensions should be a central if not sacred purpose of a *Festschrift*. The need to meditate on the constituents of teaching that have enduring impact and influence is one of the essential needs of mind and soul. Too often in our modern technologico-Benthamite age and habits we lose sight of the spiritual significance of teaching. The art, the craft, of teaching is thus devalued with telling consequences for the individual and his culture. Greatness, it seems, is too readily sacrificed to the cult of equality. Such is our concern with the democratizing process in education that we ignore the criteria of excellence. Yet the valuative task of separating the true teacher from the false teacher, like that of separating the true prophet from the false one, must not be shirked. The great teacher is a rare person. The great teacher who is a great critic is an even rarer person. The great teacher and critic who is also a great encourager of others is a unique person. Any encounter with such a teacher and critic is a privilege, which, when given, is in itself a miracle of experience.

Great writers, it can be said, heighten experience. Great teachers change lives. Exposure to the example and the testaments (oral or written, but preferably both) of a great teacher and critic is to participate in an act of consecration, in itself an incarnational process. Within this "forming" and "making" process lies a spiritual transmission. "The influence of the teacher upon the pupil, of the right teacher upon the right pupil, is not merely compared to, but even set on a par with, divine works which are linked with the human maternal act of giving birth." Martin Buber trenchantly reminds us in these words that the intrinsic greatness of a teacher ultimately lies in "pointing the way." The shaping experience of this greatness, as renewal and as affirmation, revolving around the eternal criterion, finds rest in the unity of the One.

Great teaching moves towards and proceeds from great criticism. The teacher as critic and the critic as teacher assume reciprocating roles, a posited consolidation, a mutuality. The pursuit of the one foments the pursuit of the other. No teacher without a critical position, a world view, can hope to attain in himself and in his pupils a transcending and a transforming vision of truth. The critic meditates on the discriminations, the determinations, the explorations, the scrutinies that he must finally proclaim, insofar as criticism is a proclamation of the judgments of a judging mind. The teacher as critic mediates these judgments. He conveys and passes them on in apostleship. In a very large sense he seeks to teach what he believes, his beliefs, his critiques, identifying him in both his inner and his outer selves. A great critic, it is almost needless to say, must have integrity: a scrupulous respect for what he proclaims and believes.

Integrity postulates an ethical element in the formation and ordering of a critic's judgments. It is one of the main supports of criticism. It is an impelling aspect of the critic's character, without which he would lack character. It helps to reveal a rooted personal quality, which must yet find its true *telos*, its transcending purpose, beyond personalism. Yet, as great a truth-force as it is, integrity of itself is not the final desideratum. It needs to discover its true ultimateness, its humanistic and spiritual quintessence, beyond the secular frontier of judgmental values. Indeed, judgmental values must discover their true sapiential significance, their most valid awareness and authenticity, in conjunction with and by extension to the virtue of humility. One's educational work and one's critical pursuit must ascend, synoptically, to this virtue, finding in it their integral completion as an answer to the voice of the world.

IV

These foregoing reflections are occasioned by and attain their positive and particularizing connections with a *Festschrift* entitled *Teacher and Critic: Essays by and about Austin Warren*, edited by Myron Simon and Harvey Gross and published in 1976.[1] We find in this exquisitely edited and beautifully produced book the qualities of character and intellect that distinguish Professor Warren's lifetime of work and thought and, even more, of meditation and contemplation. A teacher and a critic of extraordinary power, range, and depth, as repeatedly testified to in this book, Warren occupies a special place of honor among great American teachers and critics. The distinction of Warren's teaching brings to mind that of his own teacher and master, Irving Babbitt. The concentrated totality of his work as a critic has enduring excellence, commensurate with that of an F. O. Matthiessen and of a Lionel Trilling. Even as Warren's achievement requires equivalent honor, it also contains unmistakably distinguishing specialties.

These disclose the endowment of creativeness, but, above all, of character. It will be seen that the exceptional value of Warren's contribution is pedagogic, indeed, catechetical. "Whether theoretical or practical," he writes in one of his finest essays, "The Teacher as Critic," "the best criticism is . . . nearer to the catechetical than to the expository." A revealing remark, it illumines the ultimate direction taken by Warren in his *oeuvre*. In this ultimate direction we can discover the basic rhythms and patterns, the *données*, of his work: a call, a promise, a testimony, a commission.

Often leaping in eloquence and arresting in perception, Warren's work takes on the form of public preaching that adheres faithfully to the double discipline of language and spirituality. "With the man of integrity, his whole being takes incarnation in his every act, his every paragraph. He is always representative." This statement, which comes from Warren's voluminous journals, and is included among twenty-five aphorisms selected for inclusion in *Teacher and Critic* under the heading "Approximations," essentializes his labors as a teacher and a critic ever in search of wisdom—and salvation.

Before he retired in 1968, Warren was a university teacher of English, his career spanning nearly a half century. During this period he published seven books, including the *Theory of Literature* (1948), which he wrote in collaboration with René Wellek. (The latter has contributed a trenchant essay to this *Festschrift* on the history and nature—and on the concomitant rewards—of this collaboration.) The figures on whom Warren has written major studies are Alexander Pope, Nathaniel Hawthorne, and Richard Crashaw. His most celebrated collection of critical essays is *Rage for Order* (1947), which, with the *Richard Crashaw: A Study in Baroque Sensibility* (1939), Allen Tate rightly designates as being "among the most distinguished of this century." Its worthy sequel, published in his retirement, and Warren's eighth book, is *Connections* (1966). His two companion studies in regional culture-history are *New England Saints* (1956) and *The New England Conscience* (1966). The former is a magisterial book, central to Warren's own spiritual autobiography.

Paul Elmer More is the subject of a long essay in *Connections*; this is Warren's supreme essay, the one that, in its critical vision and style, and in its kindred spiritual-critical sympathy, breadth, and meaning, tells us much not only about More but also about Warren, whose own critical sympathy lies somewhere midpoint between Babbitt and More. It is an essay that, to apply to it words from Leon Edel's tribute, stamps Warren as "one of our modern artists of the essay, one of our masters of *mediated* utterance." Particularly for those wanting lessons in prose style, this and other essays by Warren (*e.g.,* those on Ralph Waldo Emerson in *New England Saints,* and on E. M. Forster and Franz Kafka in *Rage for Order*) will repay frequentation. In "Two Autobiographical Notes," prefacing the first part of *Teacher and Critic,* containing selected essays by Warren, he stresses his deep concern with the problem of style: "I have more and more seen that the kind of meaning I aim at is that kind which incarnates itself in style; and it is style—meaning in diction and rhythm—which is my final concern." In its majestic restraints, starkness, and economy of expression, this autobiographical essay is, for the catechumen, an illustrious model of clarity and cogency and of concentration and compression.

v

Magnanimity is a word that comes effortlessly to mind when one considers the overall value of Warren's work as a teacher. Not one of the essays of tribute to him fails to advert to this sterling quality, which Professor Myron Simon rightly connects with Warren's search "to build a community in the classroom by making the relation between student and teacher a reciprocal one." Warren gave of himself fully and selflessly to his teaching. He never held back. That is to say, he did not try to save himself from dissipating in the classroom the ideas he hoped eventually to commit to paper. In this giving of himself not only to his own pupils but also to the distant auditors who sought him out, speaking as he did to their condition, he gave constant witness to his vocation. (His extant letters provide an untapped but rich and formidable source of humane and spiritual instruction, as well as models of epistolary excellence informed by the humility that comes from the inner, or noetic, self, as it simultaneously conveys force by conviction and strength of character.)

Not unlike Babbitt, the New Humanist, Warren, the Christian Humanist, was, in his classroom, an experience, at once unusual and unforgettable, implicitly religious in origin and character. Not unlike Babbitt, he too was in no sense academic or pedantic, but, in an implicitly Emersonian sense, Man Thinking. Babbitt can be viewed as the man and teacher as moralist. Warren personifies the teacher as encourager and the critic as sage, the teacher and critic as priest. Each, in his turn and in his way, was to acquire his disciples. Though both were, in their ministries, to demand a decision for order, a reverent discipline, on the part of their disciples, Babbitt must be seen as a moral guide, Warren as a spiritual helper. Discipleship, in Babbitt's case, was characterized by a strict, even a polemical, moral theology; a law in tone and temper. But it was a discipleship with a mission that lacked an aesthetic, that lacked music, so to speak. Discipleship, in Warren's case, is characterized by a sacramental gift. It is a discipleship that binds through the ministry of Word and Sacrament. Babbitt's followers were to constitute a body of preceptors, insisting on *metanoia*. Warren's followers constitute, as the contributors here indicate again and again, a priesthood, a fellowship, and a communion, insisting on *koinonia*.

Allen Tate concludes his "Homage to Brother Austin" with these words: "He has been too busy for strife in his pursuit of truth." Clearly Warren has avoided the kind of critical warfare into which, for instance, Babbitt, in America, and Leavis, in England, hurled themselves with such amazing vigor. In some ways, Warren's avoidance of strife is to be regretted. The demonic forces that perennially assault moral life and cultural order need to be confronted at every available opportunity. No hiding in and behind a theory of literature or criticism can every hope to arrest the *furor impius* of the Enemy. The burden of judgment comprises the critic's, and the teacher's, primary responsibility; yet the critic must also have the courage to be. Such a critic belongs to the Elect, chosen and also choosing to resist the cruel demonisms that desanctify the meaning of man. Yet a great critic must finally define his mind and character, his greatness, in the special and identifying ways in which he gives shape to his principles of order. Some critics choose to be militant and polemical in the attainment of their aims. Zeal is their hallmark. Others, though they hardly deny the fact of conflict, choose to follow a different passage leading not so much to confrontations but to encounters in dialogue and understanding. These latter critics rely more on their spiritual rather than on their martial weapons. Warren belongs to this category.

No other living generalist critic is more intensely aware of his own need and search for general principles of order. Warren's view and definition of first and last principles are diligently demarcated in the overarching themes of his metaphysics of order, riveted by a New England mind, and presided over by a New England conscience, as it exerts a moral and intellectual discipline in the hard process of making judgments, defending truths, contemplating ends, resisting (in C. S. Lewis' words) a spreading "tradition of educated infidelity." Warren is an example of a modern New England saint, at once and always catholic and critical, in whom the mystical is ordered by the rational, the enthusiastic by the moderate, the moral by the ethical, the theological by the critical, the personal by the impersonal, the ecumenical by the eclectic.

Reconciliation and atonement, humility and humanity; a concelebration and a confraternity of grace: these are the main currents of Warren's life and work, and the ultimate message of a teacher and critic making his, and helping others to make their, way towards the One. Their hierarchic spiritual search is endemic to invisible warfare. Emblematized by strict conscience and good courage, this search is sustained by the virtue of magnanimity, which Saint Thomas Aquinas saw as a subdivision of fortitude. It is a privilege for all who share with Austin Warren a sympathy of vision to salute the memory of this great man of letters who died in 1986 at the age of eighty-seven.

15

Education for All Time

Irving Babbitt's *Literature and the American College: Essays in Defense of the Humanities*, first published in 1908, has been reissued by the National Humanities Institute, which is to be commended for making available this classic.[1] Although new books continue to be published concerning our educational problems, *Literature and the American College* has a prophetic relevance that makes it indispensable reading in our time. It should, in fact, be a required text for present and future educators. Indeed, it is a book that also constitutes a sacred text that deconstructionists, our most dangerous apostles of contemporaneity, shamelessly scorn. In reissuing Babbitt's masterwork, the National Humanities Institute bravely testifies to an existing voice of sanity in the intellectual community that needs to be listened to despite the din that the deconstructionists and their befuddled allies have produced and the influence that they have amassed in the educational system.

What *Literature and the American College* should conduce is renewed reflection on the crisis in education. Hopefully such reflection will go beyond the kind of instant analyses that we are now accustomed to or the kind of educational reforms that are often half-hearted and half-baked. *Literature and the American College* underlines the perennial need in education, no less than in religion, for articles of faith, those statements of belief and certitude that define an educational creed and adhere to universal principles and acceptances. Such a creed proclaims a sense of devotion, delineates standards of achievement, and points to the organic connections between past and present in relation to the future. It identifies a spirit of order and continuity that contributes to the shaping of a humane society and that provides civilizational bearings and paradigms.

What this educational creed should do above all is to show that matters of crucial importance are not the outgrowth of trends and fads, nor the results that emerge from a spiritual vacuum. It emphasizes a view of education against the backdrop of permanent things, that is, the absolutes of existence that transcend an ephemeral, mechanico-materialist world and that have a moral center and constancy. It discloses the unchanging fact that education has spiritual roots and character, has purpose and meaning exclusive of flux and transience, has its own grand design, its own *magna charta*, so to speak. That there are values that defy the idols of the marketplace and the immediate demands of clock time: this is, in the end, the overarching article of faith of an educational creed for all time. This article of faith frees the responsibility and the mission of education from those pressures of immediacy and temporality that reduce the idea of education to what is expedient and opportunistic. Education, in this respect, also connotes the true freedom that is right and truth—that which conjoins piety and discipline, the two highest qualities of intellect and spirit.

The disorder of the modern age has been mirrored to an almost savage degree in the disorder of education. And as modern society has more and more been drawn to the new gods of technology, of computers, and even of cybernetics, so too has humane education lost its true purpose and character: the indefectible rules of faith that comprise its creed and that declare its vision of what is needed to educate, and to civilize, and to save man. This loss now affects education at all levels, and it appears in sundry forms—as pragmatism, utilitarianism, relativism, nominalism, gnosticism. It has helped to dislodge the humane principles of education that have their roots in man's moral nature and in the spiritual disciplines that nourish and mold that nature. The mystery and the divinity of man have increasingly been sacrificed to abject scientific facts and to a cruel process of objectification. The moral dimension of education—that which relates to the character and conscience of man, or what might be termed the inner needs of the soul—has now been transformed into the mechanistic dimension of education that stresses the collective thingness of a society whose allegiance is to outer forms of existence, to the inorganic, the functional, the programmatic.

Education has become an ancillary agency of social reform and a means towards an end. How man is to be trained (to use that synthetic word of modern educational theorists) for entrance into a job market is today the adopted principle of education, of education that has been almost completely absorbed by the megatechnic mechanisms of power that deprive education of its moral constituents. It is the job, and not the mission, of education that now legislates needs and goals. In that phrase, "the job of education," and particularly in the first noun of that phrase, "job," we have the hard requisites of buying and selling at a profit, which process, of course, also summarizes the disintegrative crisis of education, as well as the irreconcilable differences between those who uphold the *artes liberales* and those who promote the *artes serviles*.

Education has become preoccupied with presentness and hence with the short view and with short cuts. It lacks transcendent perspective, the vision without which civilization itself perishes. An empirical educational methodology thrives everywhere, as moral issues and ultimate questions are scorned (along with the study of history, theology, political theory, and philosophy itself). Nor do we find the study of language and literature commanding the high priority it deserves. Egalitarianism pervades the curriculum as much as it does society; one subject is as good as another, it seems, as the hierarchy of studies is increasingly dismantled. The discipline of ideas, and of ideas that have consequences, hardly exists as an axiom of education. What we find in the place of a structured design in education is a kind of hotch-potch, the result of which is a new class of illiteracy. We are constantly being faced by a proliferation of parts and an eradication of the whole. We can no longer locate a center of values in the realm of education; no body of knowledge, in its continuity and tradition, is any longer commonly shared by or expected of those who are being educated.

Not unity and centrality but fragmentation and deconstruction are the two prominent conditions in education. Too, an insidious provincialism often prevails in educational institutions, if one is to judge by the demise of required courses in world literature in many colleges and universities. And a crass secularism nullifies the classical and biblical view of man. The modern secular city in its crudest forms is exalted, as the Athens, Jerusalem, and Rome of sacred history are relegated to a dead man's dump. Some cultural commentators approvingly speak of this radicalizing process as one of demystification. No other word better instances the overweening pride of a man at the most perilous point of blasphemy. No other word better embodies the arrogances of a radical modernism that seeks to destroy the foundations of our sacred patrimony. Inevitably alienation and rootlessness are symptoms of the search after strange gods, and these are precisely the symptoms of a debased educational system as we experience it.

These words may seem severe to those who will no doubt cite the large population being educated, or the large selection of courses available in every area of interest, or the large number of diverse institutions satisfying every conceivable educational need and curiosity. Yet, all the outward signs of success and opulence cannot finally hide the lack of the invisible Spirit that discloses human worth and validates the divine and unwritten laws of the universe. Civilization is not the product of the law of numbers; rather, it is the result of disciplined, selective, even aristocratic thought, of undaunted commitment, of qualitative concentration, of selfless perseverance as finally revealed in the achievements of our greatest writers, thinkers, philosophers, composers, teachers, and all the other great builders of civilization. We tend to forget that our goal should be that of educating people who will contribute to and sustain standards of civilization; who will give their loyalty to civilizing values and moral virtues, which some of our cynical educationists insist are unteachable and unachievable.

In the long run our empirical approaches to and formulas of education reflect a spiritual neutrality indifferent to and, at worst, contemptuous of paradigms of character and the counsel of conscience. Under these circumstances education increasingly discloses purely functional and technic emphases; it places its faith in quantitative, relativistic, experimental, and progressivist practices. In these emphases and practices we view the tyranny of a bureaucratic education, which has come to supplant a humane education, just as external forms of education have come to supplant internal values of education. This corrosive process ignores criteria that are time-tested and time-honored. It is a process that enshrines disconnectedness, even as any glance at our educational programs will confirm the absence of any unifying sense of relation between intellectual disciplines. A disordered and disoriented philosophy of education prevails at all levels.

Ultimately a genuine and lasting educational creed is one that distinguishes between right and wrong, between truth and error; that encourages reflection, inspires reverence, compels judgment, and teaches meaning. The teacher of the humanities is one, then, who distrusts the extremes of specialization and endorses the law of proportion. For such a teacher the goal and the office of instruction are not vocational but humanistic and moral: not that of training one for competition and power but for wisdom and character. How is character to be shaped, disciplined, improved, refined? That is a central question that the teacher of the humanities never stops asking. His concern is not local and restrictive but catholic and critical; it identifies a comprehensive orientation that accentuates education for all time, not education for a particular time. Today the tremendous advances in science make even more urgent the need to view education in the larger transdisciplinary contexts of the human spirit and human heart.

Modern education, insofar as it mirrors utilitarian and industrial theory and practice, mirrors that is to say the world of spiritless facts, needs more than ever those civilizing standards that contain the humanistic disciplines, or qualities, for which the Latin word *humanitas* is used. These civilizing standards mould not only intellect but also soul. *Humanitas* connotes a principle of education that is too often overlooked or derided: the need to scrutinize the moral cosmos in the human soul. This need is one that never ceases in relation to the human condition; it is invariably a universal need that impels man to search for an understanding of what separates the wrong life, or the wrong pattern of life, from the right life. It is the moral recovery of this humane dimension that is required in education.

It is sad that education today forgets the conception of human life and destiny—of the opposition of good and evil—that one finds in the moral imagination, which helps make men better in their cities, as the ancients said, and inspires them to grow wings to overcome gravity. Central to this conception are the dignity and the sacredness of life that one finds to be of supreme importance to the Hebrew prophets, the Greek tragedians, and the Christian fathers. In modern society human life is increasingly reduced to naturalistic formulas, functional processes, behavioristic demands, biological reality, mathematical calculation. Human life is transformed into what might be called an entropic state of consciousness, that is, a state of inert uniformity that culminates in nothingness. Such a state of degradation underlines the valuelessness of life and also crystallizes in a meaninglessness that completely negates differentiation, effort, belief.

The obsessive preoccupation with positivism, careerism, specialism, vocationalism, technicalism that we observe in our educational system is the inevitable counterpart of the entropic process. As this preoccupation has surged into prominence and popularity, moral criteria and expectations that should stand at the very heart of an educational creed and system are abrogated. The eclipse of the moral imperative compounds the eclipse of God. This twin eclipse constitutes the greatest disaster of the modern age, for in it we discern the desanctification of human life. Need one wonder, then, why the humanities have been progressively de-emphasized in the modern world? In their seed and composition, the humanities ultimately accept the idea of transcendence, the acceptance of a transcendent moral order of history as we see it advancing from Mount Olympus to Mount Sinai to the Mount of Olives.

Humane education revolves around a comprehensive perception of human meaning and destiny. Piety and moral essence, which should inform such a perception, are aspects of educational policy that are being ignored. In losing sight of this higher goal, we have manifestly weakened the entire educational process. No less than the architecture of our cities, education itself is amorphous: it also lacks soul and spirit, two words that trouble and anger many educators—and educationists. The elements of unity and harmony, which diminish what is insidious and paltry, are precisely what are not considered as prescriptive educational principles. Even when they are considered, they are reduced in significance and use. It is their absence that one finds frightening in the present situation, and, surely, that absence makes more possible the advent of so much ugly music, ugly art, ugly literature, and ugly architecture. The humane, and the humanizing, ethos is thus in retreat as we view an expanding educational wasteland around us.

To be sure, the humanities will not save the world. But without them the world becomes more barren and mechanistic. When one observes the content of school studies at almost any level today, one inevitably finds missing a humane and moral concern, or consciousness. Specialistic constructions and dimensions impede a growth of awareness, of understanding, and finally of humility. Which also reminds us that it is technique that now determines levels of existence, in short, a preoccupation with what is purely functional, with the way the knife cuts, so to speak. Man's personal, moral, and spiritual worth thus receives little attention in the educational system, and the result is very much a kind of perverse adulteration. Clearly the decline of the humanities has been commensurate with the advance of a rigorously technological society as we have progressively substituted a social and technical discipline for human and moral discipline. This dialectical substitution hastens the total decline of humanistic education and the ascent of the new education that we see all around us.

Hardened ideologies and methodologies have been steadily eroding the truly humane ethos that gives educational philosophy a spiritual basis. Whatever the extent of the annihilative process that pushes aside the moral nature of the educational task, it cannot go unchallenged. The new education that we view everywhere dramatizes its divorce from spiritual needs. That divorce entails inestimable consequences for American democracy and leadership, especially in terms of the future. "Consequences" is a word that we tend to overlook and that, more specifically, modern educational theories have slighted in pushing for immediate results and socio-temporal solutions. The fact remains that we worship time, present time, and such a worship is a worship of false idols.

In this connection it might be recalled that while Moses was delayed on Mount Sinai to receive the two tables of stone containing the written law of the Ten Commandments, his people, growing impatient, demanded visible and immediate gods as leaders. Aaron then made for them a golden calf before which he also built an altar. This biblical event personifies not only apostasy, corruption, sin, but also the breakdown of incorporeal, transcendent Spirit in life and in the world. Something of the magnitude of consequence of what happened at ancient Sinai has been occurring in modern education, in which contempt for humane principles and traditions, rooted in the Ten Words and in Spirit, has led to the adoption of a new morality. In such a situation education becomes predominantly education for the present time and for a broken world, a world of parts, fragments, moments, episodes; a world of flux in which a golden calf, now incarnated in the form of imperious technique, commands veneration. Such a world neither possesses nor conveys the insight and the wisdom that Irving Babbitt views as thaumaturgic educational values. The perils posed by such a world are in the end fateful not only for the order of the soul, but also for the order of the republic.

These reflections on some of the conditions that affect and influence education in the present time may also help to remind us why it is all the more urgent to think in terms of education for all time.

V

Spiritual Soundings

ᕿᘛᕽ

The preservation of our sacred patrimony requires tenacious commitment, for the struggle to retain even the semblance of a civilized world of dignity, reason, and order is unending. This struggle is ultimately a spiritual struggle for first and last principles, for the great spiritual possessions bequeathed to us by Athens, Rome, and Jerusalem and which constitute our "entailed inheritances" and our lasting debts to the Greek philosophers, the Hebrew prophets, and the Christian saints and martyrs. This patrimony is our main-mast and we need to steer carefully. Our conservatism is our conservatorship—and invariably our spiritual responsibility. How can we preserve and protect the great traditions of our patrimony? That is the question we must ask ourselves as we define our responsibilities in the midst of the impiety that, in its syndrome of chaos and decadence, besieges so much of modern life and its institutions.

16

Literature and Religion

Within the academic establishment, and particularly in the area of modern literary studies, the contention of some scholars and teachers that the relations between literature and religion have a deep critical and educational value has not been exactly popular. In fact, hostility to this belief has often been prevalent. In the early 1960s I myself conducted a graduate seminar dealing exclusively with literature and religion, and I can still remember, not without pain and distress, how some senior professors looked askance at my seminar. If some of my colleagues were skeptical about my course offering, they condescendingly pleaded a formalistic bias. Others, who had a lesser commitment, treated my undertaking as an abstract excrescence inevitably resulting from the influence on me of "Comparative Literature," for which I should in time be forgiven. Still others responded belligerently. One colleague scornfully remarked that I "was trying to play God." Passing by me on occasion in the corridor, during that entire semester, he bowed solemnly, but disdainfully. Even after the passage of years, during which I also examined in my teaching and writing the relations between literature and history, literature and philosophy, literature and politics, this same colleague never failed to remind me that, for *him*, my early interest in literature and religion signified a cardinal academic sin for which I was permanently branded in his eyes, and no doubt in those of his sympathizers.

If the other posited interdisciplinary relationships were regarded as being legitimate, though also possibly curious, the relationship between literature and religion clearly indicated an absolute infraction of ongoing consequence. That is to say, it was viewed as a relationship that finally disclosed, on my part, a metaphysical, in short, a religious and spiritual, predisposition that, in a strictly intellectual sense, was completely unacceptable. One could talk about literature and history, and yet be an anarchist—that was perfectly acceptable. One could talk about literature and philosophy, and yet be a nihilist—that was also acceptable. And one could talk about literature and politics, and yet be a Marxist—that was even more acceptable. But for one to talk about literature and religion and also be one who subscribed to our Judaeo-Christian patrimony—well, that was utterly unacceptable and even contemptible.

Innuendo, distrust, derision, caricature, and invective have, it seems, informed reactions to any consideration of the relations between literature and religion. There are many famous instances of the language of scorn reserved for these relations, but none can be more infamous than that employed by Mr. Michael Gold (1894–1967) in his review of various novels by Thornton Wilder that appeared in the *New Republic*, October 22, 1930, under the caption, "Wilder: Prophet of the Genteel Christ." Gold's assessment is a case study of the critical demolition of works that have religious moorings and convey religious interest and need. It belongs to the record of written criticism; and however unsophisticated, shrill and vulgar it now reads, given its socio-historical moment and antecedents—the Great Depression in America had then begun, and the Great War in Europe had not too long ago ended—Gold's review remains symptomatic of those feelings, expressed and unexpressed, that so often describe a liberal critic's response to literary and religious relations. "Mr. Wilder," Gold announces, "is the poet of the genteel bourgeoisie." Pointing to Wilder's wish to restore the spirit of religion to American literature, Gold declares that this is merely a "newly fashionable literary religion that centers around Jesus Christ, the First British Gentleman"; it is "Anglo-Catholicism, that last refuge of the American literary snob." Singling out Wilder's style, Gold goes on to indict its spiritual effeteness, its pretentious verbal patterns, its sham rhetoric. Is this, Gold asks,

> . . . the style with which to express America? Is this the speech of a pioneer continent? Will this discreet French drawing-room hold all the blood, horror and hope of the world's new empire? Is this the language of the intoxicated Emerson? Or the clean, rugged Thoreau, or vast Whitman? Where are the modern streets of New York, Chicago and New Orleans in these little novels? Where are the cotton mills, and the murder of Ella May and her songs? Where are the child slaves of the beet fields? Where are the stockbroker suicides, the labor racketeers of passion and death of the coal miners? Where are Babbitt, Jimmy Higgins and Anita Loos's Blonde? Is Mr. Wilder a Swede or a Greek, or is he an American?

This comminatory paragraph tells us more about Gold's doctrinaire suppositions and biases than about Wilder's style and meaning. In it we have a synoptic glimpse into a radical's political point of view and critical psychology. Gold, it might be recalled, was an American communist, a founder of the *New Masses*, a contributor to the *Daily Worker*, a perennial celebrant of proletarian art, and a catechumen of Walt Whitman and Karl Marx. His most friendly critics called him the "American Gorky." Gold's indictment of Wilder's novels discloses much about the ideational background of the distrust of literary and religious relations and also about the sociology of critical thinkers and practitioners in the 1930s and 1940s and later, even more dramatically, in the late 1960s and early 1970s. What Gold has to say about Wilder's religious inclinations is now a formative part of a critical (and pedagogical) pattern. It contains the representative tone and temper of the general critique of literature and religion. If it is now less irate, it is nonetheless an accepted habit and presents a seminal (and uniform) responsiveness. It constitutes a critical *Zeitgeist* that, cognitively speaking, regulates and stamps perceptions of literature and religion, and of their relations in the context of spiritual and moral meaning. Gold's critique epitomizes the "secular hypothesis"; that is, it accentuates the empirical habits of rejection in our political age, an age of disbelief characterized by "the interior disloyalty of modern times," as Romano Guardini has expressed it. Even a severely moralist critic like F. R. Leavis has in his own way assisted this "secular hypothesis" by his censure of any committed critical approach that legitimates the relations between literature and religion. In particular, he stresses that literary criticism and specifically "Christian Discrimination" are totally incompatible, "that there can be no substitute for the scrupulous and disinterested approach of the literary critic."[1]

Leavis's critical honesty is not in doubt here; he is one of the greatest moralist critics of the twentieth century. Indeed, it is the moral severity of his critical achievement that makes his remarks about the interdisciplinary relations between literature and religion all the more troubling and disappointing. Yet when one weighs Leavis's words against Gold's, however antithetical their ideological roots and positions happen to be, they convey the general lines of attack on literature and religion as a valid area of critical inquiry. What we have in the positions of Gold and of Leavis is ultimately a shared rejection of and animosity towards the relations of literature and religion. This curious alliance is especially revealing in showing how even sharply opposing political and critical positions have a way of merging in opposition to any posited significance relating to literature and religion. In that alliance and in that opposition can be seen the kind of disparate enemies opposing those who uphold the critical validity of the relations between literature and religion. Clearly, for those who do accept this validity, and who also seek to demonstrate it, critically and pedagogically, the possibility of meeting the belligerent gestures that I myself encountered in offering a seminar on literature and religion is always a very distinct one.

No matter how many journals or conferences or seminars seek to validate the relations between literature and religion, the element of distrust and ultimately of derision is immanent. Literary scholarship, we are told, if it is to be dispassionate, must exclude, or at least subordinate, religious interests, facets, ideas, essences. The critic's autonomy must not be violated by any religious consideration or capitulate to any religious principle of faith and order. Hence, when literary scholarship and criticism in any way sanction the relations between literature and religion, then it is often neither scholarship nor criticism, but a culpable form of religious discrimination, "Christian Discrimination" as it is branded.

Characteristically, when George Orwell writes that "[t]he opinion that art should have nothing to do with politics is itself a political attitude," the academy applauds him. When, on the other hand, T. S. Eliot (in his 1935 essay on "Religion and Literature") writes that "[l]iterary criticism should be completed by criticism from a definite ethical and theological standpoint," he is singled out for special attack. These reactions constitute an unfair and condescending juxtaposition, and at the same time also tell us something about the age in which we live. Ours is not only an age of politics but also an age of liberalism, of radical humanism, an age that condemns Edmund Burke's "moral imagination" and condones John Dewey's "liberalism and social action." Such an age obviously has no use for a religious perspective, let alone such a thing as religious fear. It is an age in which "the eclipse of God" has become complete and in which, to use the parlance of contemporary critics, the process of "demystification" has at long last brought us out of the medieval darkness, in which an Eliot and a Christopher Dawson would have us dwell, into the "secular city" with all of its glamor, excitement, sensation—and obscenity.

In the academy, in educational theory and practice, in theory of literature and in critical doctrine, the voices of the "secular city" and of "demystification" that we now hear coalesce shrilly in word or in work that bears the name of "deconstructionism." D. H. Lawrence, in his novel *Women in Love* (1920), prophetically evokes the conditions of this deconstructionism when he decries "the destruction of the organic purpose, the organic unity, and the subordination of every organic unit to the great mechanical purpose. It was pure organic disintegration and pure mechanical organisation. This is the first and finest state of chaos." *Women in Love* is itself a novel of crisis in which modern man's fate is one of spiritual emptiness and alienation. No other twentieth-century novel more memorably tells us of how much modern man has snuffed out the candles of belief, how much he has separated himself from the idea of the holy that, for instance, radiates F. M. Dostoevsky's *The Brothers Karamazov* (1879–1880). Indeed, no two novels better illustrate or legitimate the viable relations between literature and religion than do *Women in Love* and *The Brothers Karamazov*.

In an age in which, as Allen Tate observed nearly fifty years ago in an essay, "What Is a Traditional Society?", we have the decay of manners, religion, morals, and codes, men "are no longer capable of defining a human objective, of forming a dramatic conception of human nature." Tate goes on to conclude, much in the sense of Lawrence's decrial of "the destruction of the organic purpose, the organic unity," that man who lives in such a world "lives in an untraditional society. . . . [and] an untraditional society does not permit its members to pass to the next generation what it received from its immediate past." In such a society, whether one views its extremisms as being symptomatic of the "secular city," or of the "secular hypothesis" or of the final entry into "the kingdom of enmity" (to use the term of Nikolay Lossky, the Russian religious philosopher), the religious element, the religious sense or conception, has no place of influence and in effect there is no place for man's moral nature or, in short, for the ideas of value, of transcendence. "Morality is responsibility to a given set of conditions," Tate asserts. "The further the modern system develops in the direction that it has taken . . . , the more antitraditional our society will become, and the more difficult it will be to pass on the fragments of the traditions we inherit."[2]

The transformation, or "metastasis," to use Eric Voegelin's word, of modern society now fully confirms Tate's fears. That which constitutes the interior and invisible life, under these circumstances, steadily surrenders to the external attitude, to techniques, as these variously thrive in a situation characterized by discontinuity and fragmentation. The spiritual focus inevitably disappears as technique in whatever form ascends in importance; and the human soul is both dislodged and displaced by *Massenmensch*, about which leveling process thinkers like José Ortega y Gasset and Karl Jaspers have written with prophetic depth. Any scrutiny of the relations between literature and religion can hardly ignore the powerful historical conditions affecting and shaping human nature and destiny: mechanistic conditions for the most part that not only demystify but also desanctify human life and give the modern age a deeply irreligious cast. This irreligious cast, in all of its modern trappings, is finally at the heart of the hostility towards any intellectual discipline that is associated with religion. My colleague who asserted that I "was trying to play God" was impelled precisely by an irreligious sentiment that was at the root of his hostility.

Even those scholars who accept literature and religion as a viable interdisciplinary subject, but who at the same time disregard its moral and spiritual tangent, are in the end unaware of the real relations between the two. For literature and religion, in their unity of meaning, affirm more than just a critical dialectic; they have, in the long run, a metaphysical thrust and meaning that go beyond a purely conceptual relation. The fact is that their relationship demands in the long run much more than a disinterested method of examination and evaluation. It is an ultimate relationship that possesses ultimate essences, not only moral but also eschatological. That is, this relationship moves beyond the pursuit of purely critical and intellectual objectives; it has both an ethos and a *telos* of a higher and deeper dimension. Much more than mere literary scholarship is at issue; temporal and topical considerations are not, cannot be, the last frontier of an examination of literature and religion. The very presence of the religious factor makes secular axioms critically incomplete, even as the conjunction "and" inescapably predicates, in this special relationship, universal meanings and ramifications. As such the interdisciplinary relations between literature and religion are at the very apex of all interdisciplinary relations insofar as the critical judgments to be made, the discriminations to be etched, and the values to be announced finally return to, even as they revolve around, supernatural essences. (Both Dostoevsky and Lawrence illustrate in their fiction a "religious sense" and a "sense of ending" that involve spiritual and divine concepts. Lawrence's own assertion that the imagination is at its maximum point religious has its force of relevance here.)

At the very moment when a religious context enters both the literary and the critical function, that function acquires a higher order, higher principles, higher meaning, higher seriousness. The critical consequences of relations between literature and religion thus assume and magnify a spiritual character and impingement. These consequences speak to the human condition: speak to the soul, as it were. Noetic concerns are now necessarily joined to pneumatological essences, and in this critical confluence we view the active presence of the principle that some certain end must always be kept in view, that there are overarching spiritual significances, even resolutions, which have an intrinsic presence in the relations between literature and religion. This critical confluence, it can be said, is irrevocably antipodal to purely secular views of literature that Walter Pater, "the Oxonian Epicurus," epitomizes in his celebrated conclusion in *Studies in the History of the Renaissance* (1873) that "art comes to you professing frankly to give nothing but the highest quality to your moments as they pass, and simply for those moments' sake."

Other interdisciplinary relationships have intellectual, linguistic, and critical content and cultural lessons, but the relations between literature and religion, even as they absorb both the critical context and the cultural lessons, transcend purely temporal explication and meaning. These relations, in other words, signify more than the triad of "thought, words and creativity" and involve more than "the living principle," to use here two critical rubrics. These relations, in the end, have a spiritual orientation and belong to "the needs of the soul"; they make far greater demands upon us than those ordinarily associated with "the function of criticism"—"the common pursuit of true judgment." The critical spirit finally predicates not only what is conjunctive but also what is ascendant; it must be followed, that is, to its greatest point of understanding, of growth. It does not stop at a certain level of perceptions and judgments that have aesthetic and critical essences and transpositions. The office of criticism, as Paul Elmer More pointed out in the early part of this century, becomes at a certain point almost identical with education, and this also has a pedagogical function, which in more recent years, especially with the increase in specialization (and fragmentation) in the educational world, has been scandalously neglected or forgotten in the academy.

In this respect the critical spirit has a double function, one that has not only a judgmental but also a pedagogical dimension. There is yet a third function, the spiritual, or the sapiential, as it might also be termed, that contains and illustrates the ascendant element so well expressed in Joseph Joubert's famous words, "The true, the beautiful, the just, the holy!" It is this third function, or paradigm, that finally encapsulates the relations between literature and religion, that gives these relations a transfiguring visionary power which surpasses pragmatic, nominal, and gnostic considerations and also gives them fullness and completion. These claims are not meant to sanctify what might ostensibly be termed a religious criticism, the dangers of which Leavis sought to guard against. Criticism is not, after all, a sacramental act, though it can have a moral quality of vision, even a vision of the infinite. The American New Humanists, to recall, distinguished between critics who have intuitions of the Many and those who have intuitions of the One. "Men tend to come together," Irving Babbitt states, "in proportion to their intuitions of the One; in other words the true unifying principle of mankind is found in the insight of its sages. We *ascend* to meet."[3]

Neither the aesthetic experience nor the temporal moment is adequate in attaining the kind of critical transcendence that Babbitt has no doubt in mind. "When a man lives aesthetically," Søren Kierkegaard observes, "his mood is always eccentric because he has his center in the periphery." Kierkegaard's words help to identify the finite characteristics of a secular criticism that is measured by time, *chronos*. Such a criticism obviously restricts the range, even as it severely reduces the metaphysics of criticism. It is, in a word, time-bound: a slave of time, a prisoner of the profane world. No critic who embraces a world like this can penetrate the religious vision of a Dante or a Blake, or even what Graham Greene calls "the religious aspect" of a Henry James. The religious attitude as it is rendered in literature has universal character, which to be critically apprehended requires a synthesis of comprehension, judgment, and piety. This latter element, with its moral ramifications, extends both the critical and the pedagogical function; it consecrates and seals their mission. Piety helps us to see and enter the sacred country, with understanding, insight, and humility that deepen and cleanse the life of the mind and the life of the soul. The critical and pedagogical function is thus spiritually enlarged and illuminated precisely in those ways that Rachel Bespaloff reveals in her remarkable book *On the Iliad* (1947), and in her final summary sentence in it: "But there is and will continue to be a certain way of telling the truth, proclaiming the just, of seeking God and honoring man, that was first taught us and is taught us afresh every day by the Bible and by Homer." At once numinous and redemptive, this sentence superbly mediates the relations between literature and religion.

In the present climate of literary scholarship one does not easily come across the kind of critical ethos, or the kind of spiritual depth, that characterizes Rachel Bespaloff's study. In the academic world, that is, in the intellectual community that shapes and trains the minds of the young, this worthy ethos, as it is variously registered in *On the Iliad*, or in Paul Elmer More's *Shelburne Essays* (1904–1936), or in Austin Warren's *Rage for Order* (1948), or in Joyce Cary's *Art and Reality: Ways of the Creative Process* (1958), or in a historical work like Werner Jaeger's *Paideia* (1939–1944) is now mostly dislodged. This particular dislodgement simultaneously identifies the steady erosion of the once guiding principles and values of *humanitas* and its growing displacement today by the forces of "deconstruction" that embrace a world "without truth, without origin beyond man and humanism," in Jacques Derrida's words. "The deconstructionist theory," René Wellek rightly warns, "is a flight from reality, and from history."[4] This history, one should immediately add, is also sacred history, with its traditions and hierarchies and with its disciplines of continuity as these affect all moral and spiritual meaning. But what is not openly or consciously admitted by those who are now appalled by the votaries of deconstructionism "destroying literary studies" (the phrase is Wellek's) is that this theory is ultimately a cumulative development, a metastasis made inevitable in the modern age in which, *inter alia*, the hedonist theories of Pater and Oscar Wilde, the radical politics of Michael Gold (and those who continue to echo his Marxizing views), and the empirical morality

of Leavis have, in their paradoxical ways, defined and formed the critical *Weltanschauung* of our time, and have prepared the ground for the
deconstructionist invaders, the contemporary representatives of the
"Scourge of God."

Even Wellek's complaints come too late, lacking as they do the
moral and spiritual acceptation that must ultimately govern a "theory
of literature." Anyone who examines the dialectical methodologies
that have developed in the academy during this century should be able
to understand why the critical and intellectual imperialisms of our time
have now found their true and inevitable successors in deconstructionism. This is a fateful consequence that is a symptom and a portent
of the relativism and the skepticism of the modern age. We have seen in
the academy not only a failure of nerve but also an increase in religious
neutrality, or amorality, in concert with a critical empiricism that tries
to locate its scale of values in what is claimed to be a transcendent and
disinterested intelligence operating in critical "scrutinies," "revaluations," "interpretations," "explorations." Such a criticism seeks for
surrogate transcendences and transfigurations that are unattainable and
illusive. It is an attempt to make criticism a religion of intellect.

The point I am trying to make here is that criticism, even in its finest
hour, that plays with or accepts in any way the "secular hypothesis"
ultimately rejects the idea of the sacred: rejects what I have termed a
"reverent discipline"; rejects, in other words, the view that literary
studies must find their apogee, and thus their true humility, in the divine. (T. S. Eliot's *Four Quartets* contain the greatest paradigms of this
spiritual synthesis.) Wellek notes that "Evaluation used to be criticism's central task," but whatever the merits of this task, it also identifies the ultimate weakness of the principle that is at the center of "the
ideal of impersonal objectivity." Again, the formulaic assumption is
that criticism is disinterestedness. But we have, in this critical process,
not a line of ascent but of descent, a sharp declivity into a terrifying
abysm. In that abysm there is no Spirit, no *transcensus*, no genuine critical confluence that builds upon evaluation by reforming and spiritualizing it, giving it unity and centrality, accepting and affirming that element of piety, of the holy, that Joubert invokes.

Critical value (and valuation), in short, needs to attain its true spiritual content, its articles of faith, which liberate it from the secular dom-
ination. The attainment of this critical value requires spiritual defini-

tion complementing critical judgment. What is achieved, hence, is a standard of standards, a discipline of discipline, and a judgment of judgment. A spiritual ascension is an integral dimension, a desideratum, of a critical process that advances from a dialectical methodology to an experience of the holy that brings a special knowledge, a deeper insight, a transubstantive reality. In this respect, then, the literary, critical, and pedagogical functions, in their supreme synthesis, are not so much cleansed as they are purified and absorbed by the religious element. In art and in *paideia*, as in society and in culture, the religious aspect points to a greater spiritual transformation, to the reconciliation of the secular and the spiritual that Paul Tillich associates with "ultimate concern" and "ultimate courage." This reconciliation, this relationship, is still another instance of what I term the critical confluence that expands and deepens the meaning of existence in the selected contexts of literary and religious relations.

Religion, writes Tillich, "is at home everywhere, namely, in the depth of all functions of man's spiritual life. Religion is the dimension of depth in all of them. Religion is the aspect of depth in the totality of the human spirit."[5] Not only the relationship between literature and religion but all relationships give witness to what Tillich says here. This allness in time and in eternity is what, in the end, distinguishes and consummates the religious dimension. It is precisely this dimension of literature that needs to be perceived and analyzed in its kenotic authenticity. What we discover, in the process, has much to tell us about the human condition, about man's aspirations, his expectations, above all, his state of soul, whether in its state of damnation or in its capacity for redemption. Literature, in particular, becomes psychography. It helps render a spiritual biography of the age in which we live and which we shape; it reveals our deeper self in its inner and outer conditions.

To claim that the relations between literature and religion are merely another instance of, say, a theology of salvation is to misconstrue these relations as they unravel in the modern world. On the contrary, these relations afford one a better glimpse of the crisis of consciousness at all levels that characterizes our modern dilemma in all of its categories and conditions, as these have been variously viewed not only by Tillich but also by such critics and thinkers as Eliot, Joseph Wood Krutch, Nikolay Berdyaev, Martin Buber, Karl Jaspers, Eliseo Vivas, Romano Guardini, and Richard M. Weaver, critics and thinkers of significant if

not remarkable spiritual insight. Indeed, there is no other critical confluence than literature and religion that can better disclose to us our
interior life, now deep and hidden, forced as it has been to remain sub-
merged in an age of techniques and secular dogmas. If we are so obviously earnest in our attempts, in the academy, to examine our political
character, or our socio-economic role, or our psychological and psy-
chohistorical profile, we should be equally earnest in our attempt to
encounter our spiritual essence. But that we have largely avoided the
demands of this encounter by centering our interests on peripheral literary and critical considerations is in itself a confession of our superfi-
ciality—and our illusions. The preoccupation with fantasy literature
and science fiction is an example of our peripheral proclivity, and of
our refusal to enter the spiritual depths.

The avoidance of the religious question in its spiritual and moral demands, and in its mystery, is commensurate with the overall deterioration of first and last principles, which have been progressively displaced during the past fifty years by pluralistic distensions and
distortions. Artist, critic, and teacher, in effect, have largely abandoned any concern with ultimate concerns and with ultimate reality.
In an age in which religious feeling has atrophied, these two ultimates
are even more difficult to grasp. "The supernatural is an embarrass-
ment today even to many of the churches," Flannery O'Connor laments.[6] That the religious question itself has been subjected to attacks
and mutations from within its own structure, especially when one
thinks of liberation theology, adds even more to the diminution of the
sacramental view of life, of "that sense of Mystery which cannot be
accounted for by any human formula," to use Flannery O'Connor's
words. This diminution reflects the supra-secular spirit that now
thrives and that places great obstacles in the way of a religious attitude
as a "transcendental unifier."

In more recent years Aleksandr Solzhenitsyn has tried to remind us
of the perils of this anti-religious phenomenon, and the animus against
him, especially as found in politically and religiously liberal circles, has
been considerable. His emphasis on the idea that "Freedom is self-re-
striction," and hence on the principle that diverts man from outward
to inward development, thus giving modern man greater spiritual
depth, has not gained him many friends in the intelligentsia. When,
too, Solzhenitsyn emphasizes the pan-prophetic truth that the essential

task is not that of political liberation but rather that of the liberation of the human soul, that is, of something that "requires from each individual a moral step within his power," he is undoubtedly also challenging the postmodern world in which we live. His art pleads the case for a "spiritual realism," which constitutes a higher quality of vision that needs to be apprehended.[7]

When the religious spirit is apprehended, the imagination itself is heightened. The quest for religion in nineteenth-century Russian literature, according to Father Georgy Florovsky, radiates in the writings of Dostoevsky, Gogol, and Tolstoy. "It was their conviction," he declares, "that human life without faith is a perilous adventure which is bound to end in disaster. Man without God cannot remain truly human; he sinks and decomposes."[8] This deterioration, as consequence and symptom, is nowhere better seen than in contemporary American fiction, in which, as John W. Aldridge has recently shown, "solipsistic preoccupations of the imperial self" thrive, particularly in the novels of Joseph Heller, William Gaddis, Jerzy Kosinski, Thomas Pynchon, and John Barth.[9] Clearly, "ultimate reality" and "spiritual realism" are the victims of the postmodern and post-historical world, a world that lacks, in the words of Joseph Pieper, a "dynamic centre from which all activity springs and to which all that is received and all that is undergone can be collectively referred."[10] Such a world lacks relatedness; precludes "the great relationship," as Lawrence would have it; destroys connection between I and Thou, to recall Martin Buber's "dialogical principle."

Indeed, the connections between literature and religion underscore the living significance that, as Buber phrases it, "religion is reciprocity," that "we live in the currents of universal reciprocity." "Only connect" is E. M. Forster's primary message to us in *Howards End* (1910) and *A Passage to India* (1924), novels that illustrate dramatically how human relations fail to attain an inner and outer nexus and thus also fail to attain a higher order of being, temporally and spiritually, in which beginnings and endings coalesce. The relations between literature and religion disclose an important aspect of this nexus, even as they reveal an added dimension in the capacity for human relations that venture beyond pragmatism ("this philosophy of glamour," as Marjorie Grene labels it), beyond presentness, beyond the confines of what Kierkegaard terms the "extensive" life.

In the study, teaching, and criticism of literature, religious experience in the full variety and truth of its manifestations needs to be fathomed and assessed. But for this critical process to take place the kind
of attitude that my colleague displayed, in his claim I was playing God,
must be anticipated, and corrected. This is not an easy goal to achieve.
The distrust of religious tradition that marks modern life, especially in
the academy in which *chic* liberal views predominate, is amply evident.
The unconscienced liberalization of the curriculum, that is, the growing de-emphasis of and now the outright attack on the concept of *humanitas*, with its moral and spiritual roots, further shows how difficult
it is to legitimate the relations between literature and religion. There
is almost nothing in our blatantly secular society and culture that will
encourage this legitimation. Even in religious circles the spiritual element has its enemies.

Not spiritual discipline but eleutheromania is the presiding principle
of action in modern life. To be sure, the academy sanctions the study
of literature and religion, but generally this is a cosmetic and egalitarian
sanction of a special genre. Perhaps it cannot be otherwise. "We are
here as on a darkling plain": Matthew Arnold's words prophetically
capture a faithless generation "in its true *blankness* and *barrenness*," to
quote here a phrase from one of his letters to Arthur Hugh Clough.[11]
Perhaps, too, we cannot, and perhaps we should not, expect the critical
function or the educative process to have that "intensive point" which,
for Kierkegaard, *is* the religious life. Even in writing the preceding sentence, with all of its troubling qualifications, I myself am indicating the
doubt, both religious and metaphysical, that is an integral part of our
modern world and that makes all the more revealing Samuel Beckett's
observation that we are now experiencing the cruel impact of the absolute absence of the absolute.

Yet that doubt, by its challenging presence, also stresses for me the
breadth and depth of the religious problem as it is registered in life,
literature, and thought. And I am reminded that, for the student of
modern literature who wants to understand the religious problem,
and in turn seeks to broaden and refine his spiritual knowledge, the
will to overcome doubt and to accept the possibility of an informing
religious essence in literature discloses a formidable breakthrough, a
"reaching out after the invisible things of the spirit," to use Paul Elmer
More's words, in a world in which religious effort and demands have

often given way to slothful habits of mind and soul. "Literature," writes Charles Moeller, "becomes increasingly the witness of one world and of the other."[12] The literature that makes us aware of that "other" world in which, as Simone Weil says, "the highest things are achieved," makes us aware of the religious problem that embraces ultimate concerns and ultimate questions and gives meaning to time. In the relationship between literature and religion we can discover a revelatory critical confluence that becomes a medium for an encounter and, in effect, a conversation with God. Martin Buber captures the full spiritual measure of this intermediation when he writes: "The existence of mutuality between God and man cannot be proved any more than the existence of God. Anyone who dares nevertheless to speak of it bears witness and invokes the witness of those whom he addresses—present or future witnesses."[13]

17

Dostoevsky and the Religion of Spirit

Among the most celebrated names comprising what has been termed "the Russian religious renaissance of the twentieth century" (*Russkii religioznyi renessance XX veka*) are those of Nikolay O. Lossky (1870–1944), Sergy Bulgakov (1871–1944), Nikolay A. Berdyaev (1874–1948), Simon L. Frank (1877–1950), Vasily Zenkovsky (1881–1962), Georgy P. Fedotov (1866–1951), and Georgy Florovsky (1893–1979). The many and important works of these Russian *emigré* writers—"the successors of Solovyov," so to speak—in the areas of theology, philosophy, history, sociology, law, and art appeared outside of Russia and were essentially identified with and sustained by the tradition of Eastern Orthodoxy. That Russian Orthodox Christianity has been able to survive in any orderly semblance of continuity, that in fact there has even developed a religious revival since the Russian Revolution in 1917 (with Paris serving as the inspired center of this revival), is due almost entirely to the energy and the zeal of those constituting this great movement.

Without this movement which manifested astonishing, even miraculous, intellectual efforts not only in the form of prolific and remarkable publications (*e.g.*, a book like Father Florovsky's *Puti Russkogo Bogosloviia* [1937][1] and a journal like *Put'*, which Berdyaev edited [1926–1940]), but also in the establishment in the early 1920s of a center of Russian Orthodox religious thought at the St. Sergius Academy in Paris and a steady and active contribution to the Ecumenical movement as a whole, Eastern Christianity could never have achieved a growing place of recognition in the West. The cultural significance and contribution of the Russian Orthodox Church in exile, as it were, can as yet hardly be assessed in its overall impact. Its achievement, not to speak of its survival, in the light of the historical exigencies following the Russian Revolution—the suppression and the liquidation of all traditional religious thought and theory at the hands of dialectical materialists—is, to say the least, unique.

Also belonging to this movement was Konstantin Vasilyevitch Mochulsky (1892–1948), whose contributions in the area of literary scholarship, including his *Gogol's Spiritual Revolution* (1934), *Dostoevsky: His
Life and Work* (1947), *Alexander Blok* (1948), *Andrey Bely* (1955), all
written in Russian, constitute a substantial critical contribution to an
understanding of Russian literature. It is gratifying, therefore, that his
book *Dostoevsky: His Life and Work*, written in 1942 but not published
until 1947 by YMCA Press of Paris, is now available in English translation.[2] Mochulsky first wrote this book in the form of lectures he delivered at the Sorbonne, where he was a member of the Russian faculty
from 1924 until 1941. Since its first publication this book has enjoyed
far-reaching, even seminal, influence, acknowledged and unacknowl-
edged, among interpreters of Dostoevsky's work and thought. It comprises with Vyacheslav Ivanov's *Freedom and the Tragic Life* (1952) and
Berdyaev's *Dostoevsky* (1934) a monumental triptych that no student
of the Russian novelist can afford to miss. All three books have con-
verging viewpoints, with common emphases on Dostoevsky's prophetic and tragedic functions as a novelist. In this respect, all three critics disclose an intense preoccupation with Russian Orthodox cultural
thought as a formulative approach to their evaluation of Dostoevsky's
writings and, above all, his metaphysic. Mochulsky's volume, however, moves beyond these limitary areas of approach by concentrating
more equitably on Dostoevsky's aesthetic motivations—on Dostoevsky the artist.

If Mochulsky's book is seminal, it is also massive—nearly 700 pages
in length. Hence it entails rather laborious reading, the more so since
the author includes in his text all the irritating faults of the lecture-for-
mat: repetitiousness, excessive plot summary, too many and too
lengthy quotations. And with Ivanov and particularly with Berdyaev,
Mochulsky's penchant at times for a rather philosophically-oriented
vocabulary leads to what for some readers constitutes jargon of a sort.
Once the reader overcomes these barriers and at the same time reconciles himself to a rather lackluster style, he comes into contact with a
mind and an astuteness wonderfully and consistently revealed in profound textual explication and in synthesizing insights that break
through to the core of Dostoevsky's religious genius. Mochulsky's
book has an added advantage, too, that it can be referred to as an inter-
pretive source of reference for the student, especially in the interrela-

tionships drawn between Dostoevsky's notebooks, in which he outlined his ideas, plots, aims, etc., and the finally executed forms of his
novels. Likewise, the author's interweaving of biographical facts into
the texture of Dostoevsky's artistic achievement has its benefits, especially in the case of a novelist who "lived in literature" and for whom,
as Mochulsky stresses, the creative imagination, in its impulse and consummation, "was his life's concern and his tragic fate." "His works,"
Mochulsky states in his Preface, "unfold before us as one vast confession, as the integral revelation of his universal spirit."

What is made distinctly clear by Mochulsky is that to comprehend
the meaning of Dostoevsky's novels one must also be aware of the
Eastern Orthodox beliefs that helped to fashion, aesthetically, his
world view and his perception of man. (Another excellent book that
underlines the subtle interrelationship between Dostoevsky's aesthetic
and his ideological views is R. L. Jackson's *Dostoevsky's Quest for Form*
[1966]). Sartre's dictum that the technique of an artist must inevitably
return us to the artist's metaphysic finds in Dostoevsky, and in Mochulsky's Dostoevsky, an exceptional apogee. Surely any attempt to
separate Dostoevsky's art from his metaphysics would be crippling.
Not only must Dostoevsky's broadly Christian metaphysic be understood, but also it must be understood in its peculiarly existentialist and
Russian Orthodox implications. Thus, Dostoevsky's artistic vision is
at one with the metaphysical problems of viewing the universe and
man's place in it, of recognizing man's ultimate relationship to what
lies beyond it, to the transcending and the transcendent. "Men live and
see according to some gradually developing and gradually withering
vision," writes D. H. Lawrence. "This vision exists also as a dynamic
idea or metaphysic—exists first as such. Then it is unfolded into life
and art." No words better capture what lies at the center of Dostoevsky's art and what, in fact, impelled and crystallized it.

Mochulsky underscores precisely the "dynamic idea" that Lawrence
alludes to and that becomes the burden of Dostoevsky's vision. Particularly in Dostoevsky's case this vision never remains metaphysically
silent or neutral. As such, the metaphysical constituents of Dostoevsky's art are always in evidence; are, in essence, the things that nourish
his art as it "unfolds," and "the physical opens on the metaphysical."
In Dostoevsky the metaphysic serves as the inspiration itself, without

which the artistic imagination diminishes. His concept of Christ—the Christ of "beauty, perfection, and transfiguration"; his interest in and meditation on the Gospels; his apprehension of the endless conflict between good and evil; his affirmation of the power of resurrection, of the final triumph over death and nonbeing; his insistence, as Mochulsky observes, that "the atheistic world is decomposing while still alive. The putrefaction of souls is more horrible than the corruption of bodies"; his depiction of the fate of a mankind without God: these are some of the metaphysical elements, the organic tensions, which inhere in and inform Dostoevsky's art, in the world and among the people that he creates.

Yet, it must also be stressed that Mochulsky's Christian Orthodoxy is in no way tendentious or doctrinaire, and though he is cognizant of Orthodox ecclesiology and, above all, theology, his approach to Dostoevsky is religiously internal rather than external: mystical and philosophical rather than canonical and systematic. This is as it should be, too. Dostoevsky was, after all, a "pneumatologist" in whose art the metaphysics of Russian Orthodoxy achieve creative freedom of unparalleled power. "Behind the psychologist," he writes of Dostoevsky, "stands the pneumatologist—the brilliant investigator of the human spirit." If there is any doubt of Mochulsky's criteria for judging Dostoevsky's *oeuvre*, such doubt can be quickly dismissed when one reads Mochulsky's masterful discussion of the Elder Zossima in *The Brothers Karamazov*. Zossima, he shows, resembles in various ways such well-known Russian historical figures as Father Amvrosy, whom Dostoevsky met and revered at the great Russian monastery of Optina Pustyn, and St. Tikhon Zadonsky. In the final analysis, however, Zossima was not at all a portmanteau portrait of these religious representatives of the Russian Church. The following passage, in this connection, instances the kind of criticism that distinguishes Mochulsky's work and also provides for a much richer understanding of Dostoevsky's art:

> The writer freely reworked . . . hagiographical material and created a new type of holiness, different both from 18th century "religion of the heart" and from the Elders of Optina Pustyn. Zossima is not a representative of historical Russian monasticism; he is directed toward the future as a herald of the new spiritual consciousness of the Russian people. In his religiosity there is an enraptured sense of the divinity of the world and

the Godlikeness of man; he sees the mystical unity of the cosmos and its illumination by the Holy Spirit (Beauty); this is the source of his teaching that "all men are guilty for everyone." The Elder lives in the light of the coming resurrection, believes that creation will freely return to its Creator and God will be "of everything and in all." His faith is alien to dogmatism; his teaching about man and about the world predominates over doctrines about God; he says little about the Church and nothing about its mystical heart—the Eucharist.

The developmental pattern of Dostoevsky's writings is especially clarified by Mochulsky. How Russian romanticism was one of the fundamental ideas of Dostoevsky's work; how his journalistic efforts and interests contributed to the content of his novels; how his penal servitude came to constitute his "spiritual riches"; how his idea of Don Juanism developed dialectically and polarized into opposites, and extremes, of "eternal husband" and "eternal lover"; how his novels were written for the sake of catastrophe; how his themes of the "underground," "separation," "might," and spiritual "tyranny" evolved and concretized—these and other matters Mochulsky examines assiduously. Dostoevsky's philosophic dialectic, nevertheless, is not permitted to overshadow his artistic powers. The metaphysical dimension of his thought is all the more valued and meaningful for its artistic form, its presentation and dramatization. Thus, Mochulsky emphasizes that Dostoevsky's work can be best described as a vast five-act tragedy (*Crime and Punishment* [1867], *The Idiot* [1868], *The Devils* [1873], *A Raw Youth* [1875], and *The Brothers Karamazov* [1879–1880]). It is his *Notes from the Underground* (1864), on the other hand, that introduces readers to his philosophy of tragedy.

Dostoevsky, Mochulsky shows, lived through a period of crisis in Christian culture and even experienced it as a personal tragedy, a fact that becomes apparent quite early in his writing career, with the publication of his *Winter Notes on Summer Impressions* (1863), when he "seemed to hear the tolling of a funeral bell over Europe." Dostoevsky believed himself to be one of the few who grasped the significance of this tragedy of the Christian European consciousness, as the "old idea" vanished from the scene and God disappeared, giving rise to what some modern novelists have portrayed as "an intolerable deprivation," "an irreparable absence," as well as to the belief that, to quote Simone Weil's phrase, "matter is a machine for manufacturing good." In respect to the concomitants and the results of these phenomena in the historical situation of European civilization Dostoevsky, reacting strongly, "wept real tears." His ultimate responses, Mochulsky discloses, were rendered in his art: "The writer's 'novel-tragedies' are devoted to depicting the fate of *mankind abandoned by God*. He prophetically indicated two paths: man-godhood and the herd."

The most impressive chapters of the book are those in which Mochulsky analyzes Dostoevsky's major novels. Of course, Dostoevsky's lesser-known works are also given their proper recognition but generally in so far as they anticipate and evolve into the great novel-tragedies. *Netochka Nezvanova* (1849) is valued as "the laboratory in which the ideology and technique of the great novels were worked out." *The House of the Dead* (1862) marks the beginning of Dostoevsky's "religious tragedy." *Winter Notes on Summer Impressions* introduces readers to Dostoevsky's philosophical constructions, while *Notes from the Underground* is judged as "the greatest attempt at a philosophy of tragedy." All of Dostoevsky's works are, Mochulsky contends, "the history of human consciousness in its tragic duality." Quite rightly, too, he insists that at the base of Dostoevsky's philosophy, or better his metaphysics, there lies a "mystical naturalism," or a supreme reverence for the value of life, the "living life" that so many of Dostoevsky's characters glorify. Mochulsky's point is certainly apropos when we consider that the experience of death in Dostoevsky's novels rarely attains the prominence of that of life; and when it is given prominence it is for the purpose of accentuating the resurrected life. Unfortunately, Mochulsky does not treat the whole subject of death as found in Dostoevsky's novels with the detail that it necessarily requires. In any case, that Dostoevsky himself was more concerned with life and with man reborn discloses once again the Christian Orthodox attitude toward a Christ Risen. In Dostoevsky's art this attitude assumes its artistic relevance.

Some of Dostoevsky's most enigmatic characters are made more meaningful as a result of Mochulsky's diagnoses. The lecher Svidrigailov in *Crime and Punishment* suffers a boredom that is metaphysical rather than psychological. Prince Myshkin in *The Idiot* is an image that is not sketched nor sculptured but is *chiaroscuro*. Stavrogin in *The Devils* is Dostoevsky's vision of hell, *A Raw Youth* is that of purgatory, and *The Brothers Karamazov* that of paradise. The chapter on *The Brothers Karamazov* is particularly impressive, if not the most impressive chap-

ter in the book, in examining what Mochulsky labels "the novel's ideational architectonics and its dramatic composition." Dostoevsky's final work, Mochulsky maintains, was a synthesis, an organic unity, of
all his creative achievement. Though he had worked for three years on
his last novel, he had, in a spiritual sense, worked on it all his life. The
world of this novel had evolved through the years, absorbing the philosophical and the artistic elements of the preceding works. Thus, Mochulsky points out, *The Diary of a Writer* "is the laboratory in which
the ideology of the final novel is given its descriptive form." In *A Raw
Youth* Dostoevsky established the structure of the family chronicle her-
alding the tragedy of "fathers and children." In *The Devils* the atheist
Stavrogin's confrontation of the prelate Tikhon looks ahead to the conflict between Ivan Karamazov and the Elder Zossima, between disbelief and belief. In *The Idiot* the wronged beauty Natasya Filippovna an-
ticipates Grushenka; Rogozhin overwhelmed by eros brings to mind
Dmitri Karamazov. In *Crime and Punishment* the overstepping of moral
law forecasts a similar problem in *The Brothers Karamazov.*

Mochulsky concludes his book with the assertion that Dostoevsky
occupies a place among the great Christian writers of world literature—Dante, Cervantes, Milton, Pascal: "Like Dante he passed
through all the circles of human hell, one more terrible than the medi-
aeval hell out of the *Divine Comedy*, and was not consumed in hell's
flame: his *duca e maestro* was not Virgil, but the 'radiant image' of
Christ, love for whom was the greatest love of his whole life." The
excellence of this book is to be found in Mochulsky's ability to evaluate
the Christian metaphysics of Dostoevsky's art without imposing theological norms or "discriminating Christianly," to quote an apt phrase.
Always, too, Mochulsky is sensitive to the disquieting, the paradoxical
aspects of Dostoevsky's genius and particularly to his "prophetic
soundings in depth-psychology" (to use Father Florovsky's words).

The great Russian writers of the nineteenth century, we must come
to recognize, took part in a great "quest for religion," and they charted
this quest in their writings. As a critic who helps readers to understand
and appreciate *this* aspect of Russian literature, Mochulsky is to be specially valued. His book on Dostoevsky makes no grand claims, seeks
no final critical solutions, attempts no conversionary schemes, dictates
no final critical design. His main purpose is to illuminate the ways in
which Dostoevsky's metaphysics penetrate his art. Even those readers

and critics who sometimes question the interdisciplinary relationship between literature and religion can hardly ignore what Konstantin Mochulsky has done in this book on a writer who, caught in the infinite mystery of the creative act, labored ceaselessly for what he called the "subsurface unexpressed future word."

18

Conservatism, Change, and the
Life of the Spirit

I

The changes that now grip our lives are unfathomably swift. One may even wonder how Heraclitus, the ancient philosopher of change, would view the current juggernaut of change. No aspect of existence escapes the impact of change. To resist change or to doubt its need is often viewed as a reactionary tendency. That change can also be synonymous with social disease and cultural degeneration is a demurral that falls on deaf ears. It seems that everything must be changed if only for the thrill of change. Clearly we worship the new gods of change and to pay no homage to them carries stiff penalties. Whether it is change in literary values, in political systems, in educational policies, in cultural affairs, in religious doctrines, in moral standards—in anything and everything that relates to the virtues of character and conduct, and to the dictates of conscience—the demand for change is powerful and pervasive. We choose to equate change with the necessity of progress and enlightenment and whatever fails to satisfy this necessity is judged as archaic or backward. Nothing must stand in the way of change even when change is destructive.

Conservative beliefs and principles are now being periodically dismissed by well-known pundits and myth-makers as irrelevant in light of political changes in Soviet Russia and in Eastern Europe. "U.S. conservatism crumbles as Cold War wanes," one headline announces. "Conservatives without a cause," another headline reads, and the article that follows it goes on to announce, "The disintegration has happened much faster than anyone thought. . . . But conservatism is reactive in nature. Its idea of a program is to oppose one offered by someone else. With communism threatening to vaporize, conservatism may soon have little to react against." Even some American conservatives are asking, "What next?" with one conservative leader declaring, "What the conservative movement needs is another big push," and still another confessing dejectedly that the conservative movement lacks fresh ideas.

Such announcements as they emerge from both the Left and the Right reflect a political mindset ignorant of, if not hostile to, what can be called the metaphysic of conservatism in its historical lineage and authenticity. The heady assurances of "great simplifiers" notwithstanding, change cannot be approved as the last word; itself a dimension of the empire of change, the policy of change does not always or necessarily appreciate what is permanent and enduring. It does not appreciate, in short, a transcendent conservative vision which speaks universally, within and yet beyond measured time. "A civilization cannot feed upon perishable things," Donald Davidson reminds us. "Only imperishable things at the center can give it life."

Those politicists and ideologists who choose to ignore the metaphysic of conservatism are ultimately the slaves of time, and we must not surrender to them or to the *doxai* of modernity that they embrace. To be told that it is imperative for conservatives "to recapture the rhetoric of compassion," as "conservatism alters its course" in a New Age, must also alert us to the need to avoid any slippage of standards and principles that are lasting and absolute. We must be on guard against the "votaries of the practical, of experimentalists, of empirics," as Henry James once described them, when it comes to the maintenance of standards.

"To have standards means practically to have some principle of unity with which to measure mere manifoldness and change," Irving Babbitt avers. His words should also remind us that any betrayal of standards unleashes all those impulses of romantic progressivism that bring about mediocrity and moral sloth. Some of the major religious, social, political, economic, and educational problems that we now encounter in society are the results of precisely this surrender to "manifoldness and change." Standards of discrimination and selection, once sacrificed, further empower "the general will" with all of the corrosive effects. It is sad that the voices that are more loudly heard these days are the neognostic voices counseling change—adjusting to and enforcing it, without carefully assessing its repercussions and without, above all, measuring change in terms of moral constants. A major task remains, then, to direct attention to moral imperatives that are minimally identi-

fied in an America obsessed with the pursuit of ever-increasing perfection.

Today we are being endlessly told to surrender our traditions and
standards to a postmodern time, that is, to a now totally detached and
disintegrated modernism, a modernism made to stand on its head. This
postmodernism can be said to arise with the coming of the Great War
of 1914–1918 and the enormous human, moral, and spiritual losses, the
catastrophism, that ensued and that dramatized a fallen and corrupted
modernity of disorder and degradation. Thus the death-cry "history as
nightmare" captures the declension and the entropy of the West. And
in embodying "the fourth epoch," as that phrase is used, postmodernism can be said to signify the obscene involution of all human values,
what the novelist D. H. Lawrence speaks of as the "ecstasy of destructive sensation."

When moral concern and judgment are destroyed, and the disciplines of tradition and continuity are undermined, we are inevitably
left stranded in a world in which change is the absolute and the absolute
is change. Surely those who want to redefine and re-order conservative
criteria to fit a time of change fail to grasp the fact that existence without a moral or a spiritual or a cultural context becomes disorder, which
is negation. For them "the permanent things," no less than the "sacral
order" and the "order of things," are either meaningless or superflu-
ous, and so begins the furious search for alternatives that has especially
characterized modern society. We need only look at our educational
institutions to see some of the damaging consequences of those who
insist on having change without preservation and who would therefore
have us lose "the good of the intellect."

A genuinely rooted conservatism is morally bound to reject submission to any theory or system that invites spiritual decline. If there is
to be any kind of self-examination or self-questioning on the part of
conservatives, it must start at that point when we recognize where our
indulgences have brought us. And only when we are able to perceive
the true nature of our disorientation will we be able to relieve ourselves
of its burden of dread. At that point, too, will we only be able to measure and to judge the full meaning of change. Our task should be not
one of altering course in order to accommodate change but the much
harder task of attaining moral discovery and regaining moral supports
in a moral community. Liberalism has forgotten this supreme verity

and has, in the process, been steadily discredited. Conservatism stands to suffer that same cruel fate if it fails to reject the idols of change for what they are.

Undoubtedly there are some conservatives who find it propitious to adapt to moral and intellectual confusion in our time. These conservatives are asking to be discredited no less than, say, entire bodies of the Christian Church have been discredited, not because, as Dorothy L. Sayers wrote in *Creed or Chaos* (1949), they are bigoted about theology, but because they have run away from theology. Conservatives who run away from first principles into the camp of the modernists are trivializing their fundamental tenets. The diminution of conservative standards of thought and belief comes in the wake of endorsing secular habits and practices that embody what Father Stanley Jaki calls a "quantified reductionism." Indeed, the more this policy of accommodation is accepted and implemented the more are standards leveled— and the more we slide into the abyss of nowhere and nothing. In consequence we bring about the kind of moral vacuum in which the solipsist proclaims that some truth exists in everything and some good in every change. We thus deny nothing and accept everything, even as the pan-egalitarian "song of myself" rings out incessantly, "O my camerados . . . O Libertad." Exclusionary criteria, according to our solipsists, must be erased as we proceed to satisfy every want and whimsy; to accommodate everyone, to satisfy each and any desire, innocent or perverse; to create yet another New Deal for Americans in an age that dispenses to everyone and sundry "the happiness pill" in much the same way that machines for condom dispensers are installed in the residence halls of American universities in order to help students in "negotiating safer sex."

Undeniably we live in the most uncourageous of times, as we thrash about recasting history, attacking moral order, and politicizing knowledge in the name of change. Too easily we allow ourselves to be lured by the siren calls of those universal promisers who feed our "determination to lounge safely through existence," as Joseph Conrad expresses it. Ours is a monomania with change, with the discovery of empirical data and the application of prescriptive formulas. And no doubt, in a climate of change, we shall increasingly hear from conservatives who ask, "How do ideas relate to action?" and who lament the "difficulty of translating traditionalist conservatism into [the] practical politics."

Though we cannot shun the origins of these protesting or questioning conservative voices, we also cannot deny that a quintessentially politicized conservatism far too often merely echoes and embellishes the pragmatism and the relativism of a changing world.

If conservative principles are to have enduring validity, they need to be defended against forces that strive to invalidate or deconstruct them. And for that matter, there is a decidedly conservative morality that also needs to be defended against the Ninevehs of modern secularized society. Those who would appease the economics of change through convenient realignments and readjustments ignore the inner value of life and work. We cannot begin to answer political and economic questions until we begin to have an intelligent understanding of fundamental moral questions and, yes, religious questions. And unless we can be agreed that ultimate questions affect human meaning and destiny, we merely worship time and change and placate the demands of immediacy and transience. The fact remains that what finally distinguishes the conservative ethos from all others is loyalty to moral and spiritual principles as being antecedent to all others. When we no longer recognize and insist on this distinction we contribute to a general confusion of principles.

"Men will clutch at illusions when they have nothing else to hold to," Czeslaw Milosz warned nearly forty years ago. And, as he went on to observe in *The Captive Mind*, "The Method, the Diamat—that is, dialectical materialism as interpreted by Lenin and Stalin—possesses a strong magnetic influence on the men of the present day." Lenin and Stalin have departed from the scene, to be sure, but the Diamat has not, as one can clearly see in the testimony of our postmodern political meliorists. Today the doctrine of "socialist realism," to which men and women complacently gave obedience, persists in radically changing forms; the refusal to recognize their grotesque and decadent composition instances moral evasion of the most dangerous kind. The huge failures of the people's democracies of Eastern Europe should certainly make us wary of master builders who promote political changes without due moral regard for those norms, standards, and traditions defined by great conservative thinkers from Edmund Burke to Russell Kirk.

There can be neither collaboration nor negotiation with any political purpose that would seek dominance over the mystery of the human spirit in the name of what is often called the "politics of inclusion." No conservative, particularly in the epochal time in which we now live, can dare to forget the profound truths found in these words that the Czech playwright-president Vaclav Havel recently delivered to an assembled audience of United States senators and representatives— words that should make us pause and go slow before we celebrate the new gospel of change: "We still don't know how to put morality ahead of politics, science, and economy. We are still incapable of understanding that the only genuine backbone of all our actions, if they are to be moral, is responsibility—responsibility to something higher than my family, my country, my company, my success."

II

Havel's words help to remind us that the crisis of modernity is an inclusive one. Its power and scourge are such that even those movements that seek to defend the sanctities of tradition and the values of order find themselves increasingly beleaguered. Richard M. Weaver observes that "fundamental integrity, once compromised, is slow and difficult of restoration." He goes on to emphasize: "Teachers of the present order have not enough courage to be definers; lawmakers have not enough insight." Weaver's diagnostic observations tell us something about the depth of the malaise that afflicts society and about the difficulties of resisting our continuing plight. The absence of courage and insight, as he further indicates, in the realm of intellect and the world of politics, sharpens and accelerates the personal and public dimensions of moral crisis at the highest and most important levels, where the course of civilization itself is ultimately determined.

Clearly the materialistic tendencies of the twentieth century, especially as these have solidified since the end of World War I and as "we moderns" have embodied them directly or indirectly, are not absolute tendencies in constant evidence. Insidious and intrusive, these tendencies transpose into fallacies of the most dangerous kind that trap even those who have conviction and affirm standards conducive to what Weaver terms a "metaphysical community." One likes to think of this "metaphysical community" as a natural and inseparable extension of the conservative metaphysic and of the conservative mind. One also likes to think that, in the midst of the general disarray that characterizes our crisis, there does exist and persevere a spiritual conservatism; that this spiritual conservatism is the *fons et origo* of all conservative perspectives: a primal, permanent, intensive, inviolable force and faith, unchanging and uncompromising in its principles—at once catholic, critical, and catechetical. This spiritual conservatism, one likes to think, revolves around, is rooted in, returns to, and reveres the highest axiomatic verities, the Word of God and the Order of the Soul.

God and soul are two words that are perhaps the greatest casualties of the ongoing crisis of modernity. The interior experiences of these two words, in their living significance as the fear of God and the needs of the soul, seem to have neither meaning nor relevance. Their diminution and absence are symptomatic of the vacuum of disinheritance in which modern man finds himself. As words of prescriptive value they simply do not exist in a society programmatically addicted to the unending lures of presentism that reject those sacred paradigms of aspiration that human character requires if it is to venerate and sustain any ordering principle of divinity. The rejection of these two words now enjoys wide acceptance as even a cursory scrutiny of the social-political scene will disclose.

Far from being arrested or deterred, the "age of liberalism" has actually achieved an insidious triumph as its sophistic proclivities infiltrate every aspect of human thought and activity. This destructive process signals the advance of what Michael Polanyi calls a "positivistic empiricism," that is, "[the] idea of unlimited progress, intensified to perfectionism, [which] has combined with our sharpened skepticism to produce the perilous state of the modern mind." We can now discern a withering totalization of this advance as it absorbs and shapes both political and intellectual thought and opinion. Even traditionalist conservatism retreats in front of this peril, in fearful awe of its might. The paths of this retreat are strewn with surrenders, backslidings, defeats, and losses of unfathomable consequences. Not only a principled conservatism but also a spiritual conservatism has been debased. What we find in alarming amplitude is the gradual emergence of a conservatism susceptible to the centrifugal tendencies and aims that Polanyi designates.

Sham conservatism is a symptom and portent of the spiritual desuetude that permeates American society and culture. A tinsel, opportunistic, and hedonistic conservatism, then, is what we see around us, unable to affirm the standards and certitudes that must be resolutely affirmed if an authentic ethos-centered conservatism is to survive. This survival will not occur whatever the immediate accomplishments of, say, the "moral majority" and the "new right," which merely pursue "pragmatic significations" residing in the liberals' standard baggage of "new deals" and "new frontiers." A conservatism that lacks "ontological referents" is as spiritually barren as the liberalism it opposes. Endless "policy reviews" and "policy studies," as these thrive and govern in some conservative quarters, in the end lack a basic apprehension of the "permanent things" and are responsive to the empirical ambitions that reflect the tastes and power-drives of a technologico-Benthamite world. A sham conservatism merely temporalizes and trivializes and dissimulates spiritual laws and truths. Such a conservatism belongs almost exclusively to the world and is impervious to the primacy of God as the measure of the soul. This primacy should constitute conservatism's ground of being; should define and inform a true "metaphysical community"—at once covenantal and sacramental. That community is certainly not one that we observe in our body politic or in the *realpolitik* of contemporary conservative entelechies. A glamorous politicized conservatism, as we now view it, fails to acknowledge spiritual needs that coalesce in God and soul.

Given the large and visible popular successes of political conservatism and the vibrant images and impressions it has in recent years engendered, there is an obvious unwillingness to examine critically the true conditions of the conservative movement today. That movement, however, increasingly echoes the "secular hypothesis" and dwells in the "secular city"; it has forgotten or neglected those spiritual exercises that belief in God and in the soul demands and that a genuinely spiritual conservatism accepts. Even when this political, gnostic conservatism invokes the two holy words God and soul, it profanes them by assigning to them a spurious valuation, in short, by ignoring or eliminating the inner life of conservatism. And this dislodgement is today the greatest crisis that grips conservative life and thought. That inner life is inadequately recognized or honored by many conservative leaders and spokesmen, in word or in work. In effect the theology of conservatism has been sacrificed to the new gods and the new morality of modernity. The discipline of spiritual conservatism has been manifestly lessened by its own peculiar form of liberation theology, as it were, and by the purely quantitative point of view prevailing in the market-place of ideas.

Dislodgement leads to capitulation as the present state of conservatism reveals. Where are to be found, one must ask in "fear and trembling," the spiritual exercises in conservative experience today? How is one to resist the materialistic doctrine that assails conservative criteria and that takes precedence over God and soul? A spiritually strenuous conservatism, as Irving Babbitt would say, has given way to the spiritual idler. The consequences of this recession have led to a general confusion among conservative adherents no longer able to distinguish between what Babbitt calls a law of the spirit and a law of the members, that is to say, the confusion of the things of God and the things of Caesar. This confusion, endemic in liberalism, imperils the conservative metaphysic. Nothing could be more debilitating than the confusion of first principles.

The preceding reflections should not be construed to mean that what is advocated is an otherworldly conservatism. Yet, a conservative metaphysic that neglects or omits the teleological dimension—and that seeks to escape from "the tragic sense of life"—falls into the same trap of illusion that is intimately connected with the liberal temper. Rather, these reflections, in their corrective purposiveness, seek to emphasize the need for a binary discipline—the discipline of ideas and the discipline of transcendent belief. The forms of conservative thought as we encounter them today are too much of this world, too much an acceptance of nominalist philosophy. They lack the element of ascent and are mired in the worship of time and in an "abandoned world," Godless and soulless. This is the world of spiritual dead-ends that belongs to "an age of bad faith" in which the "gods of mass and speed" breed to bring about the consuming majoritarian nightmare that Matthew Arnold depicts: "And littleness united / Is become invincible."

Insofar as the conservative metaphysic bows to the "world-machine," it reduces itself to the non-ontological and non-organic elements that identify contemporary life in its cruel alienations. This is the post-Christian and postmodern world that arrogantly renounces the "religious sense" and denies "the idea of the holy"—renounces God and denies the soul. It is, therefore, a sad paradox that conservative leaders and thinkers sometimes fail to recognize or implement their spiritual identity and responsibility. No authentic conservative metaphysic can be operable when the discipline of God and the discipline of the soul have been ceded to the *doxai*, the dialectical structures and superstructures of modern life.

We sometimes hear the claim that we live in "a decade dominated by conservatism." But such a claim must be assessed in the light of what precisely identifies and measures the particular dominances spawned by the conservative political phenomenon. From a metaphysical standpoint that phenomenon is neither reassuring nor inspiring. Its major social-political orientation is one of program and policy and points to a conservatism that has a downward tendency. That is, the conservatism that we view in the public sector is largely socioeconomic in character; its aims are too easily influenced or tainted by the idea of mechanical progress, by that overriding belief that distinguishes a modernity that scorns divine transcendences and embraces the instrumentalist article of faith that Simone Weil sees at the center of our spiritual crisis: that matter is a machine for manufacturing good. No expression better particularizes the supreme impiety of the modern age as it moulds habits of mind, attitudes, expectations, and aspirations. This impiety has gone unchecked for too long, and this dismaying fact should trouble the conscience of conservatives who subscribe to any spiritual standard and value. The world of pure instrumentality, in which everything is subordinated to the mechanical principle to which Simone Weil refers, is a profane world that needs to be unflinchingly opposed.

The perceived public image of conservatism, especially as it is articulated and conveyed by fancy conservative journalists and publicists, is one of glitter. But all that glitters in it is not gold. Too often a cleverly packaged conservatism lacks the spiritual disciplines indispensable to a serious concern with ultimate issues that go far beyond public-policy issues. It lacks transcendence in the contexts that Saul Bellow stresses when he complains that there is now "no particular concern in the foundation of the country with the higher life of the country." Such a conservatism, to be sure, has achieved institutional prominence and electoral popularity, and its glamor has even appealed to the electronics media. It is, in an organizational and popular sense, strikingly successful. But all these external trappings do not satisfy the higher spiritual demands and responsibilities that are inherent in the conservative metaphysic.

What has been concocted for popular consumption is a kind of formalist conservatism, with an emphasis on the medium, on style, on technique, on constructs. Its spokesmen and popularizers, however capable and impressive they may be in creating a "verbal icon," seldom speak in a sapiential or soteriological sense. They acutely remind us that what we must restore to conservative theory and thought is a language that is sermonic, as Weaver would say. Within this language, and metaphysic, God and soul not only occupy a central place but also define and inform a spiritual, and visionary, conservatism. No significant restoration of an authentic conservatism in our time is possible without our giving our first allegiance to spiritual principles of order— to the life of the spirit, as Eric Voegelin insists, that is the source of order in man and in society.

We cannot escape the fact that during the past ten years or so conservatism has experienced a spiritual decline even as it has made considerable political gains. This is an aberrant phenomenon in need of amendment. For whenever the conservative idea permits its spiritual aspirations to slip away and to be dominated by political motives and arrangements it is no longer genuinely conservative. The interior life of conservatism, in effect, has been subordinated to surface-consciousness, to the external world. By putting on the character of illusion it is no longer "capable of infinity" or making "contact with nonexistent reality," to use a Voegelinian terminology. For conservatism, then, to be metaphysically viable it must return to its center of principles and recommit itself to the transcendences and values that fix its spiritual ethos, shape its work, register its vision.

"It is out of reverence for the moral ideal," José Ortega y Gasset counsels us, "that we must fight against its greatest enemies, which are perverse moralities." If we are to recover "the moral ideal" and if we are to be reconsecrated to the life of the spirit, we are in urgent need of an unconditional conservatism, lean, ascetical, disciplined, prophetic, unswerving in its censorial task, strenuous in its mission, strong in its faith, faithful in its dogma, pure in its metaphysic. It must now cleanse itself of gilded accretions, false complacencies, expedient compromises, meretricious temptations, and drifting aims before it can be filled, morally and spiritually, with "a burning fervour full of anguish," as the great mystics would say. In these uncertain times, conservatism must submit itself to an exacting *metanoia*. Only in acts of repentance will contemporary conservatism find seeds of renewal.

19

Of Things Sacred and Profane

We live in an age of deconstruction when first causes and first principles are widely scorned. Breaking up and breaking down embody active drives in the modern world. Joseph Conrad, in his novel *The Secret Agent* (1907), recreates the terror spawned by revolutionists in London who seek to destroy not only the meaning of historical time (by bombing the Greenwich Observatory) but also the meaning of the moral life. "Hopes grotesquely betrayed, ideals caricatured—that is the definition of revolutionary successes," Conrad writes at one point in *The Secret Agent*, his words well worth pondering on the part of anyone concerned with the conditions of disorder in the human world. The victims of disorder are numberless, even as the consequences of its destructive process are unending. All of modern life bears the cruel scars of this brutal process; nothing escapes its onus or its impinging power of fragmentation and annihilation. In ancient times, it will be recalled, Virgil viewed life as an ongoing confrontation between *pietas* and *furor impius*. The effects of this confrontation are telling in the development of a civilization, ancient and modern, of order and dignity.

Today's apostles of deconstruction who believe that the meaning of a text is "indeterminate," neither "correct" nor "incorrect," and who refuse to assign any preconception or assumption to a reading of a text, assert that there are no sacred texts, no sacred things, or places, or principles, or beliefs, or persons. In effect, they remind us that there is no need for what Aleksandr Solzhenitsyn speaks of as a constant need "to rise to a new height of vision." They remind us, too, that we live at a time when acts of veneration are obsolete; that we live, in short, in an age of desacralization as any look at our social and cultural map, as well as, and above all, our state of soul, will disclose. The *Oxford English Dictionary* defines desacralization this way: "Secularization; the process of rendering something less sacred," while Mircea Eliade, in his book *The Sacred and the Profane* (1959), describes desacralization as a pernicious process that "pervades the entire experience of the nonreligious

man of modern societies." In modern history the spirit of desacralization has been in steady ascent since the French Revolution, culminating
in the Russian Revolution of 1917 and the results that Dmitri Shosta-
kovich later recalled in his *Testimony* (1979): "Looking back, I see nothing but ruins, only mountains of corpses." (One who listens to the *Fifth
Symphony,* composed and performed in 1937, will detect Shostakov-
ich's protest against what he calls "the horrible extermination machine.")

Clearly, but also sadly, we see very little being done to protect our
sacred patrimony from proliferating forms of impiety. Nor, indeed,
do we see any sustained attempt anywhere around us to preserve and
venerate, in their modern contexts, those "sacred emblems" that Virgil's Aeneas had been entrusted with: "Take them as companions of
thy destinies, seek a fortress for them, which thou shalt raise of mighty
size after thy wide wanderings over the deep are over," Hector, "in
sleep, in dream," commands Aeneas. The counsels we hear in our time
are quite the reverse as we are endlessly enjoined by our liberal-pro-
gressive pundits to discard or destroy any vestige of sanctity, or any
traditions of the religious and spiritual life, or any standards of the
moral and the ethical life—of the values that, in their "fittingness" and
"obligatoriness," *are* objective, as Eliseo Vivas has attempted to teach a
spiritually disoriented generation. The burden of conservatorship that
Vivas bears and pits him against naturalistic theory underlines exactly
the underlying sense of the sacred and reverence for the "right to submit a moral claim" that reside in transcendentals. Desacralization obvi-
ates transcendentals, and this pitiable fact of our contemporary world
creates a *Zeitgeist* difficult to resist or alter. What we observe in the
body politic is increasingly a conditioned reflex: the acceptance of a
soulless and godless world. We create and promote surrogate sanctities
to no end as our "culture of narcissism" frequently confirms. Hence we
should not be surprised to learn from a recent survey that American
teenagers are concerned with sex, drug abuse, alcoholism, suicide, teen
pregnancy, and teen pornography and prostitution. Surely these concerns should tell us that something has gone wrong in our society even
as in themselves they are an indictment of the society we have made.
They are also concerns that should remind us of the ancients' warning
to us that the sins of the fathers are to be laid upon the children.

Colleagues in the academic community will dismiss my statements here as the chronic complaints of a moralist teacher. I still recall one distinguished colleague admonishing me publicly for being preoccupied with scruples and therefore not belonging to the "real world." That was fifteen years ago and that colleague, now retired, no longer meets students regularly in, say, my undergraduate course in world literature. The spectacle of my classroom would scandalize even my retired colleague, liberal in his thinking and permissive in his attitude. For in front of him he would behold thirty-five blank faces, thirty-five sloppily attired bodies, thirty-five empty minds totally unprepared for and unreceptive to the disciplines of continuity and the lessons of our sacred past that I am patiently attempting to communicate in my remarks, as it happens, on ancient Greek drama and "the tragic sense of life." No spectacle, for me, dramatizes or encompasses more symptomatically or frighteningly the spirit of desacralization than such a scene. For one perceives there and then what his pupils' concerns are insofar as they indisputably belong to the real world. When I think of my eminent colleague and those many who, like him, recognize the power of the real world, accept and flatter it—and when I think, too, of my colleagues' general refusal to combat actively that ignominious world—I realize more than ever why nothing remains sacred in that world. We continually betray the sacred. That, I am afraid, is what many teachers (and ecclesiastics) are continually guilty of in the world we make. For that which is sacred in terms of the values of insight, serenity, and wisdom is too easily surrendered to the kind of profane concerns that American teenagers acknowledge. It should be otherwise, of course, but the professoriate itself, as Henry Rago wisely remarked years ago, has progressively substituted intellectual activity for intellectual life. This cynical substitution constitutes a major impiety in the long line of impieties in our educational mess.

Increasingly, then, we have distanced ourselves from the "miraculous ground" of transcendentals. We have moved away from Plato's idealism to B. F. Skinner's behaviorism, from "Being which is the All" to "the world within the skin." Those sacred writings of the ancients that stress the soul's ascent through conversion from particular to universal form are no longer taught as part of the canon of our heritage for they no longer have, as we are told, logocentric value. Instead we find all around us the purveyors of deconstruction armed with their gospel of structuralism, semiotics, hermeneutics, Marxism. These purveyors bring us to the antipodes of human meaning, and beyond that of Western metaphysics, as they shape our modernist sensibility in all of its gnostic perversions. Everything is subject to the spirit of deconstruction. Nothing is held sacred or sacrosanct. A "radical new skepticism" is in the saddle. The critic as conservator, according to one deconstructor, is a "fundamentalist" and "foundationist" and as such to be renounced along with all transcendental conceptions. What is even more lamentable about these developments is the degree of respectful importance accorded to the spirit of deconstruction in the intellectual community. Thus, as the eclipse of the sacred proceeds furiously we move more deeply into formlessness, placelessness, meaninglessness, valuelessness—into a "cosmic chaos," to use Conrad's phrase.

To "expunge divinity" from every sacred text is a central goal of deconstructionists. That goal is also one that is subscribed to by our cultural modernists and postmodernists inspired by "prophets of extremity" like Nietzsche, Heidegger, Foucault, and Derrida. Our crisis of modernism emerges precisely from what historian Allan Megill describes as "the loss of authoritarian standards of the good, the true, and the beautiful to which reason has access, coupled with the loss of the Word of God in the Bible."[1] In many ways, in fact, this process is a part of that profane secular doctrine that the "old peasant" Jacques Maritain was to equate with the most aberrational forms of "kneeling down before the world" through the displacement of timeless truths and the reformulation of traditional beliefs, e.g., the crucifixion, original sin, redemption, immortality, hell. Desacralization and chronolatry are perhaps the most debased extensions of Enlightenment presuppositions (and, now, orthodoxies), and bring us to the nethermost point of anarchy, nihilism, and decadence, which inevitably culminates in the injunction, "expunge divinity." At the point when nothing is held sacred we have without doubt reached the most dangerous stage of transformed human meaning and history. This is the *meta*-stage, as it were, the final destruction, the final diabolism. It takes us "beyond culture," "beyond absurdity," "beyond good and evil," and "beyond freedom and dignity." It signals the death of spiritual life and of humane culture, warnings of which "prophets of our destiny" like Kierkegaard and Dostoevsky conveyed with fearless devotion. Indeed, to "expunge divinity" is the total defeat of Kierkegaard's demand that we "recollect forward." In effect we become slaves of "Being" and all its heinous impartations as we move into the very last phase of the twentieth century, "the end of the modern world," as Romano Guardini has termed its rhythm of dissolution.

These remarks should not be viewed here as examples of the trope of hyperbole. No historical situation that swiftly moves to the extermination of "the idea of the holy" can be easily downplayed or dismissed. Clear and present dangers need to be confronted directly and fearlessly. Compromises have a tendency to end in indecision and indiscipline just as we have clearly reached a point in our civilization when decisiveness and discipline are indispensable. Sentimentalism and illusion in any form can be our downfall as we engage the forces of desacralization. For those who believe in the sacred, in the divine, spiritual laws are irrevocable, even as first principles cannot be viewed as being unduly aggressive in any context. There is no end to the process of desacralization, and there can be no relenting or remitting in the struggle against it. We must either accept our religious ground of being or wallow in a spiritual swamp. The categories of the sacred and the profane are irreconcilable categories with sovereign perimeters and criteria; within each there is a fast element of definiteness, of fate, of consequence. God and the devil, Dostoevsky tells us in *The Brothers Karamazov*, are forever fighting for the soul of man. In the last analysis this fight is spiritual warfare in which sacred and profane impulses stamp our destiny individually and collectively, finally and for all time.

The crisis of modernism in essence consists of alienation, which, as Heidegger would predictably insist, further declines into nihilism. This crisis in its ontological dimensions can quite simply be seen as one in which modern man has lost both his belief in revelation and his ability to experience the sacred. Only when we have fully recognized this crisis in its double destructiveness can we become more deeply aware of a "desacralization" that belongs to a "titanic demonism." To be sure, there are those who seek to deconstruct this crisis by liberating us from the dominances of sacred texts and from transcendentals and the myths of tradition. These modernists are free (in Derrida's words) "from the classical categories of history." They accept the profane nature of their modernism in all of its crises, reaches, and offshoots; they are its mediators and legislators and mythmakers, perfectly attuned to modernist (and postmodernist) technics, interpretations, structures, mutations, disseminations, breaks, discontinuities. As commentators have noted, much of twentieth-century thought is modernist and postmodernist in its acceptive view of crisis. Yet whether it is the modernists' systematization of unbelief or the postmodernists' deconstruction of belief, the results are equivalent in their seductive didacticisms: that we reconcile ourselves to things as they are; that we learn to live without belief; that we explore the modern psychology of religious consciousness in order to attain what one contemporary sociologist terms "the triumph of the therapeutic."

Yet, for conservatives in particular, as historian Stephen J. Tonsor declares, "Unbelief is incompatible with Conservatism." When he claims that conservatives cannot be cultural modernists, that they cannot willingly be part of a debilitating temper and spirit of spiritual unrest, dejection, and apprehension, Tonsor is indicating to us that a genuine conservatism has its ground of being in the sacred. For us there can be no more valuable and necessary reminder than Tonsor's stress on those lasting principles that are the bedrock of a spiritual and visionary conservatism to which conservatives must pledge their first loyalty—loyalty to the sacred and to the eternal and total unity of spiritual life. In this connection Tonsor's words deserve careful reflection:

> They [Conservatives] are free of alienation, and they have no hopes of a utopian political order. They live with sin and tragedy not as a consequence of inadequate social engineering but as a consequence of man's sin and disorder. They believe that human institutions and human culture are subject to the judgment of God, and they hold that the most effective political instrument is prayer and a commitment to try to understand and do the will of God.

Tonsor's words, pertinent and powerful in their relation to our everyday moral life, to the very meaning and existence of spiritual community, remind us that the struggle is *not* between Eros and Death, but rather between the Sacred and the Profane. The profane spirit not only abounds and multiplies but also is too easily tolerated and accepted, and it is precisely against this corruptive modernist tendency that Tonsor protests. Thus, to cite one concrete example, Lloyd's Building, London's most radically designed postwar building, symbolizes in the most visual way a general antipathy to any centrality in form or idea, or to any expression of piety. Described by its architect as making possible "a multiplicity of readings and a richer language," it reminds us of what happens when "definite standards are swallowed up in a universal relativity," to employ Irving Babbitt's phraseology.

Clearly we have urgent need of paradigms of the sacred in order to resist the modernist condition of unbelief in a world that Samuel Beckett images as the "dimmest dim." One such paradigm of the sacred has recently been reported to us by Ellis Sandoz in his evocation of Eric Voegelin's last moments of life: "On the morning of his death he asked to be read from the Psalms, finding his final solace there in words on which he quietly expired: 'O keep my soul, and deliver me. . . .' (25:20)." If the civilizing tasks of our faith are to overcome things profane, then the need to attain the twin states of mind that a Goethe links with reverence (*Ehrfurcht*) and acceptance (*Entsagung*) remains ever acute and ever constant.

20

The Critic as Conservator

The main role of the critic should be that of a conservator: one who vigilantly upholds the values of the moral and ethical life especially at a time of history when empirical habits of inconstancy and repudiation are unrestrained. To speak of the critic as a conservator is tantamount to defining his function as one that keeps certain things safe and points the way. But it is just as important to know, too, what such a critic is not; to know that is, what negatives he actively opposes. He is not, in a word, a destroyer: one whose critical impulse is blasphemous, wantonly delighting in breaking tradition, principle, value. Or, to put it in a religious context, he is not a disbeliever: one who has neither creed nor church, neither commitment nor loyalty, absences which identify a refusal to accept values as testimonies of faith. Or, to put it in still another way, he has no concern either with character in its formation or with conscience in its refinement. This is one way of saying that a destructive critic subscribes to negations: for moral order he substitutes disorder and for reverence he posits impiety. The destructive critic rejects acceptances and affirmations; he at once denies and he profanes: that is his temporal superstructure, the imperium of one who ploughs the sea, as it were. For him there are no luminous moments, no fixed criterion, no truth of faith, no spiritual and moral equivalents, no permanent things, no fulfilling purpose, no redeeming experience.

To such nullities the critic as conservator opposes beliefs that prescribe a unifying adherence to the faculty of memory, to certitudes, and above all, to standards. As such, then, the critic is a moral conservator: he insists upon preserving a hierarchy of givens, not on what necessarily is but ought to be. Such an insistence defines and circumscribes the realm of criticism, even as it endows it with autonomous power of discrimination and judgment. To limit the exercise of criticism to the imagination, to the mere estimation of its formalistic elements and techniques, for instance, or to its meaning as self-meaning, as a mere expression of personal idiosyncrasies and esotericisms, diminishes the critical latitude. Such limitations rob criticism of its true scope, to the extent that critical withdrawals and abdications, no less than critical specializations and idiosyncrasies, contribute to the ongoing crisis of values in art as in life. The critic as conservator steadfastly refuses to isolate art from life and reality from art. He seeks to conserve distinctions of responsibility, to weigh and judge the degree to which art fails life: fails, in other words, to address itself to a moral constant, to an inclusive, related totality of existence, thought, and character. It is certainly the height of irresponsibility when the word of an artist, no matter how false, is accorded an importance incommensurate with its actual worth. In the absence of the critical estate this irresponsibility is compounded. The true critical function, with its burden of responsibility, is no less awesome than the burden of vision of the imaginative artist.

For too long the critic has been seen as a passive and inferior helper to the artist; this association has developed into a marriage of accommodation, a secondary and compromising relation, now often largely relegated to commercial and journalistic advantages. The time has come to demand of criticism more than it has provided or adjudicated—or conserved. If the artist conveys his impression of the world, the critic inspects and corrects that impression in the sense of discerning the whole of that impression in its finite parts: in the effects and consequences of its freedom as these embrace man and his world, culture and society. The artist is a free moral agent in his realization of his vision; the critic is not free for he has loyalty not to a rendering of but rather to a scrutiny of vision. That scrutiny cannot be restricted solely to the freedom of the mind but to all life-dimensions; in this particular assessive capacity the critic's concern is with many concerns. The artist seeks to bribe the attention by illuminating surfaces. The critic should seek to valuate the worth of that attention, to estimate its legitimacy and rectitude. Such a view of the function of the critic may be seen as too censorial, too strictural, but in a disinherited age, when strictures are missing, they are doubly necessary. Nor should it be forgotten that strictures and discriminations form a bilateral judgmental connection. The artist portrays the creative relation of the self to the world, the critic judges the condition of that relation in its triumphs and in its defects. The critic is not free to forget causes and effects, means and ends. History, which is his legacy and witness, cannot be inattention, which easily deteriorates into anarchy.

Needless to say, freedom must be allowed to the play of imagination
for in that freedom are defined the possibilities of vision. But freedom
itself is always subject to extremes of illusion, temptation, vulgarity,
over-emphasis, indefiniteness, enthusiasm. When freedom ignores or
violates limits, it must then be subject to a criticism that addresses itself
to beliefs, criteria, verdicts. The life of the imagination, as it both renders and affects the whole process of living, cannot be absolved from
its consequences, ethically or morally. That the poetic value is an intrinsic value can hardly alter the fact that that value is also conditional;
it, too, awaits verification. Freedom has its price. The imagination, to
be sure, though it has everything to give, cannot escape a selective process of discrimination and judgment, an applied standard of valuation
that helps to identify and define what matters and what does not matter. The critic observes, and conserves, precisely this process with its
universal laws, permanencies, consistencies, characteristics; he also actively reminds us of their viability and necessity. Though the artist, in
the intuitive process of discovery, may choose to ignore these constants, the critic believes that his task is one of conserving them. Art-
speech communicates meaning in infinity, criticism measures that
meaning in value. But to measure the worth of that meaning the critic
must have recourse to tested and established examples and fundamentals as these have endured historically. The artist cannot be the ultimate
critic of his own genius; both self-interpretation and self-verification
are critically vulnerable. It remains for the critic, ever conscious of a
structure of values that he must conserve, to judge creative discovery
and to gauge its worth. The critic who conserves also controls, guides,
explains, clarifies; his purpose is not suppressive but judgmental.

Since the office of the critic must convey value and meaning, it cannot function in a void. The critic conserves and enforces a set of informing principles, a discipline of ideas, virtue, beliefs, definitions;
conceptions and perceptions are not his only insignia. More than anything else, the critic conserves the hierarchic idea of value, that there
are tacit, paradigmatic reverences, verities, and meanings superior to
others and that these should serve as qualitative antidotes to flux, relativism, uncertainty, doubt, absurdity, in short, to the problematic human situation and conditions. Indeed, the critic as conservator is careful to distinguish between clear ideas and myths, particularly
progressivist and liberal myths with their proliferating illusions and

deceits. These myths, particularly in modern times, have violated and broken the historical and moral line of continuity and have given rise to regnant anarchies of dishumanization. As a result, crisis affects all levels and spheres of consciousness, and this crisis is an encompassing moral crisis; it is a contemporary crisis of spiritual lostness.

What most characterizes this crisis are the width and depth to which modern man surrenders to it, allows himself to fall into abysms and to embrace absurdism, the twin enemies of men's religious and humanistic identity. In modern literature, particularly, it is the excessive thrill in rendering man's diseased subjectivity that informs imaginative vision and transforms it into ugly sensationalism or into mere artistic entertainments that receive major critical acclaim, and reward. This sensationalism dictates fashions not only in aesthetics but in morals; in the end it is a sellout to majoritarian taste. Whether in the literary, educational, political, or ecclesiastical realm, this sellout is readily identifiable as the subordination of excellence, of standards, to personality, to gross behaviorism, to intellectual decadence, those general brutalities that inevitably reject the world of values. Immediacy and spontaneity are preferred to transcendence; thought and assessment surrender to blankness. Moral courage, no less than courage of judgment, is everywhere in disrepute, at the mercy of destructive forms as these endlessly develop and thrive in a society in which the creative imagination itself reflects and breeds debasement and disintegration and critical responsibility, in turn, becomes irresponsible solipsism. As the modern critic has conserved fewer and fewer values of meaning, the artist has also been increasingly unable to locate and respond to the meaning of value.

A bleak critical utterance that one sometimes hears these days is that the imagination is largely dead, that it is no longer just a matter of decline. If this claim is true, and if the resulting disillusionment it occasions is unassailable, then the critical spirit itself becomes equally immobilized. Even the possible truth of such a claim underlines the need for critical diagnosis and the recovery of the critical sense. Neither the current state of the imagination nor the state of criticism, in any case, shows the kind of greatness (let alone seriousness) that indicates patient continuance and consistency, a tradition that forms and defines a totality—and endures. Disruption and debasement, not health and vigor, characterize both creator and critic in their transient allegiances. This breakdown, seen in its processive stages, is invariably determined by an absence of informing ideas and an overabundance of behavioristic attitudes. Thus, literature becomes not a search for wisdom but a liberation and glorification of personality; that which, then, is worthy of conservation—for instance, the idea of order, of reverence, of hierarchy—gives way to what could well be designated the cheap pluralism of the relative that implies the doctrine of doubt and all its terrifying reductivist offshoots in the realm of language and sensibility. The main thrust, in short, is not towards a standard of excellence, moral as well as aesthetic, but rather towards the dark, the equivocal, the depraved, the enigmatic, the anthropoidal, the sensational. More specifically, and what might be ideologically categorized as a post-liberal, post-radical, and post-historical phenomenon, the orientation towards nihilism is an inevitable condition. In some ways, in fact, this condition is worse than death itself for nihilism is a thralldom that dictates a future without meaning and a world without end. The breakdown of art and life reaches its cruellest point of fragmentation once an insidious nihilism has emerged.

Nihilistic conditions are everywhere to be seen in modern cultural life and attitudes and are our greatest peril. Paradoxically, nihilism is our modern faith, now enormously refined and made sophisticated by diverse agencies of moral inversion: by technology and cybernetics, no less, in fact, than by philosophy and theology. In the past the religious and the clerks, who were men of learning, served as conservators of transcendental truths, but in more recent times these legatees have largely disappeared or surrendered to or joined the radical spokesmen of a new order and a new morality. The nihilism of disorder, as immorality or as nonmorality, thrives even as it is sanctioned by precisely those forces that claim to represent civilization. Nihilism feeds off and grows from those who continuously betray first principles and ultimate concerns. Perhaps one of the most disturbing phenomena is the disarray, the moral insensibility, the blankness, that characterizes the inner and outer rhythm of present-day life. There is no institution, no aspect of existence that escapes the breath of corruption. Deception, conscious or unconscious, proliferates even in the supposedly most sacred realms of existence, not only in the classroom but also in the sacristy.

In the more recent past, we tended to take some comfort in ascribing our problematic condition, in its existential essences, to an ongoing crisis. But crises come and go. What really matters is how we administer crisis, how we grapple with and contain crisis, spiritually as well as intellectually, and how, too, crisis itself is defined and portrayed—and apprehended. Crisis has too easily, and now too often, been confined to the transient concerns that make up daily newspaper headlines or that so superficially engage and enthrall the existential voyeur. Our response to crisis, unfortunately, lacks faith, sustained and organic commitment. No less than the other commodities of the marketplace, crisis is just another commercial entity that belongs to the exploitative process of production and consumption. In nihilistic contexts, hence, crisis becomes simply insipid and not epochal and is thus robbed of all possibility of transcendence and atonement.

It is the astonishing display of comfort with the nihilistic orientation that should, though it does not, trouble one's conscience. How easily and complacently, indeed, do poet and priest, teacher and critic, leader and administrator adjust to and accept the purposelessness and emptiness that discloses the triumph of nihilism in the life of man. No facet of modern life escapes these nullifying effects, of which the arts, both written and visual, become symbiotically the objective correlative. What is so menacing about this situation is the extent to which it remains unrecognized, accepted and amplified and exemplified to a point beyond good and evil. Art and criticism, as we now know them, reproduce nullity without reference to a moral center, to values that are no longer conserved but rather transvalued and devalued. The impoverishment of spiritual life inevitably robs art of its purpose and meaning and criticism of its concern and discrimination. This twin loss leads to the disorientation of humane civilization and to the advent and proliferation of those nihilisms that subsume every phase of life and thought. Art as the revealing and becoming of truth, as well as a prayer of faith, is now superseded by art as blasphemy and nullification. More and more, art does not merely recreate the symptoms of devaluation but also lavishly celebrates them.

With the critical spirit in eclipse, either as a result of its own treason or of externally applied oppression or suppression, or as a result of a combination of both, art and letters echo the new morality and language of nihilism. Politically, educationally, economically, and religiously, it can be said, the same corrosive symptoms of devaluation prevail. It is frightening to see the unchecked rapidity with which the forces of nihilism annex dimensions and realms hitherto believed to be inviolable, if not invulnerable. In the course of one century alone, the twentieth, can be seen not only a disequilibrium but also a prolific invasive nihilism, unchallenged and undaunted in its drive. It is not immoderate, in fact, to view in this radical, aggressive nihilism the vortex of a satanic satrapy.

Undoubtedly these observations will be branded as unwarranted pessimisms by the entrenched liberal and radical watchers of culture, who are in reality, consciously or unconsciously, both purveyors and apologists for nihilism. Their words, their powers, their decrees are a routine fact of life and constitute a basic policy of cultural progressivism. Their control-centers infest the political, intellectual, publishing, broadcast, educational, and religious worlds. Everywhere their attitude informs and permeates taste and sensibility and aggressively undermines, when it cannot openly defame or defeat, what might be termed the ethos of a generalist conservatism. Under the circumstances, one has every right to be pessimistic about conditions that one questions, knowing all the time that one's views will be held up to derision and intimidation, or consigned to a silent death. Ultimately, of course, it is not a matter of pessimism but a matter of courage: the opportune, and requisite, courage to challenge the powers that dismiss the inherent idea of value, of limits, of hierarchy, of virtue, in short, of first causes and ultimate ends. It is this idea of causality that the critic as conservator, both as opportunity and as obligation, seeks to protect and preserve and restore. In this task he is opposing attitudes and habits of mind that have been evolving and solidifying over the last four or five centuries, beginning with the attack on and loss of the religious idea of man and the rise of a so-called scientific objectivity.

The modern critic, no less than the teacher (insofar as both roles are, or should be, interdependent), has increasingly capitulated to and adopted desanctifying attitudes and habits, which now assume the nihilistic traits that are the inevitable consequence of the liberal-radical view, the elasticity of which, and of which it boasts, has now finally snapped. In effect, it can be remarked, the critical function, as we now know and employ it, is an index of the profane impulses of doubt, which themselves develop from utilitarian habits of mind. Moral and metaphysical principles, difficult to conserve even in the most propitious circumstances, yield to mechanico-materialistic demands. The sharp decline of humanistic commitments is a symptom of this yielding and reminds us, at the same time, that the conservation of transcending principles and commitments, in short, a devotion to higher loyalties and a recognition of higher powers, underlines the need to oppose not only the dialectics of repeal but also the politics of evasion.

The critic as a conservator refuses to be relieved from responsibility, either in the enacted form of repeal or of evasion. By continuously distinguishing between better and worse, between universal rules and private ends, and between true and false visions, he defends standards and values and traditions that might otherwise surcease. There is a tremendous need for a critical conservatorship, and, concomitantly, for an authentic critical and generalist conservatism, that provides the diagnosis and administers the discipline that the liberal-minded and the crypto-nihilist detest. We need a kind of critical greatness that transcends the little heroisms born of little minds. But if the critic is to discover and convey his real greatness (no less than the artist seeking to discover and express his true genius) and to disclose his heroic potential, if, that is, the critic is to claim his true place in culture and society as a teacher and exemplar, he will need to confront and to transcend the fashions and trends and tastes that constitute a circle of mediocrity. At no time in our intellectual, political, and cultural history has there been greater need than now to break out of this circle. That such a circle exists as it does is not difficult to discern. When critical discriminations and exclusions are allowed to or, as is too often the case, forced to lapse in the name of an orthodoxy of progress and enlightenment, *jugements saugrenus* are inevitable.

Clearly, the critical function encounters formidable difficulties in a modern technological society where efficiency and production, and their experts, are accorded a superior significance. Because the critic as conservator distinguishes principles and forms to be revered and others to be shunned his task is far more demanding. Perhaps more than anything else, in fact, what the critic as conservator best synthesizes is the dialogue between intellect and soul. But this dialogue he does not limit to literary matters alone but relates it to the whole of life. In generating and effecting such a relationship, in a disciplined cultural sense, the critic as conservator faces his greatest challenge and opportunity.

The critic as conservator recalls modern man to a loyalty to fundamental principles and values, above all, to that great law of cause and effect as it embraces the whole of existence and moulds the lessons and significance of history. This is his most sacred educative task but certainly not a simple or easy one and decidedly opposed to the main current of the age and of public opinion. The braying voice of direct social action, not the ascetic and meditative voice recalling ancient wisdom and the uses of the past, is by far the more alluring and heeded voice. Unfortunately what is too often and expediently forgotten is that the critic as conservator also has an important educational role, that of influencing one's being and life. In this respect, he disturbs complacencies and dissolves illusions; his devotion is to a higher cause outside of self. The ultimate and the transcendent dimensions of life and of belief, then, are impelling aspects of the critic as moral teacher. It is not extreme to say that the critic who embraces the responsibilities of his total role now faces a demonization of culture at all levels.

Nihilism, whether in blatant or subtle essences, objectifies this demonization in attitude, temper, practice. It identifies both the context and the text of our post-historic fate as a kind of post-liberal modernism. Insofar as the literary imagination recreates the cultural situation, when that situation lacks standards and certitudes, when, that is, it suffers from moral and spiritual ennui, when nothing has transcending value or ultimate meaning, then nihilism epitomizes a common faith. In time this faith is pervasive and insurmountable. Its barrenness prescribes its oppressive forms of rage from which there is no relief or exit. Acceptance of these forms is proclaimed not only by teachers and critics but also by political, educational and religious leaders. It is in the dark prison of these new categories, without light or love, that contemporary man finds himself and that becomes his ground of being.

Changes in and solutions to these critical conditions will not be forthcoming with any alacrity or enthusiasm. No doubt, especially from the stars on the intellectual left, we shall hear embellished calls, say, for convening still another congress of writers to deal with the deteriorating cultural bases, particularly with the problem of our written culture and of the decline of literacy itself. But no congress conducted by egalitarian voluptuaries who themselves have defaulted and contributed to and even shaped and hastened our present plight, who have in fact lost forever in their souls the Vision of the Abiding One and have for too long dishonored and degraded the Word and the Idea of the Holy, will amount to anything more than mere tokenism. Blasphemies, profanations, and hedonisms have been their order of business far too long to allow for any true amelioration or renewal. Sentimental, romantic, utilitarian theories and practices have not solved problems in the past and will not do so in the future. Enervation and indiscipline are consequences of the liberal indulgences that have disabled modern consciousness.

Indiscriminating insistence on an open society, however honestly motivated, has led to widespread misinterpretations and misapplications, now irremediably uglified in nihilisms that erode the critical spirit. This critical spirit has been secularized, devalued, gnosticized, the victim of endless dialectical shiftings and driftings that conserve nothing and destroy everything of value in the name of limitless progressivism and egalitarianism. In the critical realm today we view hucksters in positions of power and influence, no less than in education we view bureaucrats. The inevitable alliance of these intriguants, as it has maneuvered to overrun the critical and the educational worlds, accents the purely functional and operational states of mind and machines. A soulless culture and society, as it has consequently evolved and deactivated ethical and moral criteria, must surely come to a dead end in the dreariest forms of nihilism.

The modern age, or, to be more exact, the postmodern age that has emerged since the end of World War II, has seen the ascendancy of the spokesmen for abolition of all prescriptive permanencies as the movement from relativism to disillusion to denial to nihilism has accelerated with incredible speed. It is lamentable indeed that this crisis, as it has pervaded all aspects of life, has not been resisted with the kind of applied leadership that is necessary if the survival of humanistic and spiritual values is to be made possible. Cowardice and compromise have been too often the adopted policy, and expediency, when even the best lack conviction. The all too evident absence from the educational, and cultural, scene of committed teachers and critics points to the extent of the diminution of both standards and character of criticism and education.

In literary art there is to be seen a plethora of cheap entertainers whose reputations are puffed up by the media in pursuit of instant, marketable thrill and salvation; and in criticism we view the despotism of a sleazy entrepreneurship and specialization, committed to nothing except opposition to the conservation of restraining values and virtues that revolve around first principles and that are, initially and finally, predicated on the inevitable relationship between cause and effect: a relationship, of course, that subscribes to the far view of life and of the destiny of man. That neither our postmodern entertainers nor entrepreneurs are responsive or sympathetic to the necessity of this view; that, in fact, they cannot tolerate either the language or the discipline of its ethos, or even converse with it, that their hostility is ignited by vulgarity and an arrogant refusal or ignorance of that higher metaphysics of life, literature, and thought that transforms into a triadic reverent discipline: these are elements that characterize contemporary nihilism, barbaric in its attitudes and vindictiveness and unimpeded in its empire of self-seeking and self-propagation. Such a nihilism, supported and exploited by the neo-cultural heresiarchs, the royal successors of the scions of enlightenment—for it is in this line of descent that such a grim paradox finds its true symbolic consummation—provides devastating commentary on the liberal-progressivist, the so-called enlightened, view as it has supplanted the far view.

These anxious comments are not made for dramatic purposes, for the drama of nihilism as we now live it is our fate. And this nihilism as the ultimate accumulation, if not the etiology, of negations, becomes monolithic. In literature as in criticism, hence, principle and prescription, conduct and conscience, and, indeed, the sapient paradigms of character, as these finally contain a philosophy of order and an order of ideas, are no longer informing criteria of judgment and sensibility. What can be called a critical Jacobinism, and all that that opprobrious term entails, in principle and in example, dominates, particularly when one examines products of the literary imagination. These products, delivered with prolific perfunctoriness and extravagantly praised by a predictable, consistent kind of critical indiscrimination, presage moral desuetude. It is the absolute absence of what must be at the heart of the imagination, the classical elements of restraint, dignity, and tragedy (in all their subtle complexities), that points to the bankruptcy of all life-values, now so obviously renounced by our men of letters. In startling evidence in the works of those now honored with the title novelist, for instance, there is to be found the rot that, going beyond even the abnormative limits of romantic self-intoxication, propagandizes the irremediable, rock-bottom symptoms of nihilism.

The language of blasphemy, the note of cruelty, the sickness of life:

these are the rendered lifestuff of literature, now variously epiphanized by profanity, rape, defecation, mutilation, incest, buffoonery, grotesqueness, abomination—and, what is now even more portentous, palsied fantasy. In this respect, too, what contemporary novelists have done to demean the experience of love and beauty does not bear thought. Literature, with its dramatized referents of disordered corruption and the human stink, is no longer an authentic act of faith but a lacerating act of negation. It makes no attempt to understand and portray life from a comprehensive view. Since so much of contemporary literature seeks, with what should surely be condemned as a one-dimensional motivation, to obviate the tensions of existence, and thus to make the significance of life just another synonym for and a manifestation of nothingness, it is not hard to see why symbolic paradox, as a legitimate and essential property of the imagination, and surely of the craft of fiction, has been altered beyond recognition and reduced to a symbolic nihilism and all its serialized images of moral deformity and the madness of our age. In effect the symbolic imagination, with all its promise, fertility, and potency, and with its tradition of value and intrinsic meaning, that in past centuries gave rise to, and gave us, its masterpieces, is the victim of an aberrant entropy. Literature and thought that have arrived at this reprobate stage must now constitute a total process of disintegration that lacks locative meaning of value or value of meaning.

What makes an operative nihilism all the more startling are its satellite diabolisms as these now multiply and expand. At the same time, it is the continuing relinquishment of purpose and belief that characterizes breakdown. And it is the succumbing to the void that marks the sub-brutal extent of this breakdown affecting the whole body of life. As found in nineteenth- and early twentieth-century works of art, and in the social-political and social-historical life-situation as a whole, the schism of the soul was to signal, both symptomatically and even diagnostically, an increasing rhythm of disintegration. Now, in this configuration of diabolism-nihilism it is the nonexistence of the soul and the betrayal of conscience that contemporary art registers *ne plus ultra*. That this breakdown no longer excites or encounters any moral opposition instances just how much spiritual experience, whether it impels conflict or harmony, is lost.

Those once active religious quests for God, or for the soul, or for the wisdom of humility, which one must recognize as belonging to the traditional domain of the literary imagination, have come to a dead halt. Ours is the imagination of the secular city, of the City of Destruction, and all its terrors and tyrannies; the imagination as the way to the Celestial City, on the other side of the River of Death, is desolate. Certainly one of the darkest powers of the demonic is that which emblematizes inertia, abjectness, susceptibility, defeat, defection, abdication, the bottom-dog nouns of moral and spiritual paralysis. This demonization, in its nihilistic snares, is no longer a mere theory but a general phenomenon, our locusts of torment, and has now become the basis of the world and humanity. The literary imagination that emerges from such a phenomenon becomes a captive handmaiden and portrait-painter. To have reached this nadir is to signal a demonic stage that, in its ontic meaninglessness and emptiness, takes life beyond prophecy and apocalypse and proclaims the *mendacium incarnatum* that renounces the gift of grace and confirms the curse of nonbeing. These are radical teleological reflections, to be sure, but nihilism is itself that last frontier of homelessness, the omega-point of man's temporal fate. Inevitably nihilism announces the triumph of spiritual defeat.

Obviously any plea now for the restoration of humanistic, sacramental, and metaphysical ideas of value will be met by implacable murmurings and disputings. The increasing dominion of an avaricious counter-criticism (and counter-culture) underlines a situation whose end is unconditional annihilation. Ultimately an age without faith translates into a generation without grace. These twin absences embody inherent and encompassing dangers that confront any conservative critical remnant challenging insurgent nihilisms. The drastic tone of these remarks will undoubtedly antagonize the liberal whose politics and metaphysics affirm the art of the all-possible. But even this liberal attitude now finds itself threatened with total shipwreck, for in that triad of reciprocating value—life, literature, and thought—barrenness now distils into nihilism. As the religious idea of human origin and value has ceased to be a center of gravity in the world, that triad becomes bereft of antinomy, in short, of moral conflict. Contemporary literature renders precisely (and perversely) an arrogant non-apprehension of the antagonisms that are found at the heart of the world, as well as of great and redeeming ideas that serve as a guide and inspiration of life.

What we find in so much of contemporary literature is an art of disjunction, even as some writers will freely admit. But however sincere such an admission may be, it does very little for the vigorous restoration and conservation of the ennobling concepts of both a moral vision and a tragic sense. This is what makes the present crisis of civilization so overwhelming in its nihilistic stasis; what, in fact, makes it a meta-crisis and all that that extending and inclusive and ominous prefix means in terms of a brutalizing abridgement of the human prospect. We need hardly be reminded, those of us who have been thrown into the twentieth century and have witnessed its epochal upheavals and experienced its spiritual wars and disasters, that the frantic search for strange gods has gone far beyond the stage of apostasy. Nihilism, which is now our yoke of bondage and our damnation, scorns the past, neutralizes the present, contravenes the future. No promise of greatness can possibly emerge from such a predicament that is, ironically, no longer a predicament!

That man is subject to a higher law and power constitutes a spiritual truth that, when rejected, imperils all human meaning. And it is precisely such a rejection that one sees written large in so much of literature and criticism, as well as of culture and society. A dialectical form of this rejection is that attitude which seeks for a total liberation from any limitary norms that belong to and define the realm of order, what nihilistic prolocutors perceive as a pre-condition for breaking through boundaries of a so-called administered consciousness. No process, whatever its illusory masks happen to be or the adventurous promises it makes, can be more insidious as any careful look at the current state of literature and criticism will show. Systematic reductionism of the most blatant kind thus becomes the real critical impulse and principle behind the drive for a freedom that is in the end bankrupt of value. For what we today view in the republic of arts and letters, as well as, and above all, in *paideia*, is the nihilism that inevitably emerges from a displacement of the life of value and that is, in a singular way, a vitiating extension and consummation of what has been known in literary modernism as a dissociation of sensibility.

Indeed, what we now see in literature (as in so much of daily life itself), to our increasing dismay, is an utter fragmentation of sensibility that goes beyond recognition: the process of negation by deconstruction or by misconstruction, or even by both. In all of this collapse, brought on one could almost say methodically and relentlessly, moral foundations totter under the unbearable weight of a disordering positivism, with all its accumulations and entrapments. Symptomatically there is absent even an existentialist resistance (in the shape of a courage of despair) to such a disordering, as most writers and critics and teachers, not to mention political and religious leaders, listlessly adapt to the changing conditions of the nihilisms that now dictate our modern fate, or, to be more exact, our metamodernism in its extremities. This is clearly not a time for either heroism or courage in any form, if one is to judge the measure of man found in literature as the counterpart of man found in society. It is the world according to Garp, not the word of God according to Saint John, that today finds wide and immediate acceptance. It is distressful to think that in this conforming acceptance we have the spectacle of modern man sealing a second fall from grace.

The fact remains, and this is a fatal paradox, contemporary art in all of its genres accepts, expresses, and endorses negations. This capitulation, this betrayal, transforms into captivity, of which counterfeit art, unsound criticism, and decadent culture are dire consequences. All those pleas for unchecked reform and innovation, all those murky romanticisms of infinitude, freedom, egalitarianism—the new and fair deals of culture and society that have simultaneously tantalized and lied to and deluded modern man—have now necessarily and irreversibly come of age. The promised alternatives have passed from illusions to complete disillusions, which, as we see, lead straight to the demonizations that assault whatever resists an unheroic morality of decontrol and disorder. The unparalleled urgency of the present historical situation must surely supersede any counsel of sentimental complacency and compatibility that rests in the all too cavalier and glib appeals to the doctrine of renovation and adjustment, that so-called liberal middle ground of vague transcendence and of paltry indecisions and revisions. But there is no evading this urgency in which an ending of unfathomable proportions must be faced in all its eschatological dread. Still, these thoughts need not close on an apocalyptic note as long as it is even possible, and perhaps only in a small band of friends and allies living in the catacombs of the modern world, to define basic differences between a morality of aspiration and a morality of numbers.

Perhaps in the end the critic's ultimate task is that of preserving even the slightest possibility of a searching out, a dialectical testing of, the larger cause and effect. In a deep and final sense, it can be said, he fights for lost causes and beliefs; he fights to save catholic, civilized, and universal perspectives from the new, and yet old, Enemy. That fight constitutes for the critic as conservator his *sacramentum* and *praxis* and compels unceasing defiance of imperious nihilism and all its works of darkness.

Endnotes

CHAPTER I

1. Throughout all quotations from Simone Weil's writings are from *The Simone Weil Reader*, edited by George A. Panichas (New York, N.Y.: David McKay, 1977).

2. See *Christ the Center*, introduced by Edwin H. Robertson and translated by John Bowden (New York, N.Y.: Harper and Row, 1966).

3. See Preface, *The Need for Roots: Prelude to a Declaration of Duties Towards Mankind*, translated by Arthur Wills (New York, N.Y.: G. P. Putnam and Sons, 1953).

4. *Christ the Center*, 31.

5. *Christ the Center*, 75.

CHAPTER 2

1. Quoted in *Irving Babbitt: Man and Teacher*, edited by Frederick Manchester and Odell Shepard (New York, N.Y.: G. P. Putnam and Sons, 1941), 229.

2. New York, N.Y.: Reynal and Hitchcock, 1942, 300.

3. "Irving Babbitt," *On Being Human* (Princeton, N.J.: Princeton University Press, 1936), 37.

4. "Irving Babbitt," *On Being Human,* 42.

5. *New England Saints* (Ann Arbor, Mich.: University of Michigan Press, 1956), v.

6. *American Renaissance* (New York, N.Y.: Oxford University Press, 1941), 231.

7. "Introduction: Holiness in History and Holiness Today," in Roland Cluny, *Holiness in Action* (New York, N.Y.: Hawthorn Books, 1963), 10.

8. *New England Saints*, 149, 152.

9. See review of George A. Panichas, *The Courage of Judgment: Essays in Criticism, Culture, and Society* (Knoxville, Tenn.: University of Tennessee Press, 1982), in *Christianity and Literature* (Winter 1983), 83.

10. These two essays are included in *Selected Essays* (New York, N.Y.: Harcourt, Brace and World, 1960), 419–438.

11. *Memoirs and Opinions 1926–1974* (Chicago, Ill.: Swallow Press, 1975), 171. Here the original title of this essay has been changed to "Humanism and Naturalism."

12. *The Heretics* (New York, N.Y.: Alfred A. Knopf, 1962), 10.

13. "Is Humanism a Religion?" *The Bookman* (May 1929), 241.

14. "A Revival of Humanism," *The Bookman* (March 1930), 9.

15. *New England Saints*, 159–160.

16. *On Being Human*, 37.

17. *The Nation* (October 18, 1917), 428.

18. "Humanism and Symbolic Imagination: Notes on Re-reading Irving Babbitt," *The Lion and the Honeycomb: Essays in Solicitude and Critique* (New York, N.Y.: Harcourt, Brace and World, 1955), 153.

19. *Metaphysics*, 1072^b.

CHAPTER 4

1. *Henry James: Letters, Volume III: 1883–1895*, edited by Leon Edel (Cambridge, Mass.: Harvard University Press, 1980).

2. *The Philosophy of Loyalty* (New York, N.Y.: Macmillan, 1908), 139. See also Romano Guardini, *The Virtues: On Forms of Moral Life* (Chicago, Ill.: Henry Regnery Company, 1967).

3. "Robert Louis Stevenson," *The Century* (April 1888), 869.

4. *Henry James and H. G. Wells: A Record of Their Friendship, Their Debate on the Art of Fiction, and Their Quarrel*, edited by Gordon N. Ray and Leon Edel (Urbana, Ill.: University of Illinois Press, 1958), 249.

5. Quoted in "Herbert George Wells (1866–1946)," *The Dictionary of National Biography, 1941–1950* (Oxford, Eng.: Oxford University Press, 1958), 949.

6. Quoted in Rupert Hart-Davis, *Hugh Walpole, A Biography* (New York, N.Y.: Macmillan, 1952), 68.

7. Quoted in *The Diary of Arthur Christopher Benson*, edited by Percy Lubbock (New York, N.Y.: Longmans, Green and Company, 1926), 262.

8. *The Dehumanization of Art* (Princeton, N.J.: Princeton University Press, 1968 [1925]), 7.

9. *The Notebooks of Henry James*, edited by F. O. Matthiessen and Kenneth B. Murdock (New York, N.Y.: Oxford University Press, 1947), 187.

10. Quoted in Leon Edel, *The Life of Henry James: Volume V, The Master, 1901–1916* (Philadelphia, Pa.: J. B. Lippincott, 1972), 560.

11. *The Diary of Alice James*, edited by Leon Edel (New York, N.Y.: Dodd, Mead, 1964), 104. Entry dated March 25, 1890.

12. *The Notebooks of Henry James*, 187. Entry dated February 14, 1895.

13. *Joseph Conrad on Fiction*, edited by Walter F. Wright (Lincoln, Neb.: University of Nebraska Press, 1964), 88.

14. *The Letters of Henry James*, edited by Percy Lubbock (New York, N.Y.: Charles Scribner's Sons, 1920), II, 361. Letter dated March 21, 1914.

15. Quoted in "Adams, Henry," *The New Encyclopaedia Britannica: Macropaedia*, I, 74.

16. See *Henry James: Letters, Volume IV*, edited by Leon Edel (Cambridge, Mass.: Harvard University Press, 1984).

17. "Henry James: The Private Universe," *The Lost Childhood and Other Essays* (New York, N.Y.: Viking Press, 1962, c1951), 28.

18. Quoted in *The Life of Henry James: Volume V, The Master, 1901–1916*, 767–768.

CHAPTER 5

1. See *The Selected Letters of John Keats*, edited by Lionel Trilling (New York, N.Y.: Farrar, Strauss, and Young, 1951), 3, 40, 41.

2. *Phoenix II: Uncollected, Unpublished, and Other Prose Works by D. H. Law-*

rence, edited by Warren Roberts and Harry T. Moore (New York, N.Y.: Viking Press, 1970), 291.

3. *Phoenix II*, 282.

4. *The Letters of D. H. Lawrence*, edited and with an Introduction by Aldous Huxley (New York, N.Y.: Viking Press, 1932), 765. In all subsequent references this edition will be cited as *Letters*.

5. *Letters*, 312.

6. *Letters*, 382–383.

7. *Letters*, 43.

8. *Letters*, 66–67.

9. *Letters*, 68.

10. *Letters*, 89.

11. *Letters*, 79.

12. *Letters*, 110–111.

13. *Letters*, 679.

14. *Letters*, 716.

15. *Force and Freedom: Reflections on History*, edited by James Hastings Nichols (New York, N.Y.: Pantheon Books, 1943), 331.

16. *Letters*, 192.

17. See "The Hero as Poet. Dante; Shakespeare," *On Heroes, Hero-Worship, and the Heroic in History* (London, Eng: Macmillan, 1897).

18. *The Virtues: On Forms of Moral Life*, translated by Stella Lange (Chicago, Ill.: Henry Regnery Company, 1967), 2.

19. *Letters*, 23.

20. *Letters*, 152.

21. *Letters*, 137.

22. *Letters*, 199–200.

23. *Phoenix II*, 604.

24. *Letters*, 233.

25. *Letters*, 255.

26. *Letters*, 260.

27. *The Courage to Be* (New Haven, Conn.: Yale University Press, 1952), 155.

28. *Letters*, 275–276.

29. *Letters*, 348.

30. *Letters*, 444.

31. *Letters*, 386.

32. *The Courage to Be*, 176.

33. *Letters*, 304.

34. *Letters*, 294.

35. *Phoenix: The Posthumous Papers of D. H. Lawrence*, edited and with an Introduction by Edward D. McDonald (London, Eng.: William Heinemann, 1936), 673.

36. *Letters*, 383.

37. *Letters*, 383.

38. *Letters*, 407.

39. *Letters*, 385–386.

40. *Letters*, 347.

41. *Letters*, 404.

42. *Letters to Thomas & Adele Seltzer*, edited by Gerald M. Lacy (Santa Barbara, Calif.: Black Sparrow Press, 1976), 20.

43. *Letters*, 598.

44. *Letters*, 523.

45. *Letters*, 547.

46. *The Collected Letters of D. H. Lawrence*, edited and with an Introduction by Harry T. Moore (New York, N.Y.: Viking Press, 1962), II, 721–722.

47. *Letters*, 779.

48. *Letters*, 844.

49. *Letters*, 613.

50. *Letters*, 696.

51. *Letters*, 657.

52. *Letters*, 719.

53. *The Hero with a Thousand Faces* (New York, N.Y.: Pantheon Books, 1949), 390.

54. *Letters*, 719.

55. *Letters to Thomas & Adele Seltzer*, 118.

56. *Letters*, 549.

57. *Letters*, 529.

58. *Letters to Thomas & Adele Seltzer*, 155.

59. *Letters to Thomas & Adele Seltzer*, 142.

CHAPTER 8

1. "Why I Too Am Not a Neoconservative," *National Review* (June 20, 1986), 56.

2. "Notes on Unamuno," *Modern Age. A Quarterly Review* (Fall 1989), 333.

CHAPTER 9

1. Chapel Hill, N.C.: University of North Carolina Press.

2. *Contemporary Literary Critics* (New York, N.Y.: St. Martin's Press, 1977), 512.

3. Quoted in *Contemporary Authors*, edited by Barbara Harte and Carolyn Riley (Detroit: Gale Research Press, 1969), V–VIII, 1224.

4. See *Scrutiny: A Quarterly Review* (September 1949), 260–264.

5. "Diabolic Intellect and the Noble Hero: or, The Sentimentalist's Othello," *The Common Pursuit* (London, Eng.: Chatto & Windus, 1952), 142.

6. "René Wellek's History," *The Hudson Review* (Summer 1966), 325.

7. *Shelburne Essays* (New York, N.Y.: Harcourt, Brace and World, 1967 [1910]), VII, 244.

8. *Resistance, Rebellion, and Death*, translated by Justin O'Brien (New York, N.Y.: Alfred A. Knopf, 1961), 271.

CHAPTER 10

1. New York, N.Y.: Oxford University Press, 1983.

2. This is the same New Bedford for whose economically deprived "mill

hands" an influential fellow traveler of the thirties, Malcolm Cowley, accused the New Humanists of showing no compassion. What evidence, one must inquire, do we have of Cowley's compassion for the countless victims of Stalin's purge trials and liquidations? The answer to this question is provided by Arthur Koestler, in *The God That Failed* (1949): "How our voices boomed with righteous indignation, denouncing flaws in the procedure of justice in our comfortable democracies: and how silent we were when our comrades, without trial or conviction, were liquidated in the Socialist sixth of the earth. Each of us carries a skeleton in the cupboard of his conscience: added together they would form galleries of bones more labyrinthine than the Paris catacombs."

3. Knoxville, Tenn.: University of Tennessee Press, 1974, xvii.

CHAPTER 14

1. Los Angeles, Calif.: Plantin Press.

CHAPTER 15

1. Washington, D.C., 1986

CHAPTER 16

1. See "The Logic of Christian Discrimination," *The Common Pursuit* (London, Eng.: Chatto & Windus, 1952).

2. *Essays of Four Decades* (Chicago, Ill.: Swallow Press, 1968), 554, 555, 557.

3. "Joubert," *The Masters of Modern French Criticism* (New York, N.Y.: Farrar, Straus, 1963 [1912]), 55.

4. "Destroying Literary Studies," *The New Criterion* (December 1983), 4.

5. *Theology of Culture*, edited by Robert C. Kimball (New York, N.Y.: Oxford University Press, 1959), 7.

6. "Novelist and Believer," *Mystery and Manners: Occasional Prose*, edited by Sally and Robert Fitzgerald (New York, N.Y.: Farrar, Straus & Giroux, 1969), 163.

7. See especially "Repentance and Self-Limitation," *From Under the Rubble* (Boston, Mass.: Little, Brown, 1975).

8. *Mansions of the Spirit: Essays in Literature and Religion*, edited by George A. Panichas (New York, N.Y.: Hawthorn Books, 1967), 161.

9. See *The American Novel and the Way We Live Now* (New York, N.Y.: Oxford University Press, 1983). See also my discussion of this book in chapter 10 above, "Thoughts of a Dissident Critic," 132–136.

10. *Leisure, the Basis of Culture*, translated by Alexander Dru (New York, N.Y.: Pantheon Books, 1964), 78.

11. *Letters to Arthur Hugh Clough*, edited by H. F. Lowry (London, Eng.: H. Milford, 1932), 126.

12. *Mansions of the Spirit*, 60.

13. *I and Thou*, translated by Walter Kaufmann (New York, N.Y.: Scribners, 1970), 182.

CHAPTER 17

1. *Ways of Russian Theology*, translated by Robert L. Nichols, *The Collected Works of Georges Florovsky*, V (Belmont, Mass.: Nordland Pub. Co., 1979).
2. Translated, with an Introduction, by Michael A. Minihan (Princeton, N.J.: Princeton University Press, 1968).

CHAPTER 19

1. *Prophets of Extremity* (Berkeley, Calif.: University of California Press, 1985), p. xiii.

A Bibliographical Note

"Dostoevsky and the Religion of Spirit" was first published in *Comparative Literature Studies* (December 1969), 521–527; also first appearing in the same journal were "Irving Babbitt and Simone Weil" (June 1978), 177–192 and "A Failure of Nerve" (Spring 1984), 103–114.

"The Christ of Simone Weil" was first published in *Studies in Formative Spirituality* (May 1983), 229–242.

"Literature and Religion" was first published in *Studies in the Literary Imagination* (Spring 1985), 3–15.

Part I of "Conservatism, Change, and the Life of the Spirit" was first published under the title "Conservatism and the Life of the Spirit" in *The Intercollegiate Review* (Spring 1986), 22–25; part II was first published under the title "On Change and Conservatism" in *Modern Age: A Quarterly Review* (Summer 1991), 322–325.

"D. H. Lawrence: The Hero-Poet as Letter Writer" was first published in *The Spirit of D. H. Lawrence: Centenary Studies*, edited by Gāmini Salgādo and G. K. Das (London, Eng.: Macmillan, 1988), 248–265.

"An Honoring Equivalent" was first published in *Modern Age: A Quarterly Review* (Spring 1978), 195–199; the following writings also first appeared in *Modern Age*: "Bustin' Loose" (Summer 1979), 300–305; "Henry James and Paradigms of Character" (Winter 1982), 2–7, which also subsumes "Henry James's Book of Changes" (Fall 1985), 354–360; "The Critic as Conservator" (Summer/Fall 1982), 334–342; "Thoughts of a Dissident Critic" (Summer/Fall 1983), 236–245; "Unrecommended Events" (Winter 1985), 2–6; "*The New York Times* and Eric Voegelin" (Spring 1985), 98–103; "Of Things Sacred and Profane" (Spring 1986), 98–102; "Education for All Time" (Winter 1987), 2–6; "The Liberal Tone" (Spring 1988), 98–101; "Babbitt and Religion" (Spring/Summer 1984), 169–180; "The Incubus of Deconstruction" (Fall 1989), 290–293; "Metaphors of Violence" (Winter 1990), 2–6.

Mary E. Slayton has diligently assisted me in the preparation of the entire manuscript of this book. Since 1963 she has given unselfishly of her time, energy, and high ability to my mission as a teacher and critic. Her contribution to my work is inestimable.

I have to thank the University of Maryland for awarding me a sabbatical leave that enabled me to bring to a conclusion my work on this manuscript.

To the reference staff of the City Library, Springfield, Massachusetts, I extend my deepest appreciation for their kind help through the many years of the writing of the essays, many of these composed in Rice Hall, venerable and commodious and always conducive to meditation and thought.

To the colleagues and friends who have been strongly supportive of my critical ideas and beliefs and who have in different and stimulating ways prompted their formulation, of which the essays in this book are representative, I want to record here my deepest appreciation: A. Owen Aldridge, Milton Birnbaum,

Robert L. Bock, Carl Bode, T. Kenneth Cribb, Richard K. Cross, Eugene Davidson, Jude P. Dougherty, Elizabeth D. Dunlap, Harold Flavin, Stephen Gurney, Anthony Harrigan, Richard B. Hovey, Russell Kirk, Lewis A. Lawson, Marcia Lewis, John F. Lulves, Jr., Christian C. Mahler, Stephen B. Miles, E. Victor Milione, Charles D. Murphy, William S. Peterson, William F. Rickenbacker, Claes G. Ryn, Antony Thrall Sullivan, James W. Tuttleton.

To the editors and publishers of the journals and books in which these writings first appeared, I am grateful for permitting me to reprint them and, in some instances, for inspiring their composition. In each essay included here I have made changes of varying degrees in style and content. I have arranged and integrated the essays so as to fulfill the basic aims outlined in the preface. The prelusive paragraph with which each of the five major sections of the book begins seeks to announce summarily the special concerns and orientation of the essays included in the sections that make up the schema of the book as a whole. Here I also want to stress that though the essays appeared separately over a number of years—the earliest in 1969 and the latest in 1991, with the most abundant of these published in the 1980s—they have a common source in a distinctly moral concern with and measurement of conditions affecting life, literature, and thought. In their entirety these essays contain the record of a mind in which, to quote Henry James's words, "criticism *is* the critic."

The publication of *The Critic as Conservator* brings to completion the critical trilogy that has for nearly three decades occupied my attention and that tries to show not only how criticism can illuminate literary, social, and cultural problems, but also why the critic who undertakes to examine moral conditions that embrace the whole of life can help to impel the moral discovery of universal truths. The two earlier volumes, still in print, are *The Reverent Discipline* (1974) and *The Courage of Judgment* (1982). I am happy to express my thanks to the publishers who have made possible the appearance of this trilogy. In particular, I am indebted to Dr. David J. McGonagle, Director of The Catholic University of America Press, for his encouraging and helpful kindness.

Index

Aaron (Old Testament), 182
Adams, Henry, 65
Adams, John, 96
Aeneas (*The Aeneid*), 220
Affliction: and beauty, 16; of Christ, 8–9;
 and Christianity, 8–9; of the cross of
 Christ, 9; and God, 8; in the Roman
 Empire, 13; and slavery, 13; of the
 soul, 9; different from suffering, 8; of
 Troy, 11; and Simone Weil, 4, 7–13
After Strange Gods (T. S. Eliot), 20
Agnew, Spiro T., 105
Alain (Emile-Auguste Chartier), 47
Aldridge, John W.: on contemporary
 American novelists, 133–136, 197; on
 the responsibilities of the critic, 132–
 137; *American Novel and the Way We
 Live Now, The*, 132–136; *In the Country
 of the Young*, 136
Alexander Blok (Konstantin Vasilyevitch
 Mochulsky), 201
All Shook Up (Elvis Presley), 112
"Altar of the Dead, The" (Henry James),
 63, 64
Ambassadors, The (Henry James), 63
American, The (Henry James): dramatiza-
 tion of, 61–62
American Academy of Arts and Sciences,
 95, 96
American Legion, 105
*American Novel and the Way We Live Now,
 The* (John W. Aldridge), 132–136
Amvrosy, Father, 203
Anamnesis (Eric Voegelin), 107
Andersen, Hendrik C., 66, 72
Andrey Bely (Konstantin Vasilyevitch
 Mochulsky), 201
Anna of the Five Towns (Arnold Bennett),
 79
Aphrodite, 86
Ares, 86
Aristotle: and Irving Babbitt, 17, 20, 23,
 25, 35, 39, 165; *Metaphysics*, 35
Arnold, Matthew, 61, 95, 124, 198, 216
Art and Reality (Joyce Cary), 193
Asquith, Lady Cynthia, 85, 86
Asquith, Herbert Henry, 86

Attack on Literature and Other Essays, The
 (René Wellek), 116–127
Awkward Age, The (Henry James), 62

Babbitt, Irving, 98, 103, 124, 129, 135,
 146, 148, 165, 182, 186, 192, 216, 225;
 on art, 32 (Byzantine sacred), 52; and
 asceticism, 22; R. P. Blackmur on, 33,
 43; on Buddhism, 22, 23, 26–29, 31,
 32; on the Catholic Church, 25; on
 character, 43; on Christian plainsong,
 32; on Christianity, 23, 25, 31; on
 churches, 18; on criticism, 18; on
 eleutheromania, 33, 51; T. S. Eliot on,
 21, 30, 31; on evil, 25, 38–39; a *gennaios*, 17; gnosticism of, 20; on Hellenism, 51; a heretic, 20, 21; honesty of,
 19; on human limitations, 45; and humanism, 20–26 (without religion, 20);
 on humanitarianism, 24; on imperialism, 42; and the "inner check," 20, 45;
 Alfred Kazin on, 18; compared to
 D. H. Lawrence, in their "will against
 Christianity," 31; masculinity of, 17;
 F. O. Matthiessen on, 18; and meditation, 28, 29; Marion Montgomery on,
 20; moral earnestness of, 1; a moral fascist, 21; Paul Elmer More on, 18, 27;
 and Paul Elmer More, 48, 126, 135;
 and mysticism, 22, 31; Oriental admirers of, 18; on Oriental religious
 thought, 48–49; and Blaise Pascal, 22–
 23; physical appearance of, 17; and
 Plato, 17, 20; political views of, 40,
 44–47; positivism of, 17; a preacher,
 33; and Protestantism, 20, 25; and psychology, 32, 34; religio-humanistic position of, 22; and religion, 17–35 (not
 anti-religious, 18; and revealed religion, 26); and romanticism, 23, 32, 49,
 51; and Jean-Jacques Rousseau, 25 (on
 Rousseau's dualism), 42, 45, 49, 98;
 saintliness of, 1 (a "New England
 Saint"), 18, 53; and George Sand, 49;
 on "sham spirituality," 26; a spiritual
 genius, 33; on standards, 34–35, 37–38,
 41–43, 209; on unprofitable subtleties,

251

The Critic as Conservator:
Essays in Literature, Society, and Culture
was composed in 10/13 Bembo by World Composition
Services, Inc., Sterling, Virginia; printed and bound by
Braun-Brumfield, Inc., Ann Arbor, Michigan;
and designed by Kachergis Book Design,
Pittsboro, North Carolina.